SAIL AND

C000257089

THE AYLSHAM NAVIGATION

edited by

Sarah Spooner

for the Aylsham Local History Society

Research Group

AYLSHAM LOCAL HISTORY SOCIETY

www.aylsham-history.co.uk

Printed in England by Barnwell Print Ltd, Dunkirk, Aylsham

www.barnwellprint.co.uk

In memory of

Desmond Best (1924–1991)

whose detailed research on the history of the
Navigation has been an inspiration
throughout this project

Contents

Foreword and Acknowledgements

This book is the outcome of a collaboration between the Aylsham Local History Society and the Centre of East Anglian Studies at the University of East Anglia. The project aimed to investigate the history and landscape of the Aylsham Navigation from the late eighteenth to the early twentieth century. The Navigation Commissioners' minutes and account books, along with a range of other contemporary documents survive in the Aylsham Town Council Archives and formed the main basis of the research undertaken for this book. The project was made possible by a grant from Community University Engagement (CUE) East at the UEA.

The first person to research the history of the Navigation in detail was Desmond Best, for an unpublished thesis at Keswick Hall College of Education in the 1970s. A copy of his work is available in the Norfolk Heritage Centre, and was partially published in the journal of the Norfolk Industrial Archaeology Society in 2001.

The book has a number of contributors, who have written the text, helped with fieldwork, provided photographs and other images and who have helped with the process of researching and editing:

Roger and Diana Polhill, Jim Pannell, Lynda and Mel Wix, Derek Lyons, Ann Dyball, Geoff Gale, Mary and Brian Elsey, Fergus Muir, Steve Smith, Stuart Wilson, Jon Gregory, Tom Williamson. Bruce Rushin kindly provided the illustrations for some of the chapters headings and endings. The cover design is by Kerry Buck.

The text has been edited and drawn together by Sarah Spooner.

The list of people who have helped, informed and encouraged the research group is a long one. Particular thanks to Aylsham Town Council, Lloyd Mills, Aylsham Town Council Archivist, the staff of the Norfolk Record Office and the Norfolk Heritage Centre; the staff of the Norwich Castle Museum Study Centre, undergraduate students from the UEA, Ben Rust, Margaret Bird, Michael Grix, the late Tony Jubb, Tom Bishop, Mo Anderson-Dungar, Michael Sparkes, Jonathan and William Spinks, Sue and Peter Baker, Bruce Rushin, Richard Pryor, Jonathan Neville, Alan Rowlands, Thelma Morris, Geoffrey Nobbs, John Pumphry, Robert Malster, Maggie and William Vaughan-Lewis, Dr Mark Evans, and Aylsham Farm Machinery Ltd.

The production of this book is part of a wider project, the Bure Navigation Conservation Trust, which has been created to celebrate the centenary of the flood of 1912, for which various events and activities have been organised. The BNCT primarily exists to conserve and preserve the history, flora and fauna along the Navigation. One of the founding principles of the Trust was the desire not to see the remaining history lost nor habitats damaged by man's intervention. The Trust also seeks to promote the responsible enjoyment of the river for pleasure and health by local people and visitors alike by improving and extending the footpath. More details about the activities of the Trust are available online at http://aylsham-navigation.norfolkparishes.gov.uk/.

1. Introduction

A footpath runs along the course of the River Bure from Coltishall to Burgh next Aylsham in north-east Norfolk, leading through meadows, over bridges, and past church towers, converted mills and nineteenth-century cottages. It is rare to see any vessels on this section of the river, apart from rowing boats and canoes. In the eighteenth and nineteenth centuries, however, this part of the Bure was full of activity, with newly rebuilt mills grinding corn and producing paper or textiles, brickyards alongside the river, and locks being opened and closed for the passage of wherries loaded with coal, timber, bricks and other goods destined for the staithe at Aylsham, the port of Yarmouth, and the villages and towns in between.

The river between Coltishall and Aylsham was a 'navigation', that is, a stretch of river improved by various means to make it more suitable for the passage of vessels. Such schemes, which were established by parliamentary act, were common in the eighteenth century, and the Aylsham Navigation was one of several carried out in East Anglia during this period. A navigation differs from a canal in that it utilises an existing waterway, in this case the River Bure, rather than creating a wholly artificial one. The act by which it was established was passed in 1773, one stage in a much longer process. An act was often the culmination of several years of planning, and more years could pass before the completion of the improvements. Most canals and river navigations were managed in a similar way; the finance was raised by public subscriptions, donations and the selling of shares, and the finished waterway was managed by a set of Commissioners who collected the tolls, leased warehouses and wharfage and who were responsible for the upkeep and maintenance of the waterway. In all of these respects, the Aylsham Navigation was a typical eighteenth-century navigation. Its end, however, in August 1912, was rather more dramatic than many of its contemporaries, when the infrastructure of the Navigation was damaged beyond economical repair by flooding on a huge scale.

This history is based on detailed archival research and fieldwork to reconstruct the operation of the Navigation, and to assess its impact on the economic, social and physical landscapes of Georgian and Victorian Norfolk. However, the Aylsham Navigation also has a much wider relevance in the story of water transport and the economy of this period, and detailed research on a regional case study can thus add to our understanding of the national picture.

The Eighteenth-Century Economy

The period between 1760 and 1830 was one of unprecedented population growth. In 1750 the population of England had risen to around 7 million, by 1801 it was 9.2 million and by 1831 it had reached 14 million; doubling in a period of just over 80 years.[1] The population was also becoming increasingly urbanised, and a new breed of towns was

---

1   Porteous, J.D. (1977) *Canal Ports: The Urban Achievement of the Canal Age*, p.3.

emerging. In the 1780s Norwich had a population of 40,000 people, and remained a large and prosperous urban centre, but by the end of the eighteenth century it had been eclipsed by Manchester, Birmingham and Liverpool, each supporting populations of at least 70,000. This rapid expansion of industrial urban centres was in turn closely linked to agricultural change and innovation. The burgeoning population needed to be fed, and although some foodstuffs were being imported, most was home produced. Crop yields soared in this period, driven by improved methods of agriculture which included parliamentary enclosure, the introduction of new crops and crop rotations, the application of manures and fertilisers and the more effective drainage of soil. The impact of these changes was not felt to the same extent in all parts of the country though. Both the industrial and the agricultural revolutions of this period could be considered to be regional revolutions, varying in their effects both geographically and chronologically. Parts of the north, the Midlands and the south-west became more industrialised, but East Anglia remained relatively unaffected by these changes. It was in the east, however, that revolutionary changes in agricultural production were most noticeable, led by the great landowners like Thomas Coke at Holkham, but also driven by the enterprising activities of smaller farmers and estates owners, such as Randall Burroughes near Wymondham.

The men, and more occasionally women, who drove forward both the industrial and agricultural revolutions were also part of a culture where 'improvement' of all kinds was celebrated and encouraged. Improvement became a by-word in the eighteenth century for anything that was modern and exciting; new roads, factories, science, steam power, canals, crops, architectural design and decoration, landscape design, literature and methods of education, all of these were embraced by eighteenth century men and women as being capable of improvement and as essential components of the modern, rational world. The Aylsham Navigation was conceived and constructed in this period of feverish activity, when to be involved or associated with any kind of 'improvement' was the mark of an enlightened and patriotic member of Georgian society.

Transport in the Eighteenth Century

Water transport was critical to the emerging industrial economy of Georgian England. Rivers and canals are often referred to as the railways or motorways of the eighteenth century, and although such comparisons can seem a little trite, the importance of waterways should not be underestimated at either a national or a local level. In order to understand the vital importance of waterways in supporting the emerging industrial economy, it is also necessary to examine briefly the state of the eighteenth-century road network.

The quality of road transport varied enormously across the country. Each parish was responsible for the upkeep of its own roads, which meant that the condition of individual roads could vary widely at both a local and county level. The Turnpike Acts from the late seventeenth century onwards helped to improve the condition of major arterial routes; pre-existing roads were taken under the management of a turnpike trust, a toll was charged for passage along the turnpike, and the money was used to pay for the maintenance of the road. The first turnpike road in Norfolk was from Wymondham to Attleborough in 1695, roughly along the course of the present A11, but no other acts were passed until 1768 when the road from Thetford to Newmarket became a turnpike.[2] After this, many of the other major roads in Norfolk were improved by this method under the supervision of turnpike trusts. From 1780 onwards most of these turnpike roads were 'macadamised', a process that involved cambering the road and covering it with a layer of broken stone and gravel. This method was popularised in Britain by Thomas Telford and John Loudon McAdam and provided a drier and harder road surface which increased the average speed of coaches and other traffic.

These improvements meant that private coaches and mail coaches had much quicker and easier journeys around the country by the late eighteenth century; mail coaches leaving Norwich for London now took about 12 hours to complete the journey compared to up to two days a few decades earlier.[3] However, it was still expensive and time consuming

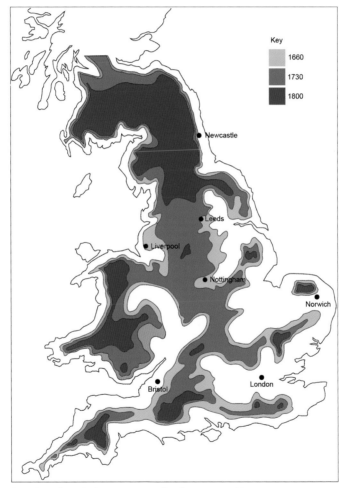

Areas of England and Wales which were 15 miles from navigable water in 1660, 1730 and 1800.[4]

2   Joby, R. (1993) 'Turnpike and Roads' in ed. P. Wade Martins, *An Historical Atlas of Norfolk*, p.146.

3   Ibid.

4   Based on Willan, T.S. (1964) *River Navigation in England: 1600 – 1750*.

to move bulky goods around by road. Coal, bricks, tiles, lime and other heavy cargoes all had a relatively low unit cost in relation to their bulk and it remained more cost effective to transport these types of goods by water. The main road from Norwich to Aylsham, the line of the modern A140, was, however, not improved under a Turnpike Act until 1796, nearly 20 years after the construction of the Aylsham Navigation.

It was water transport, therefore, which helped to support and stimulate demand for heavy goods, and in particular for coal. The largest and most successful towns and cities of the eighteenth century were situated on the coast, or at least, on large navigable waterways which were easily accessible from the sea, such as London, Bristol and Newcastle, and in the case of East Anglia, Norwich, Kings Lynn, Yarmouth and Ipswich. However, despite a lengthy coastline and a large number of navigable rivers, many places in England and Wales could not be reached by water transport. This was particularly true of parts of the Midlands, the north-west and much of Wales. It was rather less true of East Anglia, where only places in central Norfolk and the high claylands of Suffolk lay more than fifteen miles from either the coast or a navigable waterway. However, even the accessibility of those areas lying within this fifteen mile zone could be improved, either by upgrading an existing waterway, or by the construction of a wholly artificial waterway, or canal.

In the late seventeenth and early eighteenth centuries there was a flurry of river navigations. In 1660 there were nearly 700 miles of navigable waterway in England, but by 1700 this had increased to nearly 1,000 miles, and when Daniel Defoe toured the country in the 1720s he found 1,160 miles of navigable rivers.[5] During this period, then, nearly 500 miles of river were improved by various means, the most important of which were the Navigations authorised by Act of Parliament, and supervised by teams of Commissioners. This was a considerable achievement in itself, opening up large areas of the country, particularly in the north, to inland water transport for the first time. This period did not see any major technological innovations in river improvement, and owed more to the financial revolution of the late seventeenth and early eighteenth centuries. The wealth of the gentry and the mercantile classes was increasing, and the development of a reasonably reliable system of credit and shares meant that the money needed for large-scale and expensive ventures could be found more easily than in the past.[6] In addition, the demand for coal was growing slowly and steadily across the country, and it was only by using water transport that coal could be moved around efficiently and cheaply over long distances. This period was the first phase of a revolution in inland water transport.[7]

However, despite these efforts, in the second half of the eighteenth century many areas of Britain were still some distance from navigable water. During the second phase of the water transport revolution, in the late eighteenth century, artificial canals addressed this need, building on the existing network which had been created earlier in the century.

The majority of canals were created between 1760 and 1840, with a peak of frenzied

---

5   Ibid., p.133.

6   Ibid.

7   Porteous, J.D. (1977) *Canal Ports*, p.10.

activity in the 1790s; the period of so-called 'canal mania'.[8] Some of the figures associated with this period are astonishing; 38 separate Acts of Parliament were passed for canal schemes between 1793 and 1794, and in 1793 over 60 different canals were being constructed.[9] One of the earliest, and best known, canals was the Bridgewater Canal, built in 1759 for the Duke of Bridgewater from his coal mines in Worsley into the centre of Manchester.[10] The early canals were mostly unadventurous in engineering terms, compared to later examples, using the existing contours of river valleys and avoiding cuttings where possible, as with the Chesterfield, Oxford and Trent and Mersey canals.[11] In the late eighteenth century, rather than working with the natural topography of the landscape, canal engineers such as Thomas Telford began to try to overcome it, using lock flights, tunnels and deep cuttings to go straight through or over obstacles, rather than around them.[12] It was in this period that three canals crossed the Pennines, linking the textile towns of Yorkshire and Lancashire together, and the classic canal landscapes of the Worcester and Birmingham, the Grand Western, the Llangollen and the Shropshire Union were created.[13] It was the eighteenth century that cemented the navigable waterway as a key part of Britain's infrastructure. But some further canals were built in the early nineteenth century, such as the Tame Valley Canal and the Birmingham New Main Line, which likewise incorporated impressive feats of engineering.[14]

The Aylsham Navigation occupies a middle ground between these two phases. The first known reference to any attempt to improve the course of the River Bure dates from 1708 when the churchwarden accounts include a payment of £13 for 'viewing and measuring the river in order to make it navigable'.[15] It is not clear what became of this early survey of the river, but in 1722 a more definite attempt was made with the support of Sir John Hobart of Blickling Hall. A new survey was carried out by a man named Ashley who agreed to complete the scheme for £2,000.[16] It is possible, although difficult to prove, that this was Henry Ashley, who was involved in the navigation of the Great Ouse at St Ives in Cambridgeshire, and who was also the 'undertaker' of the Lark Navigation between Mildenhall and Bury St Edmunds in 1701.[17] However, despite the support of Hobart the 1722 scheme also came to nothing. Given the more general burst of improving activity along England's waterways, it is perhaps not surprising to find a scheme being proposed along the Bure. Elsewhere in East Anglia the Rivers Waveney, Yare, Stour and Colne were all improved in this period, and a number of other schemes were proposed along the Gipping and the Blackwater.

---

8   Crowe, N. (1994) *Canals*, p.17.

9   Ibid., p.9.

10   Ibid., p.17.

11   Ibid., p.21.

12   Ibid.

13   Ibid., p.22.

14   Ibid.

15   Norfolk Record Office (NRO) MF 717/9 & 718/1

16   Best, D. (1976) *The Aylsham Navigation*.

17   Skempton, A.W. (2001) *Biographical Dictionary of Civil Engineers, Volume 1: 1500-1830*.

The Act for improving the Bure to Aylsham was passed in 1773. The detailed process of obtaining the Act and beginning to plan the improvements is discussed in the following chapters. The important point, however, is that the Aylsham Navigation falls after the main period of river navigations and before the canal mania of the later eighteenth century. It could, therefore, be viewed as lagging several decades behind the trend for river improvements, but it also prefigured the huge changes which were to come in the decades after 1780, and allowed Aylsham and the villages along its course to participate more fully in the developing economy of the late Georgian period.

The history of canals and navigable waterways as stimulators of urban growth is a subject that has been comparatively neglected. Typically such waterways attracted industrial and urban growth to their banks, and gave formerly landlocked towns, like Aylsham, a much needed economic boost.[18] Although settlements at the head of a navigation or canal usually developed into towns, new settlements sometimes appeared at nodal points on the network, particularly at junctions where goods would be transferred to the road network.[19] In Buxton a small area of settlement developed in the area around Buxton Mill from the late eighteenth century onwards, away from the centre of the existing village and almost entirely focussed on the Navigation.

Canals and Navigations in East Anglia

Although the national context of the development of industry and water transport is important in understanding the history of the Aylsham Navigation, it is also absolutely critical to place it within the regional, East Anglian, context. There were very few true canals in the east of England, but there were a number of river navigations and improvements which are comparable to developments elsewhere in the country.[20] As we have seen, East Anglia was not a landlocked region, and the long sea coast meant that many of the river navigations linked to the sea, rather than to other inland waterways.[21]

East Norfolk was particularly important in the development of water transport in the eighteenth century. The port of Yarmouth was a major stopping point on the east coast trading route, and was linked to a series of rivers which allowed access further into Norfolk and Suffolk. The Yare and Wensum linked Norwich, one of the largest and most important provincial cities, directly to Yarmouth. The Waveney formed the boundary between Norfolk and Suffolk, and the Waveney valley had been an important centre of the textile industry throughout the post-medieval period. To the north-east of Yarmouth the Bure and the Ant linked the north-east of the county with the coast. Boyes and Russell have suggested that this network of rivers meant that East Norfolk was 'a water-based economy, with every village or parish having its own staithe, broad or river'.[22] The ease of water transport in east Norfolk was partly the result of a number

---

18 Porteous, J.D. (1977) *Canal Ports*, p.32.

19 Ibid., p.39.

20 Boyes, J. and Russell, R. (1977) *The Canals of Eastern England*, p.9.

21 Ibid., p.10.

22 Ibid., p.108.

of schemes of improvement in this area in the eighteenth and nineteenth centuries, including, of course, the improvement of the Bure, which forms the focus of this book.

The first act to improve the River Waveney was passed in 1670, and led to the construction of three locks between Bungay and Beccles. The Navigation between Beccles and Bungay survived into the twentieth century, and was closed in 1937.[23] The Yare, between Norwich and Yarmouth, was constantly affected by the build up of silt, and Acts were passed in 1698, 1722, 1747 and 1749 to try to solve this problem. In 1772 another Act stipulated that some of the toll receipts had to be reserved specifically for the maintenance of bridges, quays and the harbour at Yarmouth.[24] The main problem was that Yarmouth was the *only* outlet to the sea. In 1814 a group of Norwich merchants asked the local engineer William Cubitt for advice. Cubitt suggested dredging a channel to the south of Breydon Water to open up a new route to the sea, thus avoiding Yarmouth. Naturally, the town objected strongly to the scheme as this would mean vessels bypassing Yarmouth. A further survey found that the proposed cut would lead to the silting up of the harbour at Yarmouth. Cubitt therefore proposed an alternative route to the sea via Lowestoft.[25] Despite huge opposition from Yarmouth, in 1827 an Act was passed to create a new cut on the Yare to Lowestoft. The Haddiscoe New Cut was opened in 1832 and the whole navigation from Norwich to Lowestoft was finished in 1833.[26] Almost immediately, however,

Canals and River Navigations in Norfolk and Suffolk.[27]

23 Ibid., p.112.

24 Ibid.

25 Ibid., p.113.

26 Ibid., p.117.

27 Information taken from Wade Martins, P. ed. (1993) *An Historical Atlas of Norfolk*, and Dymond, D. ed. (1999) *An Historical Atlas of Suffolk*.

the navigation faced competition from the railways and the Commissioners found it difficult to repay the government loans which had funded the project.

The North Walsham and Dilham canal is the only wholly artificial canal in East Anglia. It follows the course of the River Ant from Dilham to Antingham via the town of North Walsham.[28] An Act was passed in 1812, despite some opposition from locals in Dilham and Worstead who feared the collapse of their trade once North Walsham was situated on a navigable waterway. By 1824 586 shares had been sold, raising £29,300 for the construction of the canal.[29] However, construction was delayed by a claim for damages by Isaac Harris Lewis, the owner of a staithe at Dilham. Lewis alleged that his trade would be materially damaged by the canal as the works would leave his staithe isolated, and he was awarded £1,500 in recompense.[30] In April 1825 the excavation of the canal began with 100 labourers brought from Bedfordshire under the direction of an engineer called Millington.[31] The canal was officially opened in August 1826, with a series of six locks and a rise of 58 feet. The main goods carried on the canal were corn, flour, coal, oil cake, manure and timber.[32] Interestingly, the coal trade was never particularly profitable on the canal due to the proximity of the coastline; it was cheaper to land coal on the coast and transport it overland to North Walsham.[33]

The River Stour, which forms the county boundary between Suffolk and Essex, was the subject of various attempts at improvement. Two schemes in 1638 and 1658 came to nothing, but in 1705 an Act was passed to improve the Stour to Sudbury.[34] The exact date of completion is unknown, but coal was being carried along the Navigation to Sudbury by 1709.[35] A mixture of flash locks and pound locks were constructed, and a towpath was laid out along part of the Navigation, something which would cause problems for the Commissioners in later years.[36] In the late eighteenth century the Stour Navigation was revitalised by the passing of a new Act in 1781 which appointed new Commissioners, and the amount of tolls taken doubled from £700 in 1782 to £1,400 in 1817.[37] As on the Aylsham Navigation, coal was one of the most important cargoes, as well as grain, flour, malt and bricks produced in the surrounding area. Bricks were particularly important, and were made in the brickyards near Ballingdon before being sent to London by water.[38]

---

28 Boyes, J. and Russell, R. (1977) *The Canals of Eastern England*, p.126.

29 Ibid.

30 Ibid.

31 Ibid., p.127.

32 Ibid., p.128.

33 Ibid., p.130.

34 Ibid., p.78.

35 Ibid., p.82.

36 Ibid., p.79.

37 Ibid., p.83.

38 Ibid., p.88.

The Ipswich and Stowmarket Navigation which followed the line of the River Gipping was first proposed in 1719, but it was not until 1789 that the project was revived, with local landowners securing an Act in 1790.[39] Although the Commissioners hoped to have the work completed within a year, there were a number of problems with surveyors and engineers, and it was not until 1793 that the Navigation, complete with 15 locks, was opened.[40] The toll records for the Navigation have not survived, but other evidence suggests that the main cargoes were agricultural produce and coal.[41] The River Blyth between Halesworth and Southwold was improved after an Act was passed in 1757, and the Navigation opened in 1761.[42] This was always a small scheme, with only four locks, but the trade gradually increased during the late eighteenth century, with toll receipts peaking in 1793 at £280.[43] As the Blyth was a tidal river the Commissioners faced a number of problems which other river navigations in East Anglia did not have to contend with. The gradual silting up of the harbour at Southwold meant that the Navigation was completely blocked in 1839, and it was discovered that the reclamation of the saltmarshes for agriculture in the late eighteenth and nineteenth centuries had lessened the effects of the tides which had previously helped to scour out the harbour.[44]

Studying the Aylsham Navigation

Our understanding of these navigation schemes relies on the survival of contemporary records, and in the case of Aylsham and the Bure it is fortunate that the Navigation archives have been retained by Aylsham Town Council. These comprise a detailed series of account books, minute books and other material dating from the very beginning of the scheme in the early 1770s to its end in the 1910s. These archives, and others held by the Norfolk Record Office, have been examined in detail by members of the research group from the Aylsham Local History Society, and form the main source for much of what follows. Alongside this documentary evidence, this book is also based on the evidence of the landscape itself, and on the surviving structures along the course of the Navigation which have been investigated by the research group, and considered in light of what is contained in the archival evidence.

Canals and navigable rivers share a common vocabulary; locks, bridges, lock keeper's cottages, wharves, quays, staithes and warehouses are found alongside almost all of them. Yet, regional and local differences of topography, building material and chronology meant that there could be significant variations in the appearance of the infrastructure, a variety that can also be seen in matters of finance, administration and maintenance. The Aylsham Navigation shared this vocabulary, and the construction and maintenance

---

39 Ibid., p.90.

40 Ibid., p.92.

41 Ibid., p.94.

42 Ibid., pp.99–104.

43 Ibid., p.106.

44 Ibid., p.107.

of the locks, bridges and staithes along its length are examined in detail below, as are the surviving traces of these structures on the ground.

The opening chapters of this book detail the early years of the scheme, in which the Act was passed and the funds raised before construction could begin. This is followed by a detailed examination of the Navigation from Coltishall up to Aylsham, divided into geographical sections based on the location of key features, such as mills or locks. The second half of the book takes a more thematic approach, with sections on trade, maintenance and wherries for the whole history of the Navigation. The final chapters examine the impact of the floods of 1912 and what can still be seen on the ground today.

2. The Plan for the Navigation

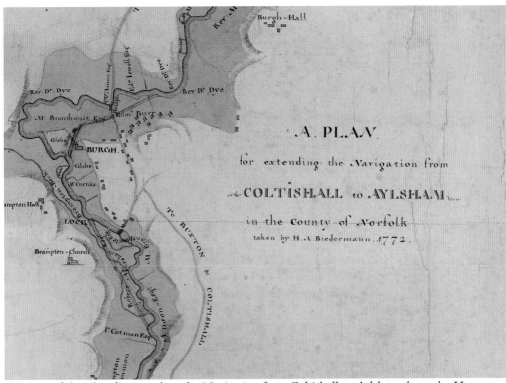

Part of the Plan for extending the Navigation from Coltishall to Aylsham drawn by Henry Augustus Biedermann in October 1772.

Behind a protective curtain in the Aylsham Town Archives hangs the copy of a map 1.5 m long that meticulously depicts the River Bure from Ingworth to Coltishall. It shows the plan to extend the Navigation of the Bure, indicating canals to be cut to straighten the waterway, the locks and bridges to be built, the water levels needed and the estates of the landowners along the river. The survey was made by Henry (originally Heinrich) Augustus Biedermann in October 1772. Biedermann was born in Germany at Blankenburg (probably Blankenburg am Harz) in 1743–1744. He was surveyor and draughtsman to Duke Charles of Brunswick from about 1760 to 1765.[1] We have no exact record of when he first came to England, but he was married to Mary Allridge in London at Marylebone in February 1768 and a daughter was baptised in Hillingdon in November 1770. In February 1769 he is recorded as at Uxbridge as an inventor who had produced a 'detailed general description of a machine for cleaning and deepening the bottom of Harbours, Ports and rivers'.[2] Later, as indicated below, he was associated with the Anson estates.

---

1 Eden, P. (1976) 'Land surveyors in Norfolk 1550–1850' in *Norfolk Archaeology*, vol. 35, p.130.
2 National Archives – ADM 106/1175/118 H.A. [Het] Biedermann; Polhill, R. (2012) 'Mr Biedermann's Invention' in *Aylsham Local History Society Journal*, vol. 9, pp.141–145.

The survey was arranged by John Adey, an established solicitor in Aylsham, in whose hand we have a detailed account of all the expenditure accrued before the Navigation was enacted by Parliament.[3] He was born in Lichfield in 1736, the son of Joseph Adey, born in 1704, and his first wife Mary.

The Black Boys Inn, Aylsham, in 1814, by Humphry & John Adey Repton, reproduced from a private collection. John Adey, Clerk to the Commissioners and brother-in-law of Humphry Repton, lived in the house on the left with a portico, now Barclays Bank.

Joseph was a lawyer and Town Clerk of Lichfield from 1746 until his death in 1763. He became bankrupt in late 1762 and when his estate was put up for auction it was bought by Thomas Anson and included the family house in Tamworth Street.[4] John was made a Master Extraordinary in the High Court of Chancery in early 1761. In 1762 he registered his address for a mortgage he took out on a family property in Lichfield as 'late of Lichfield, now at Furnival's Inn in London'. This was no doubt to support his young professional career and the subsequent bonds show him to be in London in 1763, but by May 1764 he was in Aylsham, the bond witnessed by the local excise officer, John Urrum.[5]

In November 1764 John Repton, the father of the noted landscape designer Humphry Repton, leased considerable property in Aylsham, first the prestigious No. 1 Market Place, now Barclays Bank and about 50 acres of land, and secondly an adjacent property

---

3   ATCA, Mr Adey's Bill, c1770s.
4   Reade, A. (1923) *Johnsonian Gleanings Part 4*, pp.133–146. Maggie and William Vaughan–Lewis have kindly researched the association between the Adey, Repton, Anson and Johnson families in great detail for this project. They will publish their findings in more detail in due course.
5   NRO AYL 1019.

in Hungate Street, now Norfolk House.[6] The Aylsham Poor Books record Messrs Adey & Baker occupying the Norfolk House property in 1765. Over the next few years John Adey progressively took over more of Repton's properties and bought out Baker's share of his practice. In July 1769 he married Repton's daughter Dorothy at St George Tombland and the following year seems to have moved into No. 1 Market Place. There seems little doubt that John Adey was set up in Aylsham through John Repton's benevolence.

John Repton was born in Lichfield in 1715, son of Humphry and Mary née Loat(e).[7] Humphry had a butcher's premise in the centre of Lichfield and came from a line of butcher-yeomen (not from a clerical family of Norton le Moors who had a son born in Sandbach in 1714).[8] John was appointed as an Excise Officer in Suffolk in July 1737 at the age of 22.[9] He married Martha Fitch in January 1740 and after various postings was promoted to Senior Examiner of Sudbury in 1746 and of Bury in 1755.[10] Later that year he was posted to Bedford, but before he settled he was appointed Collector of Lichfield. He may not have even taken up the appointment as in August 1755 he was made Collector of Norwich and the Port of Yarmouth to succeed Richard Dauber who was promoted to Secretary of the Excise in Scotland.[11] At the age of about 40 his domain stretched from the north Norfolk coast into the hinterland south of Beccles and Bungay and further west. This was one of the most valuable collections nationally as so much dutiable manufacturing was carried on there.

John Repton was notably solicitous for the prospects of his children. Norwich was on the threshold of a boom in its export of fine cloths. His elder son, Humphry, was sent to school in the Netherlands in 1764 and at 16 his father apprenticed him to a Norwich firm that specialised in fabric export. Humphry was temperamentally unsuited to the trade. He was much more interested in cultural pursuits leading to the inference of an early biographer 'that the exercise of his talents for poetry, music and drawing, occupied more of his time than was quite consistent with the views of his affectionate, though, in this case not very discriminating [father]'.[12] After his marriage in 1771 his father made over sufficient capital for his son to set up as a merchant, but Humphry was already looking to change his career, influenced by Robert Marsham and particularly by Nathaniel Kent, the new agent for the Anson estates in Norfolk.

Thomas Anson (1695–1773) had his principal estate at Shugborough some miles north-west of Lichfield and was an enthusiastic proponent of the Trent and Mersey Canal that

---

6   NRO Aylsham Manor Court Books.
7   NRO AYL 80. Family notes by John Repton's grandson, William Repton of Aylsham, fix the date of John's birth to 1715.
8   Misinformation from IGI family research.
9   The National Archives (TNA) CUST 47/167.
10 TNA CUST 47/185–187 and 195–196.
11 TNA CUST 47/212.
12 Loudon, J.C., ed. (1840) *The Landscape Gardening and Landscape Architecture of the late Humphry Repton Esq.*; Daniels, S. (1999) *Humphry Repton: Landscape Gardening and the Geography of Georgian England.*

ran past his estate there, started in 1766 and just completed in 1772.[13] The Trent and Mersey Canal was the second of the great canals in the Midlands that linked up navigable rivers. The Bridgewater Canal was completed in 1761 and James Brindley was the engineer employed on both, from which he established a considerable reputation. The major phase of canal building was still in its infancy, but the potential and feasibility were widely appreciated. Thomas Anson had been MP for Lichfield from 1747 to 1770 and had considerable wealth and influence through his wife, the sister-in-law of the First Earl of Macclesfield.[14]

The fortunes of the Anson family had been considerably augmented by Thomas Anson's brother George, who had a successful career in the navy, culminating in a circumnavigation of the world and capture of a Spanish treasure ship. Considerable estates had been acquired in Norfolk after the death of the Earl of Yarmouth in 1734 and around 1757 from the Coke and Paston families including land along the Bure. As noted above Thomas Anson had supported the Adey family after the bankruptcy of Joseph Adey in 1762. Very near the end of his life in 1773 he leased to John Repton the Oxnead Hall estate that had formerly been part of the Paston holdings.[15] He was a member of the Dilettante Club in London and thus a close associate of Horace Walpole of Strawberry Hill, the cousin of Horatio Walpole of Wolterton. In the latter part of the 1760s he appointed Nathaniel Kent to manage his Norfolk estates.

Nathaniel Kent, born in 1737, had spent his early life in government service and was secretary to Sir James Porter in Brussels.[16] In the mid-1760s he had studied farming practices in Flanders and failing to get a new appointment in 1766 he was advised to embark on a career as an agricultural adviser and improver, starting with the estates in Lincolnshire of the Speaker of the House of Commons, Sir John Cust. When he came to Norfolk for Thomas Anson he resided at Hevingham Hall. This was close to Stratton Strawless where Robert Marsham, now 60, had a wide circle of acquaintances that shared his interests in natural science, particularly botany, agricultural improvement and woodland management. Kent was befriended by the botanist Benjamin Stillingfleet (1702–1771), who had been William Windham's long-term tutor and a close associate of Robert Marsham.[17] In 1760 Stillingfleet had published a book on wild grasses as indicators of soil types and clues to land management, ideas that Kent eagerly adopted and developed. Stillingfleet was also a close associate of Thomas Anson and a significant beneficiary of Anson's will. From about 1770 Kent was also involved with the management of young William Windham's estate at Felbrigg and published his influential *Hints to Gentlemen of Landed Property* published in 1775. Kent and Humphry Repton became lifelong friends.

---

13 Burton, A. (2005) *The Canal Builders*.

14 Oxford Dictionary of National Biography online.

15 NRO AYL 91/2.

16 Horn, P. (1982) 'An Eighteenth-Century Land Agent: The Career of Nathaniel Kent (1737–1810)' in *Agricultural History Review*, vol. 30, pp.1–16.

17 Ketton-Cremer, R.W. (1944) *Norfolk Portraits*.

Although plans by proponents of the Aylsham Navigation have not survived in written form, the relationships between these families suggest that the Lichfield families provided the impetus for the local gentry, notably Horatio Walpole of Wolterton and his father-in-law Robert Marsham of Stratton Strawless, to start the venture. John Adey undertook most of the administrative work for the rest of his life.

John Adey put a notice in the Norwich Mercury and Norfolk Chronicle on 17 and 24 October 1772 to advertise a meeting at the Black Boys in Aylsham on 27 October addressed to 'gentlemen whose estates lie contiguous, or who are interested in an extended Navigation'.[18] The meeting opened the subscription for funds to pay for 'surveying the river, taking levels and preparing Plans and Estimates'. On 31 October and 7 November the papers carried a report of the adjourned meeting signed by the Earl of Buckinghamshire and a notice for the next meeting on 24 November. This was addressed to 'Owners and Occupiers of Land', and others interested therein and to consider a plan and estimate 'to carry the said Navigation from Coltishall up the River Bure as far as it shall be determined practicable and expedient'.[19] Adey noted of this meeting that the proposal for the 'Navigation approved and voluntary subscriptions opened when drew [sic] and got some signed by several Gentlemen present'. The newspaper reports on 28 November and 5 December, signed by Lord Walpole, says that £640 had been received and notes that new subscribers can approach 'Mr John Adey who keeps the subscription book'.[20]

The next meeting was notified for 15 December to 'further proposals …that will reduce the present estimate by at least One-third, by introducing smaller craft, contracting the canals and saving expense of a Bridge'. This was the significant meeting that decided to abandon the extension of the Navigation from Aylsham to Ingworth shown on Biedermann's map, thus saving the cost of cutting a number of canals and making a new bridge for wherries to pass Aylsham. The meeting at the Black Boys on 15 December was minuted by John Adey, the first entry in the Minute Books preserved in the Aylsham Town Archive. Lord Walpole took the chair as he was to do for all the meetings in the first year. The meeting was largely concerned with allaying concerns raised by landowners along the river and significantly agreeing to an extra bridge. Woolsey Bridge, as it came to be known, would provide a crossing over the proposed new canal below Aylsham Lock from the island created between the canal and the old river.

The report of the December meeting gave notice of the fourth meeting to be held on 12 January 1773. The report notes that 'the daily increase of gratis contributions that now amounts to £1,000.…is a manifest Proof to the great Utility thereof'.[21] John Adey kept various records of the 'intended trust' and calls upon new subscribers to apply. The notice of the next meeting states its purpose as being to present and sign a petition to be presented to Parliament. A postscript announces that Mr William Palgrave has been

---

18 *Norwich Mercury and Norfolk Chronicle*, 17 and 24 October 1772.
19 Ibid., 31 October and 7 November.
20 Ibid., 28 November and 5 December.
21 ATCA, Commissioners' Minutes, December 1772.

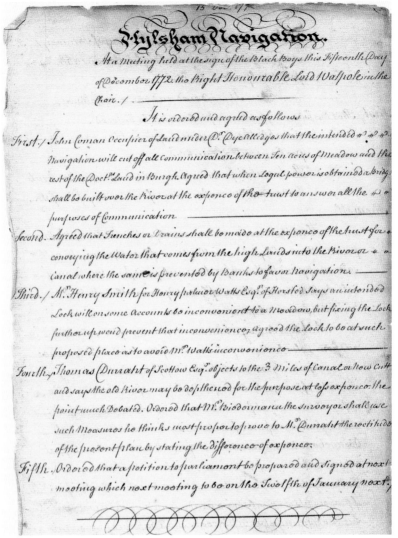

The first page of the Commissioners' Minute book, with the details of the meeting held in the Black Boys in December 1772.

appointed at Great Yarmouth to receive contributions, as the latter port 'will be greatly benefitted'. William Palgrave (1745–1822) was a corn and coal merchant and Mayor of Great Yarmouth in 1782–1783 and 1805–1806.[22] Subscriptions, in the meantime, had risen to £1,140.[23]

---

22 William Palgrave (1717–1780), his uncle, was a corn and coal merchant in Coltishall with his brother Thomas and sworn in as a Commissioner of the Aylsham Navigation in August 1775. His nephew, William Palgrave (1745–1822), son of Thomas, dwelling in Yarmouth, was sworn in as Commissioner in September 1784 with a clearly different signature. Margaret Bird kindly provided details of the Palgrave family.

23 ATCA, Commissioners' Minutes, 1772.

For the meeting of 12 January John Adey drew up a petition that was duly signed by those present.

> The humble petition of several Gentlemen, Merchants, Traders and Manufacturers of the County of Norfolk …That by a Survey which has been made of the said River it appears that the Navigation is capable of being extended up to Aylsham aforesaid and made safe and convenient for Boats Barges Lighters and other Vessels; although in some parts of the River there are Shallows and other Obstructions the removal whereof would be attended with great expense; which your petitioners are informed will be avoided, and the Navigation made shorter and more beneficial to the publick, if proper Cuts or Canals were made, ….[the Navigation] will be very great Benefit and advantage to your petitioners and to all persons having estates in that Neighbourhood and will tend to the Improvement of Trade and Commerce, and be of public Utility.[24]

After the meeting Adey wrote to Sir Edward Astley and Mr Thomas de Grey, the current Members of Parliament for Norfolk, asking them to submit the Bill. He also wrote a long letter to Edward Barwell, one of the Clerks at the Houses of Parliament, and a few days later sent him a fair copy of the draft to be presented to the public meeting on 22 January. In the interim he also rode down to Yarmouth, staying overnight, to get more subscribers signed up. A draft of the Bill as agreed on 22 January was sent to Edward Barwell to be revised 'reducing the substance as much as possible'.[25]

By February the proponents were sufficiently confident to consider the tolls and 'opening a subscription of 5% upon the credit thereof'. The Act was duly given Royal assent on 7 April 1773 and on 12 August the Commissioners were sworn in. They were listed as 'The Right Honorable Horatio Lord Walpole, Robert Marsham senior, Robert Marsham junior, William Wiggett Bulwer, Peter Elvin junior and Thomas Robins Esquires, The Reverend Richard Baker Clerk, Thomas Blake, George Hunt Holley, John Smith, Bell Cook, Edward Piggon junior, William Pepper, Richard Robins and James Curties Gentlemen'.[26] John Adey was appointed Clerk to the Commissioners and was paid £304 3s 2d for his expenses. This would have been around £20,000 in modern currency, but that included £218 7s to Edward Barwell for soliciting the Act through Parliament, two visits to Yarmouth and London and much detailed administration.[27] Thomas Durrant was appointed Treasurer and these two officers had the main responsibility for running the business for many years.

Tenders were then sought for building the locks and bridges according to the revised plan. The sealed tenders were to include two proposals, one in which the contractors would provide all the materials and the other for building the Navigation with all materials provided by the Commissioners. In September and October Biedermann

---

24 Ibid., January 1773.
25 Ibid.
26 Ibid., August 1773.
27 National Archives Currency converter.

was asked to stake out the land for the canals and estimate the cost. It looked as though the total cost might exceed 6,000 guineas (£6,300).[28] This was a problem because the Act allowed no more than £5,000 and there was some fear that a new application to Parliament might be needed. By November the survey had proceeded sufficiently to start arrangements for purchasing the land needed for the canals.

Name	Acreage (acres, roods, perches)	Purchase Price (£ s d)	Notes
Henry Palmer Watts	1r 9p	£6 15s	Cut at Coltishall
Thomas Durrant	1r 28p	£9 2s 6d	Cuts Buxton–Hautbois
Warnes Charity	2r 14p	£15 6s 3d	Canal at Aylsham
Robert Marsham	2r 20p	£14	Cut at Burgh
Rev. Mr Villiers	1a 2r 17p	£35 15s	Cut at Burgh
Thomas Drake		10s per annum in lieu of a bridge at Mayton Hall	
Rev. Bartholomew Dye	2r 17p	£10 18s	For canal at Burgh
Mrs Mary Hammond	1a 3r 10p	£52 13s 9d	For land at Aylsham
John Peterson		30 years purchase for the present rent of his meadow at Aylsham	
Robert Marsham	2r 20p	£14	For cut at Burgh
Rev. Mr John Wright	1a 24p	£30	Meadow of Burgh Glebe
Miles Branthwayte	2r 28p		in Burgh to be exchanged for land bought from Rev. Wright
Edmund Burr	1r 30p	£12 6s	Cut in Burgh
Corporation of Norwich	2r 14p	£15 6s 3d	For land at Mayton Bridge

Land Purchased for the construction of the Navigation in the 1770s.[29]

Although the call for tenders to construct the Navigation had been requested in August 1773 it was not until 16 June 1774 that the Commissioners were in a position to offer a contract to Samuel Robinson of Houndsditch, London, and James Frost of Norwich to complete

---

28 ATCA, Commissioners' Minutes, September and October 1773.
29 Information taken from ATCA, Commissioners' Accounts, 1773.

the Navigation for a sum of £4,200.[30] The work was to include digging the canals, deepening the old river, building the locks and bridges and 'perfectly compleating of the Navigation according to Mr Biedermann's plan and subject to his inspection by 31st October (except the making of a road at Mayton Bridge, a road at Buxton Mill and the Quay at Aylsham)'. As it was already June the schedule was clearly unrealistic and as Robinson did not attend the next meeting on 25 June his contract was revoked. Instead an agreement was made with Biedermann to superintend the work until its completion for a sum of £200.[31] This was essentially a two-year contract as elsewhere Biedermann is said to have had a salary of £100 a year and in December 1774 he was paid £50 for a first instalment.[32]

Having failed to find a national contractor the Commissioners offered the work out piecemeal locally, a strategy increasingly adopted as successive crises arose. The plan seems to follow the system established by James Brindley for the new large canals in the Midlands.[33] First bridges needed to be built where roads were to cross new cuts. Then work started at the lock furthest downstream so that boats could be used to bring in materials and, where necessary, remove spoil. In July 1774 the two new bridges were commissioned at Burgh and Mayton. At the end of August the new lock at Horstead was commissioned and work started in November and completed in March 1775.

The cost of digging the canals was by far the largest expense. In June 1774 Biedermann was instructed to 'prepare Barrows and all the materials necessary to be used in making the Navigation'.[34] In August landowners were warned of 'the immediate damage they will sustain on account of the land that will be covered by the soil thrown out of the canals'.[35] The treasurer was ordered to pay Biedermann £30 a week 'toward carrying on the work' for a period of six weeks, a grant raised to £50 in August, back to £30 in November and up to £50 in February. The fluctuations might have been budgetary, but more likely reflected greater availability of manpower after the harvest and after the worst of the winter. Canal diggers would be paid between about 1s and 1s 3d a day, so there was probably a workforce of about 100. The trench had to be cut to a depth of about 4 feet and the soil barrowed out. If the soil was porous the floor and walls had to be lined. In the Midland canals of this period water was added to a mixture of sand, clay and marl and puddled into the floor by treading and thrown against the walls. For much of the Navigation some treading of the clay floor might have sufficed but some marl was brought in at least for the locks at Horstead and Buxton, provided by John Pike, a Horstead farmer and overseer for the parish ratebook.

Despite calls for promised subscriptions to be paid up anxiety was growing that the works were costing too much. In November 1774 the minutes note that 'Biedermann before he contracts or puts out any future extra work for the Navigation shall acquaint or lay a Plan & Estimate of the same before Thomas Durrant Esq Treasurer for his Approbation' and 'lay a true and just account of the Money Expended by him and of

---

30 ATCA, Commissioners' Minutes, June 1774.
31 Ibid.
32 ATCA, Commissioners' Accounts, December 1774.
33 Burton, A. (2005) *The Canal Builders*, Tempus, Stroud.
34 ATCA, Commissioners' Minutes, June 1774.
35 Ibid., August 1774.

Year	Name	Amount (£ s d)	Notes
1774	Henry Biedermann	£1154	Digging canals, salary and overall supervision
	James Frost	£260	Horstead Lock
		£81 2s 9d	Mayton Bridge
		£54 8s 11d	Extra work on Mayton Bridge
	Thos Harvey & Wm Gill	£81 2s 9d	Burgh Bridge
		£54 6s 2½d	Extra work on Burgh Bridge
June to July 1775	Henry Biedermann	£1370	Digging canals, salary and overall supervision
	George Smith	£22 4s	Oxnead canal
		£37 14s 8d	Hautbois & Lamas canals
	John Ives	£89	Canal work at Aylsham
	Thomas Emerson	£63 5s 3d	Aylsham canal and river Aylsham–Burgh
	Thomas Ward	£20	Brampton canal
	James Allen	£6 10s 3d	River work Oxnead Bridge – Burgh Mill
	James Frost	£84	Extra work on Horstead Lock
		£50	Ditto
	John Neve	10s 6d	For inspecting Horstead Lock
	Thos Harvey & Wm Gill	£41 9s 11d	Planks & deals and work done
	William Gill	£40 3s 8d	Planks & deals
	Christopher West	£24 19s 4d	Woodwork and materials
	William Carter	£8 19s	Wood and carpentry for barrows
	John Beverley	£1 11s 9d	Blacksmith's bill
	Alexander Watts	£22 13s	Carting to Horstead Lock
	Thomas Fuller	£8 15s 6d	18 chaldrons of lime
	John Pike	£7 7s	Marl and clay for Horstead Lock
Sept to Nov 1775	Henry Biedermann	£70	Digging canals, salary and overall supervision
	George Bourne	£361 12s 6d	Oak timber for Buxton Lock & Bridge
	Sam & Wm Hurry	£169 1s 3d	Timber, including Riga Fir

	John Chamber	£5 11s 10d	Sawing planks for Buxton Lock & Bridge
	Guy Murray	£5 19s 3½d	Ditto
	Thomas Emerson	£14 9s 4d	Making Back Drains
	James Allen	£12 12s	Ditto
	George Smith	£9 14s 2d	Banking and cutting Back Drains
	Weyman Bushell	£5 5s	Filling old river & drainage at Lammas Common
	Thomas Ward	£29 0s 6d	Work at Buxton
	John Coman	£4	Making road at Woolsey Bridge
	Stephen Hammond	£8 19s 6d	Masonry
	William Carter	£8 19s	Carpentry
Feb to March 1776	Daniel Denham	£11 1s	Probably working with James Allen
	William Gill	£38 7s 10d	Probably lock and bridge work
	Thomas Harvey	£4 11s 9d	Ditto
	John Baldry	£5 11s	
	John Neve	£4 5s	
	Christopher West	£12 9s 10d	Carpentry
	Stephen Matthews	£1 11s 6d	
	William Chase	£3 13s 6d	Advertisements
	John Crouse	£4 12s 2d	Ditto
	Alexander Watts	£14 11s 6d	Carting wood from Horstead to Buxton
	William Pepper	12s 10d	Dydling (cleaning) river at Buxton Common
August 1776	John Smith	£400	Contract
		£160	Repairing Horstead Lock
1778	John Smith	£400	Contract
	John Adey	£9 2s	Advertising
	Alexander Watts	10s 6d	Wooden trunk [pipe]
1779	John Smith	£250	Contract
	John Green	£90 4s	Contract
	John Ives	15s	
	Thomas Harvey	£8 11s 10d	

Work contracted on the Aylsham Navigation 1774–1779, taken from the Commissioners' Accounts. Most of the work was contracted to the 'engineers' Henry Biedermann and John Smith, but the incidental work contracted to local businesses and craftsmen gives an idea of the diversity.

the Navigation Work done by his direction at the next Meeting to be audited & settled by the Commissioners'.[36] And in January 'ordered that Mr Biedermann the Surveyor leaves his Book of Accounts with Thomas Durrant Esq Treasurer till the next Meeting for his inspection'.[37] In the same month they were paying directly to George Smith & Co. 'for work done at Oxnead Canal & other work at the old River between Buxton and Oxnead and for temporary canals as appears by Surveyors Account'.[38] This would probably have been in preparation for the next project of building Buxton Lock.

In the first half of 1775 quite a lot of work was commissioned or at least planned despite the shortage of funding. Much of the expenditure, nearly £1400, was channelled through Biedermann, who may have had a workforce under his immediate direction. At the same time the Commissioners were increasingly giving small contracts to local businesses and craftsmen and keeping an eye on the work themselves. In June 1775 'the Commissioners present finding an inspection of the Works necessary do hereby adjourn the Meeting to the White Horse at Hautbois at nine o'clock in the morning of Wednesday the Fourteenth instant & from there to the Black Boys in Aylsham but should Wednesday prove rainy the Meeting is then adjourned to the subsequent Day'.[39] In later years, when the Navigation was more established, an annual inspection became a regular feature as required by the Act of Parliament. When the Commissioners met for the General Meeting in August the Treasurer was left with a balance of just £244 17s 7½d, of which £50 was needed for Mr Biedermann's half-year salary. Later that month 'it was ordered that this Meeting be adjourned [to 20 September ....] to determine whether or no to proceed with the Work of the Navigation'[40].

At that meeting it was 'ordered that for the present the Lock at Horstead shall be shut up, and that Mr John Colls of Horstead shall immediately put a lock upon the same – that against the Meeting Mr Biedermann the Engineer shall form an Estimate of a Sum at which he will undertake the whole of the remaining work he either to give sufficient security for the performance or to receive only Six Hundred pounds when he has expended Nine Hundred and in the same proportion till the Work is perfected and that no further Work shall be done in relation to the Navigation until the next Meeting'.[41] The November and December meetings were mainly concerned with ratifying part payment to numerous creditors. In February 1776 £120 was borrowed on the security of the timber bought for Buxton Lock, the clerk was 'to apply to Thomas Durrant Esq Treasurer to advance £120 at 4% upon Timber purchased by the Commissioners in lieu of £400 proposed on 29 January last to be advanced by said Mr Durrant on said Security'.[42] The credit was used to pay off a number of small

---

36 Ibid., November 1774.
37 Ibid., January 1775.
38 Ibid.
39 Ibid., June 1775.
40 Ibid., August 1775.
41 Ibid.
42 Ibid., February 1776.

outstanding bills. By the time of the General Meeting in August 1776 the balance of funds was down to £6 7s 11d.[43]

AYLSHAM NAVIGATION.

MR. JOHN SMITH, (Engineer of the Loughborough Navigation, in the County of Leicester) having at the last Meeting agreed with the Commissioners to finish and complete the Aylsham Navigation by and from Coltishall to Aylsham Bridge, conformable to Act of Parliament, he will immediately proceed with the Work: The Subscribers to the Donation Agreement, dated 24th of Nov. 1772, who have not paid their Donations, and the Subscribers to an Agreement dated 14th of Feb. 1776, for the further advancing Money on the Credit of the Tolls at five per cent. are desired to pay the whole of their Donations and half of their Subscriptions to Thomas Durrant, Esq. Treasurer, Roger Kerrison, Esq. or Mr. John Adey, on or before the 5th of April next.——The next Meeting of the Commissioners will be held at the Black Boys in Aylsham, on Monday the ninth of March next, at Ten o'Clock in the Forenoon.

JOHN ADEY, Clerk.

Aylsham, 26th Feb. 1778.

A notice showing John Smith, engineer of the Loughborough Navigation, engaged to complete the Aylsham Navigation and efforts to raise money.

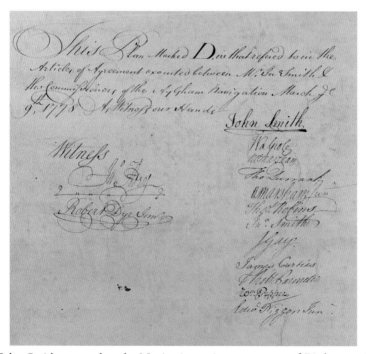

Contract for John Smith to complete the Navigation written on a copy of Biedermann's survey map. Note that John Smith, the Commissioner, was also one of the signatories.[44]

---

43 ATCA, Commissioners' Accounts, August 1776.
44 ATCA, Biedermann's map, 1772.

It was ordered that 'Mr Kent be desired to apply to Thomas Gilbert Esq Member for Lichfield to recommend a person to survey the state of the Navigation and report his opinion of the expense that will be necessary to make the Navigation perfect from Coltishall to Aylsham'.[45] No further work was done for eighteen months. Biedermann had supervised the work on the Navigation until the funds ran out in 1775, but was also doing survey work for Sir Harbord Harbord in Woodbastwick, Stanninghall and Frettenham in 1773. He seems to have lived at Woodbastwick for some years, where he is recorded as taking on apprentices in 1778 and 1786.[46] He was employed at Holkham in 1779 and made a map of Wells in 1780 and Warham St Mary and All Saints in 1783. Later he did enclosure work particularly for the Dashwood family in Hertfordshire and Oxfordshire, settled at Tetbury in Gloucestershire and died there in 1816. He was naturalised in 1804, but retained the German spelling of his name.

At the statutory General Meeting on 6 August 1777 insufficient Commissioners turned up to make a quorum and John Adey, the clerk, had to enlist the conditions of paragraph 3 of the Act and insist on a meeting in three weeks.[47] At this point of crisis a new subscription was raised, discussed in detail below. Presumably as a result of Nathaniel Kent's enquiries, John Smith was enlisted from the Midlands. John Smith followed his father of the same name as an engineer on the canals of the River Nene from 1758 to 1761, and on the Cod Beck, Rippon Canal and River Swale in 1767 to 1771.[48] In 1772 he had surveyed the Went Canal project and the Market Weighton Canal, but lost control of the latter project to John Grundy, who submitted a better plan, but remained as assistant engineer until 1775. He came to the Bure with considerable experience and submitted an estimate in October 1777 to complete the whole Navigation for £2,951 and further money was raised to cover the cost.

In February 1778 preparations were made for the new season, a notice was put in the papers chasing up the promised loans and publicising the contract with John Smith signed in March. Tenders were sought for the work and John Ives was commissioned to 'find up the Barrows, Boards & the Utensils belonging to the Commissioners & report their number and condition & places where they are to be found'.[49] By the beginning of March 1779 the work had progressed well, the locks at Buxton and Oxnead both complete, but as usual the Commissioners were short of funds and anxious about further bills. They asked for a second opinion and 'it appears to the Commissioners from the Information of Mr John Green of Wroxham that Mr John Smith the Engineer of the said Navigation has done work on the Navigation to the amount of Three Hundred pounds and upwards more than what is now due to him according to his Article with the Commissioners'.[50] £150 was paid immediately and later in the month a

---

45 ATCA, Commissioners' Minutes, August 1776.

46 TNA, Board of Stamps: Apprenticeship Books, Series IR1.

47 ATCA, Commissioners' Minutes, August 1777.

48 Skempton, A.W. (2002) *A Biographical Dictionary of Civil Engineers in Great Britain and Northern Ireland Volume 1 – 1500–1830.*

49 ATCA, Commissioners' Minutes, February 1778.

50 Ibid., March 1779.

formal arrangement was devised to include John Green as a partner in the enterprise, 'whereas Mr John Green of Wroxham in Norfolk Bricklayer has agreed to enter into Partnership with Mr John Smith the present Engineer & has contracted to compleat the Navigation from Horstead Lock to Aylsham Bridge according to the Stipulations of the said Mr Smith which partnership we the Commissioners present do approve'.[51] The Commissioners agreed to further payments and the clerk was directed to press subscribers to make their contributions.

Good progress seems to have been made through the summer and toll receipts amounted to £148 by the end of the year. Nonetheless by the General Meeting in August 1779 the financial situation was again dire and a further 'loan in aid' had to be raised from the principal proponents of the Navigation. Some panic ensued the next month as reported at the September meeting, 'Mr John Smith Engineer having on or about the first day of this instant September deserted the work of the said Navigation & left the County of Norfolk – Ordered that Mr John Adey causes Advertizements to be immediately inserted in the York and some of the London Newspapers for the said Mr John Smith to return and finish the said work on or before the 10th day of Oct. next agreeable to his contract with the Commissioners of the said Navigation dated 9th March 1778'.[52] A survey of the Navigation from 'end to end' was commissioned and John Green instructed to complete the work.

The work was in fact mostly done and John Smith was soon tracked down. He had been working on other contracts to improve the drainage of fenland adjacent to the River Witham between Lincoln and Boston and in April 1776 started to make 9 miles of the River Soar navigable from the Trent at Redhill to Loughborough. In November he was back in Norfolk and commissioned to continue 'to depthen and take out shoals reported & as appears by a survey of the Navigation'.[53] The finishing touches to the Navigation were made over the next few years, but the Navigation is generally considered to have been opened on 20 October 1779.

By now the lives of the proponents had moved on considerably. Thomas Anson died in 1773 and his estates in Norfolk were inherited by his nephew George Adams, who changed his name to George Anson. Nathaniel Kent continued to manage estates for the Anson and Windham families into the 1790s and by then had a major land agency business, with two partners, in London. The peak of his career came with the management of the royal estates at Windsor and Richmond from 1791 to 1797. He remained actively engaged with several other Norfolk estates and wrote a report on the county for the Board of Agriculture published in 1796. He was active to the end of his life in 1810 and left a profitable business to his son. John Repton died in Norwich in January 1775. He was buried with his wife Martha, who had predeceased him in December 1773, in St Michael's, in Aylsham with a fine memorial. Windham, Kent and Marsham helped to shape Humphry Repton's career as a landscape gardener and in 1778 he abandoned his Norwich business, moving to Sustead with his wife and young son, christened John Adey Repton.

---

51 Ibid.
52 Ibid., September 1779.
53 Ibid., November 1779.

Repton greatly admired John Adey for his 'honesty and Christian spirit'.[54] In 1775, as the principal executor of his father's estate, he was administering the Oxnead Hall estate under a deed of family arrangements between himself, his sister Dorothy and John Adey (the other executors), in accordance with the terms of the lease to his late father John.[55] His sole brother John, having come of age, took over the family lease of the farm. John junior was singled out for praise by Arthur Young and Nathaniel Kent in their reports on the agriculture of Norfolk for his crop rotations, seed drilling, land drainage and 'his books kept with uncommon accuracy and care'.[56]

In 1781 John Adey was appointed a Commissioner for the King's bench, Common Pleas and Exchequer Courts. He was also a Clerk of the peace for Norfolk and again in 1781 was Under-Sheriff for Norfolk, extending his legal role to county matters. He continued as a Clerk of the Navigation until the end of his life in 1809, assisted from 1806 by his partner William Repton, Humphry Repton's younger son. He and Dorothy (died 1822) had no surviving children and were buried in St Michael's, Aylsham. Their memorial includes the epitaph that 'the union of this affectionate pair was blessed with an uninterrupted happiness of thirty nine years'.

The Parliamentary Act

The Act of Parliament runs to 19 pages with some 56 paragraphs. It was drafted by John Adey in the days after a Petition to Parliament had been signed at a public meeting at the Blackboys Inn on 12 January 1773.[57] He records that 'attending said Meeting when petition was signed entered in the Book and ordered that Letters should be written to Sir Edward Astley and Mr de Grey [MPs for Norfolk] to present same to Parliament and that Bill should be prepared against next Meeting'. On 15th January he rode to Yarmouth 'getting petition signed by several of the Gentlemen there out two days Horse and Expenses £1 6s'. Then there is a more substantial claim for £10 10s for drawing up the Bill folio and a further £2 2s for making a fair copy and sending to Edward Barwell, a Clerk at the Houses of Parliament. On 22nd January he entered 6s for 'attending said Meeting when Bill was read over and ordered to be sent to Mr. Edward Barwell to consider and settle same'. On the 25th he took the coach to London, accompanied by Henry Biedermann, and was away for six days 'attending Parliament upon the Petition'.

In February and March the public meetings finalised the rates for tolls and the interest of 5% per year to be paid on the subscriptions. On 18th February the Bill was 'read and settled'. This entailed two further journeys to Yarmouth 'with subscriptions to advance Money on the security when got 9 subscribers to same'.

---

54   Daniels, S. (1999) *Humphry Repton: Landscape Gardening and the Geography of Georgian England.*
55   NRO, AYL 1019 and AYL 91/2.
56   Young, A. (1804) *General View of the Agriculture of Norfolk*, p. 252.
57   Copies of the Act are preserved in the Aylsham Town Council Archive.

A N

A   C   T

F O R

Making and Extending the Navigation
of the River *Bure* (commonly called
the *North River*) by and from *Coltiſhall* to *Aylſham Bridge*, in the County
of *Norfolk*.

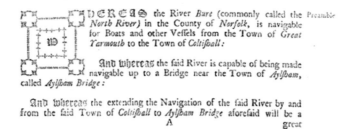

WHEREAS the River *Bure* (commonly called the *North River*) in the County of *Norfolk*, is navigable for Boats and other Veſſels from the Town of *Great Yarmouth* to the Town of *Coltiſhall*:

And whereas the ſaid River is capable of being made navigable up to a Bridge near the Town of *Aylſham*, called *Aylſham Bridge*:

And whereas the extending the Navigation of the ſaid River by and from the ſaid Town of *Coltiſhall* to *Aylſham Bridge* aforeſaid will be a

A   great

The first page of the Act of Parliament for the Aylsham Navigation, 1773.

The Bill received its second reading on 16th March and on 20th March Adey took the coach to London and stayed for 19 days 'attending the soliciting and passing the Act', the period when the Act would have been printed and needed proof reading. Biedermann joined him on the 5th April to assist in the preparation of the Bill. The Act received Royal Assent on 7th April and it just remained to pay the 'carriage of parcels and Acts' and to pay off Mr Barwell's bill of £218 7s, about £13,000 in modern currency.[58]

It seems John Adey should be given most credit for drafting the Act, working out its many complex provisions and guiding it through the public meetings and the

---

58   National Archives Currency converter.

somewhat corrupt Parliamentary process. There is little doubt that Thomas Anson saw a draft as there is a specific clause that 'a Wooden Pipe or Trunk lying across the said River between Oxnead and Buxton Mills, which serves as a Drain to certain Meadows belonging to Thomas Anson, Esquire, should be placed lower'.[59] He is the only individual mentioned in the whole Act. When it came to construction, the locks were to be built of wood, with the exception of Burgh Lock, which was to be made of brick – and Thomas Anson's estate had a brick kiln conveniently close.

The main provisions of the Act were to set up an administrative framework, control the waterway and manage the finances. A summary is included as Appendix 1.

The Navigation was to be run by a board of Commissioners, who would be eligible only if they lived in this part of the county and had an estate to the annual value of £100 or a personal estate of £3,000. The Commissioners had powers, taken on oath, to use the waterway, contract the construction and upkeep, and audit the finances. They had to meet at least annually, with a quorum of seven, and were provided with legal procedures to create by-laws and resolve disputes. The staff, a Collector of Tolls, Treasurer, Clerk, Surveyor and any other necessary officers, were to be on oath and appointed and dismissed at the discretion of the Commissioners. The Commissioners were not to have other vested interests and were to defray their own expenses.

The Commissioners were empowered to acquire land but adjured to respect local property during the construction of the necessary canals, bridges, locks, gates, wharves, warehouses, lock houses, towpaths and drains. In case of objection a series of legal procedures were specified up to a hearing by Sheriff and jury. They could enforce millers to control the flow of water for the passage of vessels, set posts to mark water levels, open and close locks as needed, and make provision for repairs. Users of the waterway were to give account of lading, identify their vessels and pay their tolls. There were penalties for any misuse. Liability for damage was subject to inquest.

The construction of the Navigation was to be funded from donations and loans (described as subscriptions). The Commissioners were allowed to acquire £5,000 and work was not to start until that sum was raised. The expense of construction and maintenance, together with the annual repayment of 5% on the loans, was to be met by charging tolls. The toll rate for different goods was specified: 1s per ton for coal and building materials, 1s 6d for corn, timber and other commodities. Tolls were reduced to two–thirds for goods passing through the locks only at Buxton and Horstead. No tolls were to be charged for manure, marl and other material for improving the land, nor for materials to maintain the waterway. The accounts were to be kept in a book and annually verified by the Commissioners and Treasurer. The 5% dividends could be assigned by will or notification to the Clerk.

In the nineteenth century some dispute arose over whether the Commissioners or the landowners should maintain the banks along the waterway. The Commissioners resorted

---

59 ATCA, Act for Making and Extending the Navigation of the River Bure, 1773.

to taking legal advice, the upshot of which was that the Commissioners agreed to keep weeds and debris out of the water and the landowners were required to remove herbage from the banks. It was slightly ironic that the dispute arose with the landowner at Oxnead who was a successor to Thomas Anson, who was such an enthusiast for canals.

The only evident mistake was to restrict the Commissioners to borrowing up to £5,000 with no work to be done until that sum raised. The work eventually cost £8,886 4s 5¼d, about £560,000 in modern currency. The optimistic forecast was no doubt needed to get the project started and a need to revise the Act was avoided by converting some of the subscriptions into donations, a public-spirited gesture by a number of gentry.

The Subscribers

> And be it further enacted, That it shall be lawful for the said
> Commissioners…to borrow and take up at Interest any such … Sums
> of Money as they shall think necessary for the Purposes of the Act, not
> exceeding the Sum of Five Thousand Pounds, and to assign over the said
> Tolls…not exceeding the Rate of Five Pounds per Centum per Annum …
> to such Persons or their Trustees as shall advance the same.[60]

Henry Biedermann estimated in October 1772 that it would cost £4,006 5s 4½d to construct the Navigation. Once the petition to Parliament had been accepted a public meeting at the Black Boys on 18 February 1773 agreed that £5,000 should be borrowed against 5% interest paid from the proceeds of the tolls.[61] Theoretically, the loan would be repaid in twenty years. In reality there were several complications.

The money would be needed only progressively as the construction proceeded.[62] At the first Annual General Meeting in August 1773 a first call was made for 10% of the pledges to be delivered by the next meeting on 7 September. At that meeting John Adey was reimbursed the £304 3s 2d for soliciting the Act through Parliament as described above. There were also small bills for stationery and in November Henry Biedermann was paid £20 for his survey of the year before. The main construction was started in the summer of 1774 and two more calls were made for 10% in May and August that year. The three final calls for the residue were made for 20% in October and 25% in November 1774 and February 1775. A sum of £3,900 had been pledged by 39 subscribers paying £100 each over this period. There were a few defaulters so the total money received came to £3,600. To make up the shortfall from the £5,000 a Donation List was opened in November 1773 for smaller contributions between £5 and £50. This raised £311 5s in 1773, mainly from local merchants and farmers, £80 in 1774 and £460 in 1775, by when the gentry were being asked for larger gifts from £50 to £100. By 1775 it was clear

---

60 Ibid.
61 ATCA, Commissioners' Minutes, February 1773.
62 The information for this section is taken from the Minutes and Account Books of the Aylsham Navigation in the Aylsham Town Council Archive.

that the costs of construction would considerably exceed the original estimate. A little revenue had accrued from the tolls collected on the lower stretches of the river from Buxton to Coltishall, but by August 'it was ordered that the Meeting be adjourned [to 20 September] to determine whether or not to proceed with the Work of the Navigation'.

By August 1777 work had ceased, Horstead Lock was closed, Biedermann had left, and the funds were exhausted. The Commissioners agreed to open a New or Second Lending List, but first needed to circumvent the statutory limit of £5,000. They did this by converting part of the original loan to donations. So in August 1777 the following order was included in the Minutes, 'Ordered that Mr. Adey inform the Subscribers on the lending List that the money for completing the Canal cannot be raised without each Subscriber abating 30% of his original Subscription & to report their Answer at the next Meeting & it is further ordered that each original Subscriber has a preference in subscribing his rateable share to the new Subscription to compleat the whole wanted if desired'. A number of gentry in particular converted their entire holding to a gift at this stage.

In October 1777 it was noted that £2,951 was estimated by John Smith, the new engineer, to complete the work. The £450 of donations agreed in November 1772 could be deducted to give £2,501, but that added to the £3,600 raised by subscription still exceeded the £5,000 permitted by £1,101, and it was this sum that had to be abated.

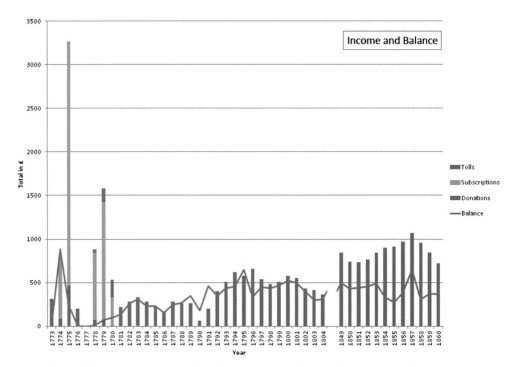

Income (from tolls, subscriptions and donations) and the balance (after payments for construction and maintenance) between 1773 and 1860.

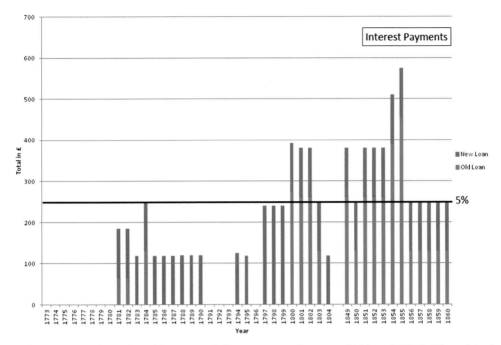

The interest paid on the Old Loan and the New Loan between 1781 and 1860. The original agreement was to pay 5% a year, but the payments had to be deferred to a considerable extent and it was not until the 1850s that 5% was paid regularly on all loans.

The sum of £2,501 now needed was raised over the next couple of years, although John Adey had to write more than once to subscribers asking for the payment of arrears. Some further donations were also received, £20 10s in 1776, £70 in 1778 and £60 in 1779. The new subscribers were offered two sweeteners. In August 1778 it was agreed that 5% would be given to them 'before any Interest shall be paid for the said Money which have been before lent', i.e. prior to subscribers of the old loan. Then in November 1778 it was 'approved of for all Subscribers to pay the whole of their contributions on or before the first day of February next and that the Subscribers to the Second Lending Agreement deduct the interest at the rate of 5% for the first Call of the said Subscribers from the date of the receipt to the 5th of January next', pre-empting their first returns.

At the AGM in August 1779 there was still a shortfall and another £120 was needed, 'whereas certain Subscribers to the second lending List having made default…the Right Honorable Lord Walpole Robert Marsham Esq Robert Marsham Junior Esq George Hunt Holley Esq Mr John Smith Mr Robert Parmeter Thomas Durrant Esq and Mr James Curties have agreed to subscribe the sum of £20 each to supply the deficiency'. This was called the 'loan in aid' and was to be repaid in the same manner as the second lending list or 'new loan'. A list of all the donors and subscribers is given in Appendix 2.

So by 1780 the original £5,000 account was balanced as follows,

Old Loan £3,600 abated to	£2,610
Second or New Loan in 1776	£2,270
Loan in Aid	£120
Total	£5,000

The whole construction up to August 1779 had cost £8,886 4s 5¼d, the excess over the original estimate of £4,006 5s 4½d made up partly from tolls on the lower part of the Navigation, but largely by donations and new subscriptions. The Commissioners started to pay interest on the second lending list and the 'loan in aid' in 1780 and on the first or 'old loan' in 1782.

Although the terms of the loans required a repayment of 5% a year the payments often had to be deferred or reduced, as indicated on the graph, due to the costs of maintenance or reduced tolls. The new loan and loan in aid (NL) continued to be given preference to the old loan (OL). Payment on the old loan lagged behind until 1855, after which it was paid regularly for the previous year until all repayments diminished in the 1890s. The capital was repaid on the new loan by 1800 and on the old loan by 1817. The Commissioners began to default on the interest payments in 1893 and they ceased altogether in 1897.

3. Mills and Locks

The location of watermills was critical in determining the course of the Navigation. There are five watermills along the Navigation above Coltishall; Horstead, Buxton, Oxnead, Burgh and Aylsham itself. All of these mills are on sites which probably date back to the medieval period, although the built structures that are now visible date to the eighteenth and nineteenth centuries. The history, architecture and millers of each mill are discussed in detail in later chapters, and this section will introduce some important themes and technical developments of the eighteenth and nineteenth centuries.

Until the very late eighteenth century water was the most important source of power, and was used to drive mills for a variety of purposes, principally the grinding and processing of grain, but also for the production of paper, textiles and in the iron industry.[1] All of the mills along the course of the Navigation were corn mills, with the exception of Oxnead which also functioned as a paper and textile mill during its history. There are two key factors which are critical for understanding the history of watermills. The first is the type of water wheel used in the mill, and the second their position on the river and any associated changes made in the watercourse.

Waterwheels

The mill machinery was powered by the movement of water onto and through the wheel. The efficiency of the mill was determined by the direction, volume and consistent flow of the water when it entered the wheel. The simplest and most widely used type was the undershot wheel. The water hit the paddles or blades at the bottom of the wheel in the same direction as the flow of water. Undershot wheels were simple, cheap to install and were suitable for use on any watercourse with a consistent flow of water. They were not, however, very efficient. In the 1750s the civil engineer John Smeaton conducted a range of experiments on model waterwheels, and calculated the efficiency of the average undershot wheel at just 22%.[2] In the 1820s a French engineer, J.V. Poncelet refined the design of the undershot wheel by introducing curved blades or paddles which reduced the amount of water that bounced back off when it hit the blades of the wheel. Poncelet claimed that this improved the efficiency of the undershot wheel to 65%.[3] Undershot wheels require a fairly long leat to build up the speed of the water. They are sometimes found in conjunction with complicated series of leats and sluices to control and improve the flow of water and therefore the efficiency of the wheel.

---

1   Cossons, N. (1975) *The BP Book of Industrial Archaeology*, p.67.

2   Wenham, P. (1989) *Watermills*, p.36 and Cossons, N. (1975) *The BP Book of Industrial Archaeology*, p.70.

3   Cossons, N. (1975) *The BP Book of Industrial Archaeology*, p.70.

The overshot wheel was more efficient and utilised buckets rather than blades or paddles. The water fell into the buckets at the top of the wheel and the weight of the falling water turned the wheel. Critically, overshot wheels turn the opposite direction to undershot wheels.[4] In 1759 Smeaton concluded that 'the effect therefore of overshot wheels, under the same circumstances of quantity and fall [of water], is at a medium double to that of the undershot'.[5] Overshot wheels require a small but steady supply of water and are typically found in conjunction with millponds where the water is dammed from a number of watercourses.[6]

The final main type of waterwheel was the breastshot wheel, which was also constructed with buckets rather than paddles. The water entered the wheel just above the axle in a 'high' breastshot wheel and below the axle in a 'low' breastshot wheel. This made the wheel turn in the same direction as an undershot wheel and the opposite direction to an overshot wheel. Breastshot wheels were generally associated with a good, well controlled supply of water and a long leat (an artificial or modified channel which supplied the mill with water).[7]

Most waterwheels were built of wood, although by the eighteenth century some were being constructed from cast iron.[8] Most of those along the Navigation appear to have been hybrid wheels, constructed out of both wood and cast iron.

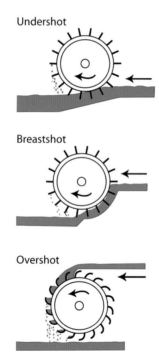

Undershot

Breastshot

Overshot

Different types of waterwheel in use during the eighteenth and nineteenth centuries.

---

4   Wenham, P. (1989) *Watermills*, p.36.

5   Smeaton, J. (1814) *The Miscellaneous Papers of John Smeaton, Civil Engineer*, p.49.

6   Vince, J. (1970) *Discovering Watermills*.

7   Wenham, P. (1989) *Watermills*, p.37.

8   Vince, J. (1970) *Discovering Watermills*, p.6.

Location of Mills

The basic requirements for a watermill were a head of water to drive the wheel and a watercourse with a consistent and controllable flow. On small or inconsistent watercourses the water would have to be dammed and collected in a large millpond in order to build up enough power to turn the wheel.[9] This was not the case on the River Bure, which did provide a constant flow of water. Rivers in East Anglia, however, are generally not very fast flowing, compared to those in the north or the west of the country, and so generated a reliable, but relatively low head of water. This meant that the cheapest and easiest type of mill to build would be one with an undershot wheel and a short leat taking the water to the wheel. This is the pattern of all the mills on the Navigation, with the exception of Buxton. Aylsham, Burgh, Oxnead and Horstead all had undershot wheels and were built across the course of the river itself, with the wheels housed internally within the mill building.

The exception to this is Buxton Mill, rebuilt by William Pepper in 1754. This is also built across the course of the River Bure, but unlike the other mills Buxton was powered by a breastshot wheel and an overshot wheel working in partnership. Overshot wheels were quite unusual in Norfolk and only a handful of others have been recorded. Both breastshot and overshot wheels needed a much greater head of water than an undershot wheel, and longer leats were usually constructed to create enough flow to turn these more efficient wheels.[10] Buxton Mill is the only mill on this section of the Bure to be associated with a long, artificial leat which predated the construction of the Navigation by about thirty years.

All the mills on the Navigation were rebuilt in the late eighteenth and nineteenth centuries, but their location across the channel of the river meant that they blocked the course of the river for any potential water traffic, so during the planning and the construction of the Navigation new cuts had to be made to bypass all the mills. This means that some of the most complex stretches of the Navigation are found in the immediate vicinity of the mills, which will be considered in more detail in the chapters to follow.

Locks

Five locks were constructed along the course of the Navigation, all of which, with the exception of Aylsham Lock, were located close to the watermills. Although the course of the Navigation did not include dramatic changes in topography, the landscape of the Bure valley is gently rolling, which necessitated the use of locks. Biedermann, in his survey of October 1772, had calculated that there was a fall of 35 feet from Ingworth to Coltishall. He recommended a series of seven locks, each measuring 54 feet in length and up to 12 feet wide, with a rise of 5 feet at Horstead and Buxton, 5 feet 6 inches at Oxnead, Burgh and Burgh Hall, 5 feet at Aylsham Lock and 3 feet 6 inches at Ingworth. Almost immediately the Commissioners decided to economise and the proposed lock at Ingworth was never built.[11]

---

9   Cossons, N. (1975) *The BP Book of Industrial Archaeology*, p.77.
10 Ibid.
11 ATCA, Commissioners' Minutes, October 1772.

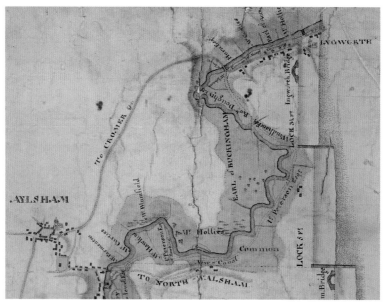

*Biedermann's map of 1772 shows the scrapped section of the Navigation,
showing the proposed lock near Ingworth which was never built.*

In November 1774, once construction had started, the plans were again modified. The lock near
Burgh Hall was moved further upstream towards Aylsham, and the proposed lock near Burgh
Bridge was scrapped.[12] Confusingly, Aylsham Lock was often also referred to as Burgh Hall Lock
and the perception that two locks had been built was perpetuated on Faden's map of 1797,
which shows two locks near Burgh. The local craftsmen had no experience of lock building.
In March 1774 it was ordered 'that a proper person be sent over into Suffolk or elsewhere to
inspect & Measure a Lock take an Account of the Scantling [the size of timber] & enquire the
real Value'. James Tomison, an Aylsham carpenter, was duly despatched to Suffolk and paid £5 5s
in June 'for his journey into Suffolk & settling a Model for the Locks'.[13]

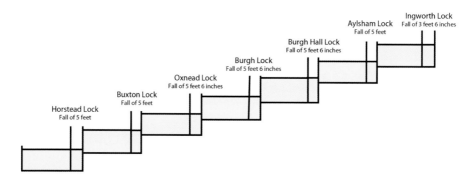

*The falls between each lock taken from Biedermann's survey of 1772. The locks at Ingworth and
Burgh Hall were never built.*

---

12 Ibid., November 1774.

13 Ibid., March 1774.

4. Coltishall to Hautbois

Horstead Mill as it might have been, depicted by Peter Dunham.

In 1770 river trade from Yarmouth terminated at Horstead Mill. In earlier times small cargo vessels had traded further and in the Roman period to the small town at Brampton. In 1685 an account of the manor of Mayton noted that 'the Manor house stands upon the river that runs to Yarmouth which is navigable within a mile of the said house, bearing vessels of great burthen which bring up coal & divers other commodities from the said Town & carry down it corn, Timber, billet and what else the Country affords at very cheap rates to the great benefit of the Country especially of such places as are near it. It is thought that in time the river may be made navigable to the said Manor house which will be a huge advantage to the estate'.[1]

Horstead, south of the Bure, Coltishall, on the slope to the north, and Hautbois, west of the bridge that joins the other two parishes, were flourishing centres of trade in the 1770s. The light chalky soils on the slopes away from the river provided good yields of wheat and barley, though Dr Charles Grape, the rector of Horstead, writing in 1789, remarks that 'the land of Horstead is very hungry and will eat a deal of Muck'.[2] Turnips

---

1   Millican, P. (1937) *A History of Horstead and Stanninghall Norfolk*, p.6.

2   Ibid., p.146.

grew well to the benefit of folding sheep. On the more clayey soils towards the river oats were grown and the meadows used for hay and pasture.

Horstead Mill was the last mill on the Bure before Yarmouth. John Colls, at 23, had taken the lease of the mill from King's College, Cambridge in 1767 and was also a farmer and merchant. Henry Palmer Watts owned Horstead House and the large estate running down to the mill. He probably erected the house on Hall Field to the south east and let this with the surrounding lands to John Colls. This was said by Dr Grape to be some of the best land in the parish. A son, John Langley Watts, was a Norwich merchant, alderman and Mayor of Norwich in 1774 and another son went into partnership with John Colls in the next decade. Upstream was Horstead Hall, the residence of Thomas John Batchelor, now about 33, with another large estate running down to the river. Beyond that, across the parish boundary, was Mayton Hall, purchased by George Anson, the circumnavigator, in 1734 and inherited by his brother Thomas Anson, who, as we have seen, seems to have inspired the Navigation.

By the 1770s the production of malted barley was a major local industry, well documented in the diaries of Mary Hardy.[3] Her husband, William Hardy, now in his early 40s and recently retired from the excise service, was a prosperous Coltishall brewer, maltster, farmer, and owner of a number of properties. He and Mrs Rose Ives, another Coltishall brewer, resident at Coltishall Hall, produced a great variety of beers and ales that were widely carted to towns as far away as North Walsham, Aylsham and Edgefield. However, the specific requirements for individual outlets were not suitable for bulk transport by wherries. She died in 1780 and Chapman Ives, attorney, farmer, maltster and brewer continued the business into the next century. William Palgrave, who died in 1780 at the age of 62, lived at Coltishall Manor and was a maltster, coal and corn merchant, with his own staithe. He was in partnership with his brother Thomas, who died in 1775 and whose son, William, was in the same trade and mayor of Yarmouth in 1782–1783.[4] William Palgrave and his eponymous nephew were both Commissioners of the Navigation. This was one of several merchant families with businesses in Coltishall and residences or family connections in Norwich and Yarmouth.

The considerable trade in agricultural products included the extensive working of marl pits and numerous lime kilns. Maps of the estates of Mayton and Horstead Hall from the seventeenth and eighteenth centuries show numerous cuts into the chalk ridge. The main workings were a little downstream towards Belaugh, served by a complex of channels linked to the river. The residual workings of these pits later became known as Little Switzerland. Marl and other fertilisers became a valuable cargo for the Navigation and were exempt from toll charges. There was a fulling mill for thickening woollen cloth in Horstead, but by the 1770s this was probably in decline and certainly by 1809 it was said to be very ancient and dilapidated. Boat building was stimulated by

---

3   Margaret Bird, pers. comm. Extracts from Bird, M. (forthcoming) *The Diary of Mary Hardy 1773–1809. I. Public house and waterway.*

4   Margaret Bird, pers. comm.

the special requirement of small wherries for the planned new Navigation and Wright's boatyard in Coltishall may be envisaged as a significant beneficiary.

The Canal and Lock at Horstead

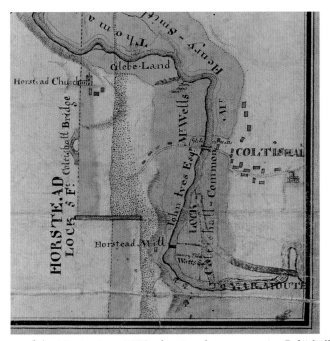

Biedermann's map of the Navigation, 1772, showing the new cuts in Coltishall and Hautbois.

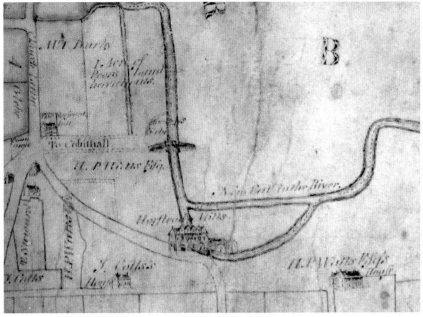

Dr Grape's map of Horstead drawn in 1788, reproduced with permission of the late Tony Jubb. Horstead Mill is clearly shown astride the river, with the straight new cut to the north.

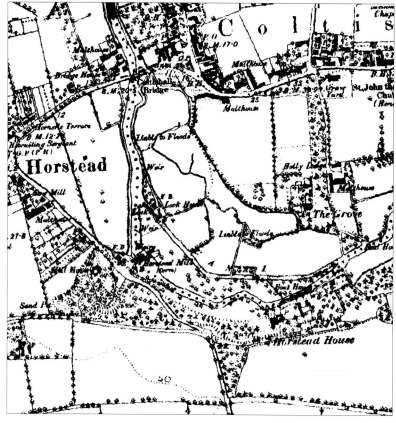

Horstead and Coltishall on the Ordnance Survey six-inch map, 1880s.

Construction was started at Horstead so that the new lock could be used to bring up materials for work further upstream. Biedermann's map of 1772 shows two canals from the proposed lock to the river beyond, one straight down through Mr Watts' meadow and a longer one eastwards through Mrs Smith's meadow. This version of the map was used as a contract to employ John Smith, the engineer, to finish the work in 1776 and bears his signature with those of several Commissioners. It is possible that the longer canal was added to the map at this later date. At the initial meeting of the Commissioners in December 1772, Henry Smith, agent for Henry Palmer Watts, asked for the lock to be moved closer to the mill so that the bypass did not cross as much of Watts' meadow. In August 1774 landowners were warned of 'the immediate damage they will sustain on account of the land that will be covered by the soil thrown out of the canals' during the digging of the cut.[5] At the end of August it was 'ordered that the Lock near Horstead Mill be put down as soon as possible and that the Communication for the Water be immediately opened between Coltishall Common and the River below Horstead Mill along a Ditch which parts Mr Watts' property from the property of Kings College'.[6] Henry Palmer Watts made a further protest; he now wanted the canal from the dam at Horstead Mill, originally planned to empty into the river below the mill, to be extended

5   ATCA, Commissioners' Minutes, August 1774.
6   Ibid.

40

across Coltishall Common and through the property of Mrs Smith to the river lower down. The Commissioners agreed to do this, subject to Mrs Smith's approval, on the understanding that Palmer Watts would pay one hundred guineas towards the cost. Unsurprisingly Palmer Watts wriggled out of this, and the claim was reduced to £50 in September. By January 1775 the Clerk wrote in response to a letter from his son, John Langley Watts, that it was 'wholly repugnant... that the Commissioners have determined to enforce the said agreement and demand the fifty pounds agreed to be paid'.[7] There is no evidence that the money was ever received and in fact John Langley Watts had died in November 1774.

The carpenter James Frost from Norwich won the contract to build the lock at Horstead (Coltishall and Horstead were interchangeable names but what was later called Coltishall Lock was generally referred to as Horstead during the eighteenth century). An interim payment of £130 out of a total bill of £260 was paid to Frost in October 1774, presumably for materials. In November an inspection by the Coltishall merchants John Neve [or Neave] senior and John Neve junior was ordered to make sure it was made from 'good sound Heart of Oak and free from Sap'.[8] Other timber had been purchased in Yarmouth from William Hurry, who was paid for Riga Fir timber for the construction of the lock and bridge in Horstead and Coltishall. John Colls, the Horstead miller, had to be compensated for the loss of water during the period when the lock was being built.

The diary of Mary Hardy, the wife of the Coltishall brewer, records that the Hardys, with Mr and Mrs and Miss Smith, went up to the 'New River' to see the lock on 29 November 1774. They brought two bottles of gin and Mrs Ives, another Coltishall brewer, gave the men a barrel of beer for tea. Thomas Neve, the White Horse innkeeper, 'forced them to Drink it abroad' – outside. This was the first day of digging the lock itself. Mr Smith is probably John Smith, the local school master and an acquaintance of the Hardys.[9] The lock was completed in March 1775. Mary Hardy's diary recorded that 'Mr Ansells *Grampus* went through the new Lock to Day, being the first [wherry] that ever went through that Lock'.[10]

---

7   Ibid., January 1775.

8   Ibid., November 1774.

9   The several Smiths mentioned in this section seem to be partly related and partly unrelated according to Margaret Bird, pers. comm. Henry Smith was an attorney in Great Hautbois and estate manager for Henry Palmer Watts. John Smith, the Commissioner, might be the brother of Henry the attorney; this John was in 1772 head of Caius College, Cambridge, and served for some time around then as Vice-Chancellor of Cambridge University. Mrs Margaret Smith (née Atthill) was the widow of Joseph, brother of Henry the attorney and John the Vice Chancellor. She was the owner of the property at the downstream confluence of the old river and the new canal, at what was the head of the Navigation at that time. John Smith, the schoolteacher in Coltishall and visitor to the Hardys died in 1784. John Smith the engineer came from the Midlands. No other information has been found on the contractor George Smith.

10 Grampus is another name for a dolphin.

However, there were problems with the lock almost immediately. The Commissioners ordered that the lock should be shut in the same year it was opened, and in 1776 there is an enigmatic reference to the lock having blown up, making it necessary to build a dam. In the summer of 1777 it was ordered 'that Mr Durrant cause the Horstead Lock to be inspected and if it appears that it can be made passable that he causes the same to be done at his Discretion and that he shall repay himself for the Money he expends thereon out of the first money he receives for Tolls which are to be taken to the extent of the Act'.[11] In December 1777 it was recorded that 'the Gates... have been Broken & suffered great mischief from the Keelmen passing thro' with their vessels in the night Time'.[12] A curfew was imposed from 8pm until 6am until 25 March and from 10pm to 4am from 25 March to 29 September, and the miller John Colls was responsible for locking the gates at night. John Smith, who had replaced Henry Biedermann as the engineer, was paid £160 for the necessary repairs.

Horstead to Hautbois and Mayton Bridge

The waterway from Horstead to Hautbois was an early source of tension between the Commissioners and local landowners. In 1772 Thomas Batchelor, of Horstead Hall, objected to 'the whole navigation'.[13] Dr Charles Grape, the rector of Horstead, noted in his parish register a little later that the new Navigation was 'to the Prejudice of the Trade of Horstead Mill....and to the Great Damage of T.J. Batcheler, Esq's meadows & royalty from Colteshall to Meyton Bridge. The land being frequently flooded & The Fish & Swans Disturbed or Stolen'.

At the first public meeting in December 1772 Thomas Durrant, who was to become Treasurer in August 1773 and a major landowner around Scottow, had suggested it would be more economic to deepen the river between Horstead and Hautbois rather than cut a three-mile canal. The revised route is partly shown on Biedermann's map below, showing the section from Horstead to Hautbois.

Mayton Bridge dates from the sixteenth century, and its brick arches spanned the course of the old river. The bridge was unsuitable for wherries and other large vessels to pass underneath. The Commissioners therefore decided to bypass the bridge with a new canalised section and a new bridge. It is unclear from the minutes and accounts of the Navigation why the old bridge was not demolished and replaced. In July 1774 the new bridge was built by James Frost of Norwich at a cost of just over £80.

By March 1775, when the first wherries went through Horstead Lock, it was possible to start collecting tolls at Buxton. This was entrusted to William Pepper, the miller at Buxton, and £20 was collected before the Horstead Lock had to be closed in September. A further £46 was collected in 1776 before financial problems brought activities to a halt and Pepper defaulted on submission of the toll takings. In August 1777 John Colls was appointed to collect the tolls at Horstead and the lock had been repaired.

---

11 ATCA, Commissioners' Minutes, August 1777.

12 Ibid., December 1777.

13 Ibid., February 1772.

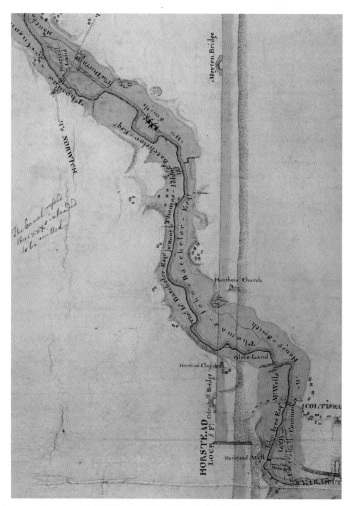

Biedermann's map of 1772 showing the Coltishall to Mayton Bridge section.

A year later a meeting was arranged for 14 September 1778 at Horstead. It was to 'fix a Navigation Mark at the said Miller [sic] and Examine the said Navigation from the lower End of the farther Canal at Horstead below Horstead Lock into Buxton Mill Damm & to make their Report at the next Meeting whether or no the same is Navigable for Boats, Barges and other Vessels of Sixteen Tons burthen drawing Three Feet & half Water'.[14]

In November it was ordered that the 'full tolls granted by the Act be paid by all Vessels Navigated beyond Meyton Brook and that the same be made known to the Collector'.[15] It was also ordered that 'Water Marks be fixed upon the posts of the Upper Gates of Horstead Lock and that the Highwater mark be cut Thirteen Inches lower than the upper side of the Top bar of the upper Gate & the low Water mark Six Inches lower as agreed upon by the Commissioners and Mr John Colls'.[16] By the time the Navigation was officially opened in August 1779 the collection of tolls was regulated, £69 collected in 1779 and £187 in 1780.

---

14 Ibid., September 1778.

15 Ibid., November 1778.

16 Ibid.

The Staithe at Mayton Bridge

The construction of the new bridge was followed by a staithe in 1780, when it was ordered that 'a Gate to be placed at the Entrance into the new staithe at Meyton Bridge and the same be kept locked [at night] for the better collecting of the Money'.[17] John Bell of Little Hautbois was appointed staithe-keeper and paid 5% of the tolls. A new by-law required 'that every Boatman on the payment of one shilling may discharge Freight or Loading upon this new Staithe', with a penalty of a penny an hour for staying more than one day.[18]

At the same time James North was asked to make a 'Survey & Plan of a way on the South side of the Canal leading from the said Navigation Bridge at Meyton to a Meadow of the Corporation of Norwich divided by the Canal'.[19] This related to a dispute in 1779 involving Thomas Durrant, the Treasurer, and the Corporation of Norwich over a small piece of land next to the new Mayton Bridge. This land formed part of a farm that had been left to the Corporation in 1694 by Reverend Warnes, the money from which was to be distributed among the poor in Norwich. In order to create the new cut and bridge, bypassing the old Mayton Bridge, it was necessary for the Navigation to carve through the meadow belonging to the Corporation. In 1774 the Corporation conveyed two roods and fourteen perches to the Commissioners of the Navigation in order for the new cut 'then staked out' to be excavated, but under the strict provision that the land was only to be used for the completion of the Navigation and for no other purpose.[20]

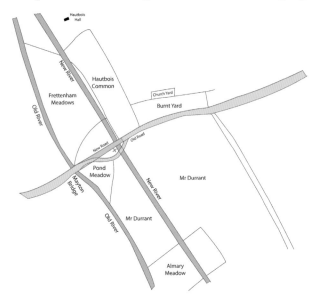

A sketch map of the disputed site of the granary/staithe marked with a red cross. The old road is shown in orange and the new road across the new cut in green.[21]

---

17 Ibid., September 1780.
18 Ibid.
19 Ibid.
20 NRO MC1604/1/1.
21 Based on NRO MC1604/1, a 1774 sketch map of the area.

A map surveyed by Joseph Rumball in 1773 shows the intended cut, and the line of the new road to be made from the old bridge to the new one over the canal.[22] This arrangement cut off a small portion of the Corporation's meadow, leaving it isolated on the far side of the new road. It was this small piece of land that was to become the subject of the dispute.

The Corporation leased the Warne's Charity land to Thomas Drake, who applied for permission to build a new granary on the meadow next to the new road, which was granted. On the 24th February Thomas Durrant stopped his coach next to the half finished building and started pulling down the walls, arguing that it was built on land purchased by the Navigation. Drake promptly set his men about rebuilding the walls, but on the 1st March Durrant, along with a number of other local men, demolished them once again. Drake rebuilt his granary for a third time, but on the night of the 5th March it was pulled down by a local bricklayer called John Pratt. Pratt confessed to the action, swearing that he had done it under orders from Thomas Durrant.[23]

Drake appealed to his landlords, the Corporation of Norwich, who met with Durrant to try to resolve the issue. Durrant refused to accept any wrongdoing, insisting that the piece of land in question was the property of the Navigation, and that he was acting within the law by taking down a building illegally erected by Drake. The Corporation, and Drake, disagreed, and maintained that at the time that the granary was built the land had still been in the possession of the Corporation. A resolution could not be reached, partly due, it appears, to Durrant's refusal to let independent 'gentlemen' give their opinion, and in November 1779 a warrant was issued for his arrest.[24]

When the case was brought before the Assizes in August 1780 various witnesses gave evidence about the demolition of the granary, but the key witness seems to have been Biedermann himself. Biedermann testified that the land in question had been staked out by him as being for the Navigation, and that he had intended it to be a staithe. He claimed that the stakes had then subsequently been moved after the sale had been made, which had misled the Corporation and Drake into thinking that the land was still in their possession. The Corporation had paid a surveyor to measure the width and depth of the channel to prove that the two roods and fourteen perches purchased by the Navigation were wholly taken up by the new cut. Biedermann argued that the passage of wherries had widened the channel, thus invalidating this measurement, and that the two roods and fourteen perches had included the land in dispute. The case went in the Commissioners' favour and the staithe at Mayton Bridge remained in operation.

The Nineteenth Century and Beyond

Although the Navigation was officially opened in August 1779 and tolls were being collected on a regular basis, the Horstead lock continued to give problems. Throughout the

---

22 NRO N/MC/1/60.
23 NRO MC1604/1/1.
24 NRO MC 1604/2.

1780s it needed recurrent repair assigned to Thomas Harvey, the millwright at Aylsham. In 1788 arched beams had to be put into the structure in order to prevent the side walls from collapsing. An inspection in 1791 reported that it was in 'such decay and bad Condition that it will not answer to repair it other wise than by such repairs as shall be absolutely necessary to keep the same at work and together until a new Lock can be built'.[25]

In anticipation of this Thomas Harvey acquired for the Commissioners 'two Pumps or Screws called Archimedes Screws with their Apparatus for the purpose of raising Water'. They were bought from John Berne Petre of Westwick for £17 17s. In August the Commissioners decided to defray payment of interest to the subscribers to allow for the costs of building the new lock if a Committee found 'it is absolutely necessary'.[26] In September balks of fir timber were bought for making a dam in preparation for building the new lock and Thomas Harvey was paid for various other machine wheels and water wheel planks. Despite the funds allocated and considerable outlay a major rebuild was postponed. The inspection of July 1794 reported that 'the Lock at Horstead in so ruinous a state that it will not answer to repair it and that a new Lock shall be built near where the old one stands to be begun early in the next Spring and finished as soon as possible'.[27] The advantage of building the new lock to one side was that the old one could be used in the interim, except for a relatively short time when the channel was reconnected. Digging the new channel cost £47 17s 11d and £14 15s was paid to Henry Palmer Watts for 39 perches of land. This time 160,000 hard bricks were bought as well as 55 balks containing 1,645 feet of fir timber. Only 2,000 bricks were left over and sold to John Colls for £2 13s in 1796. The work cost nearly £800, was all done under the supervision of Thomas Harvey in 1795 and the bills submitted in December.[28] The local craftsmen seem to have had considerable problems in devising a satisfactory design for these unfamiliar structures, but few further repairs were recorded until the 1880s, when leakages were noted, and the 1890s, when water levels were too high. In 1903 and 1906 the lock doors had to be removed for repair. By this time, the lock was being recorded as 'Coltishall Lock' and pleasure craft were passing through without paying a toll. In May 1909 the Navigation was closed for three weeks as the lock had to be pumped out for necessary repairs, which were closely inspected over the next two years.

Henry Palmer Watts died in 1780 and Horstead Mill itself was rebuilt in 1789 by Henry Palmer Watts junior and John Colls. The partnership was dissolved and the mill advertised for sale in 1797 in the Norfolk Chronicle, where it was described as a 'spacious new built Water Corn Mill... built on an improved plan'.[29] The Colls family continued to run it until the 1830s, Richard inheriting when John Colls died in 1806.[30] White's Directory of 1836 records Cooke & Gambling as corn millers and the Cooke family continued until the 1880s.[31] By 1892 Benjamin Barnard was the miller for East Norfolk Roller

25 ATCA, Commissioners' Minutes, April 1791.

26 Ibid., August 1791.

27 Ibid., July 1794.

28 ATCA, Commissioners' Accounts, December 1794.

29 *North Norfolk Chronicle*, 8th April 1797.

30 Millican, P. (1937) *A History of Horstead and Stanninghall Norfolk.*

31 White, W. (1836) *History, Gazetteer and Dictionary of Norfolk*, London.

Mills until the mill was bought freehold from King's College by Robert John Read in 1910. Apart from a short wartime period of flour-milling between 1915 and 1918, animal feeds alone were produced from the early 1900s, possibly as a result of the loss of water transport after the 1912 flood. Milling continued until the mill was destroyed by a disastrous fire on 23 January 1963 and now just the lower parts of the building remain. However, the complex water system and the lock survive in good condition.

In 1847 there was a review of the administration of the Navigation following the resignation of Samuel Parmeter as Treasurer because of his vested interest in a railway scheme. The Commissioners decided to appoint a Superintendent to act as Clerk of the Works and also supervise the collection of tolls. At the same time the wharf at Yarmouth was closed and Coltishall became the centre of administration. John Mace was appointed in 1848, provided with a cottage at Horstead Lock, paid £30 per annum and 5% of the tolls. He resigned in 1861 and was replaced by his son William in 1862. By 1869 the Commissioners were dissatisfied with his work and he was replaced by Elijah Bircham of Norwich, who served until the flood of 1912. Frederick Stevenson was the last wharfinger, kept on until 1920. A delegated group of Commissioners made an annual inspection of the Navigation, generally in July. They had their own lighter and usually breakfasted at the White Horse in Coltishall and took luncheon on board.

The bridge over the canal at Mayton built in 1774 had a short life span. The builders were carpenters and it is likely that all the early bridges were made of wood, the main structure of 'Sound Oak Body Timber' and filled in with fir, either from the local estates or, as recorded for the lock and bridge at Buxton, brought up from Yarmouth in beams not less than 24 feet long and 12 inches square. It seems likely that the piers on either bank, known as wings, were made of brick, as at Aylsham Bridge, but there is no clear evidence for this in the documentary record. The erection of the bridge was an easy matter, for these bridges were built on dry land before the channel was linked to the old river, but in May 1775, only a year after its construction 'it was ordered that the Surveyor cause a New Land Tie to be fixed at the Meyton Bridge across the road to support the Wings....as the old one is broke by the weight of the earth above'.[32] Further land ties had to be found by William Gill junior for rebuilding the bridge in 1792 at a cost of £92. The blacksmith was paid for 'Bolts Screws Spikes Hooks and other Iron Works used at Burrough Lock Meyton Bridge and Oxnead Lock'.[33] In 1841 the bridge was again considered dangerous and William Thorold advised on work which was undertaken by Robert Mack and J. Johnson for £313, including the cost of diverting the river and the construction of temporary dams. This was a huge expense; the Commissioners had declared balances in hand of around £600 in 1839, falling to £483 in 1840 and then to £278 in 1842. This work seems to have solved the structural problems and no further repairs were needed for over forty years. Nothing visible remains of this bridge and as it was less attractive than the sixteenth-century road bridge nearby no images seem to have survived from the nineteenth century. The increased use of traction engines caused concerns about stresses in 1911 when a notice was placed near the bridge stating that it

---

32 ATCA, Commissioners' Minutes, May 1775.
33 ATCA, Commissioners' Accounts, 1792.

was not advisable to cross the bridge in a traction engine; an extremely heavy and slow moving beast.

Wherries waiting to be loaded at the malt house staithe beside the Rising Sun in Coltishall, c1914. Photograph by Walter Rout, reproduced with permission of Poppyland Publishing.

Olga Sinclair opened her history of Coltishall, *When Wherries Sailed By*, with 'as many as twenty wherries would drop down on a single tide, so the old wherrymen recalled'.[34] There were staithes at the Rising Sun Inn, at the end of Mead Loke and beyond the lock and bridge at the White Horse Inn. Other wherries took coal on to Bream Corner for the lime kilns at Hautbois and served the Navigation up to Aylsham. A huge amount of coal was brought up for the maltings, but large quantities were also used domestically. The turnpike road from Norwich to North Walsham was opened in 1797 and the trade directories of the nineteenth century record a regular service of carriers plying to Norwich three or four times a week. The railway arrived in 1879, the station north of Coltishall on the line from Wroxham to Aylsham. However, up until this point the waterway provided by far the most effective means of bulk transport.

The population of Coltishall expanded by nearly 50% in the first half of the nineteenth century, partly from an increased birthrate, but also from people moving in from the smaller villages. The census records 601 inhabitants for Coltishall in 1801 and 897 by 1841. The 1841 census showed that only about half the people then living in Coltishall had been born there and that those under the age of 15 accounted for a very large proportion of the population.

34 Sinclair, O. (1987) *When Wherries Sailed By*.

Horstead Mill from the air in around 1960. The lock-keeper's cottage constructed on the Navigation in the early nineteenth century, is just visible in the top left. Reproduced with permission of Jonathan Neville.

The malting industry thrived throughout the nineteenth century. It was the cornerstone of the Coltishall economy and by the 1880s employed more than 100 men in some 18 malthouses along the banks of the Bure.[35] Malt was produced mainly from September to May for export to Yarmouth and for local use. Brew houses were often associated with the malthouses and public houses were provided with a wide range of products over a considerable part of north Norfolk. When the estate of Robert Hawes was auctioned in 1841 it included the farm residence, brewery, malthouses, cottages, land and 53 tied inns and public houses in Norfolk.[36] There were no less than nine public houses in Coltishall in the 1880s to serve the hot and thirsty malting gangs and a predominantly labouring community. The marl industry continued through much of the nineteenth century. Marl from pits on the eastern side of the North Walsham Road north of Coltishall was partly used on the fields, but mostly burnt in the village kilns. The Rev. John Girling was appointed rector of Hautbois in 1859 and soon developed a rich seam of marl in a meadow near the rectory. He built three large lime kilns for his own workings and had more brought over from the Coltishall extraction pits. A 100 yard cut was made from the Bure to facilitate loading the wherries and bringing in coal to fire the kilns.

---

35   Bond, R. (1986) *Coltishall – Heyday of a Broadland Village*.

36   NRO MS 7351 7 D.4

View from Coltishall Bridge, looking upstream, with wherry at the premises of R.S. Amies, Corn & Seed Merchant. Courtesy of Norfolk County Council Library and Information Service.

By contrast Horstead remained very much a small separate community with employment mostly on the large estates. Some other employment was provided by the mill, the smithy, the lime kilns and marl trade. The Recruiting Sergeant on the village green was the only public house, established in the sixteenth century and given its present name some time after the Restoration. The population grew only slowly: 503 in 1836, 565 in 1881 and 613 in 1901.

Coltishall has been considered the oldest boat-building centre in the Broads.[37] Some eighty wherries were built in yards along Anchor Street with an average of one new wherry turned out each year from the 1860s to the end of the century. As noted in the chapter on wherries, the Wright family had been boatbuilders in Panxworth and Coltishall since the eighteenth century. Four members of the family were Coltishall boatbuilders or watermen in 1841 and a further three generations were involved here or in Norwich up to 1861. John Allen started his business in 1864 and through four generations dominated the trade until the closure of Clifford Allen's yard in 1974. The last trading wherry to be built in Norfolk, the *Ella*, was launched at Coltishall in 1912, but from the 1880s Allen's yard was busy turning out sailing yachts for leisure use and providing a continuous service in maintenance and repairs.

The population of Coltishall increased a little from the middle of the century up to the 1880s, but by 1901 the figure of 916 was little different to the count of 907 in 1851. The railway, the development of larger, more efficient plants for processing grain and the decline of the marl trade all had an effect on the prosperity of the villages. Villagers had to turn increasingly to tourism and jobs within commuting distance.

37 Bond, R. (1986) *Coltishall – Heyday of a Broadland Village.*

5. Buxton to Oxnead

A watercolour of Buxton Mill by Bruce Rushin.

Between Buxton and Oxnead is one of the most attractive stretches of the River Bure, with the most significant bend in the course of the river near Lammas. This section of the river contains a few artificial cuts and two locks at Oxnead and Buxton Mills. The engineering associated with the Navigation, however, is rendered potentially confusing by an earlier scheme of improvement along the river between Oxnead and Buxton carried out by the miller of Buxton, William Pepper, in the 1750s.

Biedermann shows the location of the new cuts to be made, cutting off awkward bends in the river along the great curve between Buxton and Oxnead. These are all relatively small-scale cuts, and the most complex stretches occur in the immediate vicinity of the two mills, which both had to be bypassed by the course of the Navigation. Biedermann also shows the 'new canal of Mr Peppers Over-Shot Mill' running roughly parallel to the river, although slightly higher up the valley side. The meaning and significance of this 'new canal' will be discussed in depth below.

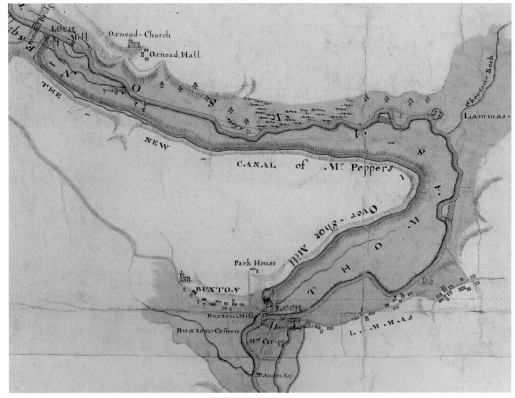

Biedermann's map of 1772, showing the section from Buxton to Oxnead.

Construction: 1774 to 1778

The first work to be carried out on this stretch of the river was the excavation of the new cuts, which were underway in November 1774, supervised by Biedermann. The Commissioners paid George Smith 'for work done at Oxnead Canal & other work at the old River between Buxton and Oxnead and for temporary canals as appears by Surveyors Account'.[1] In February 1775 Biedermann was asked to provide a plan and to estimate the cost of making a new canal along Lammas Common instead of using the old course of the river, but nothing ever seems to have come of this proposal, and the cuts were made along the existing river instead.[2]

In February 1775 Thomas Durrant requested a 'Modell of a Lock & Bridge to be made for the Buxton Mill' and tenders were put out in March. In May the Commissioners agreed with Mr George Borne of Coltishall to provide 'sufficient quantity of sound oak Body Timber for Compleating a Lock & Bridge' at Buxton at a cost of just over £300. It was also agreed with Samuel and William Hurry of Yarmouth to provide fir timber, costing £1,269.[3] Nobody came forward to bid for the tender and by June 1775 Biedermann was told to employ two pairs of sawyers to cut out the oak and deal then lying in a field near Buxton Mill, and to sell off the chips from the sides of the oak timber. The timber from the Hurrys was still at Coltishall and a

---

1 ATCA, Commissioners' Minutes, November 1774.
2 Ibid., February 1775.
3 Ibid.

team of horses was to convey it to the field where the oak timber for Buxton Lock was laid. This suggests that it was still impracticable to bring building materials upstream by water, which had been one of the main reasons for starting construction at Coltishall. In September small sums of about £5 were paid to John Chamber and Guy Murray for sawing the planks and it was ordered 'that no further work shall be done relative to the Navigation until the next Meeting'.[4] In February 1776 £120 was borrowed on the security of the timber bought for Buxton lock, and the credit was used to pay off lots of small outstanding bills.[5]

No further work was carried out until February 1778 when preparations were made for the new season. Tenders were sought for bricks suitable to build the lock at Buxton, for a supplier of lime and for somewhere to deposit the earth that was to be extracted from the new cuts. Oak and deal timber was to be ordered from the timber merchants, Hurry, Borne and Neave in Great Yarmouth and Mr Tomison was to oversee the quality and delivery.[6] The timber at Lammas on the land of John Wright, still unsold in October 1777, was to be restacked 'into as small a space as possible', and new arrangements were made with James Fuller, the present tenant of the land where the building materials were stored. John Ives was commissioned to 'find up the Barrows, Boards & the Utensils belonging to the Commissioners & report their number and condition & places where they are to be found'. They also ordered a notice to be put in the Norwich papers to the effect that 'the Commissioners expect on the 25th instant to complete a contract for finishing the Canal to Aylsham'.[7]

AYLSHAM NAVIGATION.

ANY Perfons having hard burnt Bricks, either Red or White, proper for the Purpofe of Building Locks, are defired to fend in their Propofals before the 20th of this Inftant February, to Mr. John Adey, of Aylfham, for the Delivering of a fufficient Quantity at Buxton Mill, to build a Lock there; and Perfons delivering fuch Propofals, will pleafe to fpecify the Dimenfions of their Bricks. And any Perfons having Brick Earth caft, by them, are alfo defired to fend their Propofals for delivering well burnt Bricks, not later than June next, made of Earth new caft; and the Commiffioners will be ready at the next Meeting, to be held at the Dog in Aylfham, on Wednefday the 25th of this Inftant February, at Eleven o'Clock in the Forenoon, to receive Propofals for cafting a great Quantity of Brick Earth, at any Place between Buxton Mill and Wroxham Bridge, on any Ground not more than a Furlong diftant from the Line of the River. And as the faid Commiffioners expect at the next Meeting to a compleat Contract for finifhing the Navigation to Aylfham, an Order will foon after be made for paying the Whole of the Subfcriptions into the Hands of Roger Kerrifon, Efq. Banker, in the Name of Thomas Durrant, Efq. Treafurer of the faid Navigation.

JOHN ADEY, Clerk.

Aylfham, Feb. 5, 1778.

Advertisement for building materials for the lock at Buxton in the Norfolk Chronicle, February 1778.

4   Ibid., September 1775.
5   Ibid., February 1776.
6   Ibid., February 1778.
7   Ibid., October 1777.

At a meeting in August 1778 the Commissioners proposed to hold a meeting at Horstead Mill that September to 'fix a Navigation Mark at the said Mill and Examine the said Navigation from the lower End of the farther Canal at Horstead below Horstead Lock into Buxton Mill Damm & to make their Report at the next Meeting whether or no the same is Navigable for Boats, Barges and other Vessels of Sixteen Tons burthen drawing Three Feet & half Water'.[8] The mention of the dam at Buxton Mill may indicate that the lock was still under construction, rather than referring to the millpool.

The lock at Oxnead was not completed until November 1778. The mountings for the gates on the downstream side were set at an angle from the upright so that on opening they would swing slightly upwards, probably in an attempt to clear silt which might have accumulated here. This would also mean that the pressure of the water within the lock gates would force the gates downwards, making a better seal and counteracting the lifting effect of the water when the lock was filled.

Maintenance 1793 to 1910

Not long after construction was completed, there were problems with both the locks and the bridges. Flood damage in the winter of 1779 meant that John Smith was required to 'Didle and take out the Great Filth & Rubbage washed into the mouth of the Canal below Oxnead Lock by the drawing up of the Oxnead Mill Floodgates'.[9] There was also maintenance work to be done on the bridges and the inspection of March 1793 revealed that 'thorough repair' was needed for the locks at Oxnead and Buxton and the bridge over Buxton Lock. Bills totalling over £150 were paid for land purchase, masonry, timber, damming and levelling and blacksmith's work at Buxton.[10] It was necessary to make 'coffin dams' (sometimes also called cofferdams) above the lock chambers. A cofferdam was a temporary enclosure which allowed the lock to be drained, allowing the repair work to take place in a dry environment, rather than in the water. In July 1793 arrangements were made with a number of local craftsmen to make the dams above each lock, to provide 'hard Burnt bricks' and mortar, to take down the old walls and clean the old bricks for reuse, for putting in scaffolding, rebuilding the walls, and then back filling and removing the dam wall.[11] The lock at Oxnead also needed new wood and ironwork for the gates, which were to be dressed with pitch and tar. Reclaimed shipwreck timber was used as well as new deal timber. At the end of a long list of payments is 'also a small Bill of £1 7s for 2 Men [for 18 nights] attending Oxnead Dam from Blowing up & for 2 Hogsheads of Terras etc'.[12] By November 1793 bills were being paid for these major investments, but the Treasurer was under pressure to pay the interest on the second Subscription List which had been due in 1791 as soon as he was 'in cash by £700'.[13]

---

8   Ibid., August 1778.
9   Ibid., November 1779.
10 Ibid., March 1793.
11 Ibid., July 1793.
12 Ibid.
13 Ibid., November 1793.

The Commissioners decided that the existing bridge over the Bure at Oxnead would be adequate to serve the Navigation. However, by 1788 they had decided that 'the county bridge at Oxnead is not of a sufficient height for craft belonging to the Navigation to pass under without injury to same'.[14] In the 1880s the bridge was damaged by the passage of traction engines, and the Commissioners debated whether to use ironwork to strengthen the bridge. Oxnead Park Bridge, close to the Hall itself, was also a source of problems for the commissioners. Built by the Anson family, it proved too low for vessels and had to be raised in 1806. The Ansons and the Commissioners agreed to share the costs of its maintenance, but this proved to be an ongoing issue. In 1884 Sir Henry Stracey still owed the Commissioners money for repairs carried out nine years earlier.

After these major repairs in the late eighteenth century, only relatively minor work was carried out in the nineteenth century. At Buxton a lock gate had to be replaced in 1840, and both upper gates were replaced in 1865. The brickwork and piling of the lock at Oxnead needed attention in 1869, 1871 and 1883 but it was not until 1905 that the doors had to be taken off for the lock to be completely dredged. The lock chamber survives in relatively good condition, and is now almost empty of water. Most of the visible brickwork appears to date from the repair work carried out in the late nineteenth century. Low water levels were a problem at Buxton in 1892, and again in 1904, when the wherry *Cyprus* was stranded for a day because of low water below the lock at Buxton. The next year, the Commissioners were blaming the miller at Buxton for water levels that were too high. As at Mayton, traction engines had become a serious problem by 1910 when warning notices were to be placed on both sides of Buxton bridge.

William Pepper and Buxton Mill

Among the better known men who were the original Commissioners of the Navigation was William Pepper, variously described as 'miller', 'mealman' and 'flour merchant' on his memorial in the church of St Edmund, Old Costessey.

Mostyn Armstrong, who published his History of Norfolk in 1781, two years after Pepper's death, was clearly impressed by his achievement.

> At Buxton is a large water-mill, planned and executed by the late ingenious Mr William Pepper: from many curious parts of its construction it well deserves the attention of strangers; part of it is worked by the River Bure pushing under the wheels, and part by a canal brought from Oxnead, which turns an overshot wheel. The building makes a very handsome appearance upon the river and is an ornament to the county.[15]

Armstrong did not find any other mill on the Navigation worthy of comment, or Pepper's other mills at Bawburgh and Costessey, so the mill at Buxton must have been remarkable, with the head of water almost doubled by the combined flow of the river and Pepper's own canal. William Pepper was thus able to install one of only six overshot

---

14 Ibid., September 1788.
15 Armstrong, M. (1781) *The History and Antiquities of Norfolk*, pp.126–7.

wheels identified in Norfolk, which was no easy task in an area with no significant hills, and where a sufficient head of water had to be contrived.

Biedermann's map shows the course of 'the New Canal', which was taken off the river just below Oxnead Bridge (and just upstream from the site of the lock). The canal roughly followed the course of the Bure, but was dug higher up the valley side. It is unclear from the surviving documentary evidence when this canal was constructed, but Pepper rebuilt Buxton Mill and the adjoining millhouse in the latter half of the eighteenth century which may suggest a similar date for the canal.

Pepper was both a subscriber and a Commissioner of the Navigation, and the minutes make it clear that his canal was already in existence in 1773. Thomas Durrant had to be assured by the Commissioners that the Navigation would use the 'old river' rather than 'Mr Pepper's Cut' which implies that there had been a suggestion that the Navigation could be taken along Pepper's canal. In the end, however, the Navigation was taken along the course of the river, perhaps because the possible disruption on Pepper's canal may have lessened the efficiency of the overshot wheel. In 1782 Pepper's nephew and heir, George Watson, advertised the remainder of the Buxton Mill lease after his uncle's death. He claimed that 'the said mills are capable of performing more work than in any in this part of the kingdom'.[16]

As well as being a Commissioner of the Navigation, and a technologically advanced miller, Pepper was also responsible for collecting tolls from wherries that had been able to reach Buxton through the lock at Horstead. He contributed £28 from tolls collected up to March 1776 and at the General Meeting in August 1776 he was ordered to pay £46 3s 3d 'being part of the tolls collected since the last Meeting'. By this time the balance of funds was down to £6 7s 11d. However, in 1777 it was ordered 'that Mr Wm Pepper discontinue the collection of the Tolls of the Navigation and that Mr John Colls of Horstead Mill collect the Tolls at Horstead Lock when the same is reopened until there is an order of the Commissioners to the contrary'. By this time William Pepper no longer attended meetings of the Commissioners and he was persistently pursued for the relatively small sum of £41 7s 3½d he was considered to owe for collecting tolls to the end of his life in 1779.

Pepper's canal terminates near Buxton Mill House in a complex series of ponds which are most clearly shown on the Tithe Map of 1842.[17] This extraordinary group of artificial channels survives in earthwork form underneath a later plantation. The Tithe Apportionment records them as fishponds, but their shape perhaps also suggests an ornamental use, or use for wildfowl shooting. In the 1780s when the lease for the mill was advertised, the extensive gardens and pleasure grounds surrounding the mill house were noted in the Norfolk Chronicle, which made no mention of fishponds. It is unclear how these ponds were connected to the mill. They are not shown on Biedermann's map of 1772, and so may be later, although this map cannot always be relied upon for

---

16 *Norfolk Chronicle*, 21 September 1782.
17 NRO DN/TA 612.

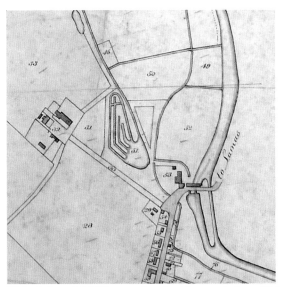

Buxton Mill on the Tithe Map of 1842, reproduced with permission of Norfolk Record Office.

its depiction of features not immediately connected to the Navigation. Biedermann, however, does clearly show that Pepper's canal was connected directly to the mill at Buxton, and given that the main purpose of the map was to give an accurate depiction of watercourses, it seems likely that there was a direct connection. The earliest map which does show the ponds is the 1809 Enclosure map, but this does not show how the ponds were connected to the mill.

Pepper's canal near Oxnead in May 2011.

The watercourses around Buxton Mill were quite complex, and all designed to regulate the flow of water in the channels around the mill. This is most clearly shown on the Ordnance Survey six-inch map, published in the 1880s.

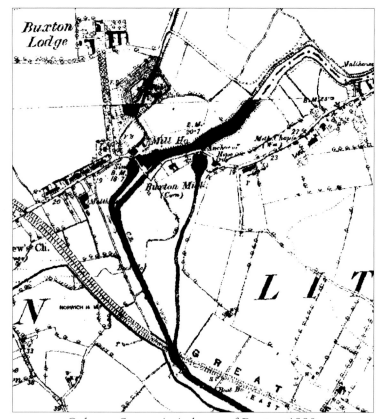

Ordnance Survey six-inch map of Buxton, 1880s.

The mill straddles the natural course of the river, and the lock was placed immediately adjacent to the mill building, with a short, straight cut from the lock to rejoin the main channel of the river a little further to the south. Upstream of the mill, a sluice near the Anchor of Hope public house controlled another artificial channel, shown on the 1880s Ordnance Survey map with a large pool immediately next to the road. Biedermann's map of 1772 shows this as a proposed new cut, although the course in the modern landscape is more sinuous than all the other cuts made on the Navigation. This rejoins the river much further to the south, near the present railway bridge, and was clearly never intended for vessels, but purely for water management.

In the first half of the nineteenth century the mill was run by the Gambling family. In 1841 John Gambling, then aged 50, was recorded on the census as the miller at Buxton. His son, Horace Gambling, had taken over the mill by 1861, where he lived with his growing family, a governess, a cook and two other servants. Horace Gambling moved to Gorleston, near Great Yarmouth, and was recorded there in 1871 as a miller, merchant and shipowner employing 35 men. Little is known about his business in Gorleston, but

The natural course of the River Bure (on the left) and the eighteenth-century bypass cut (on the right) to the south of Buxton Mill (the white building visible in the distance) in September 2011.

he perhaps continued to trade along the Navigation, particularly as other members of the Gambling family were maltsters in Buxton.

Oxnead Mill

The system of cuts and watercourses around Oxnead Mill is complex and closely linked to the history of the mill itself. A new cut bypassed the mill, leaving the course of the river just after Oxnead Bridge and rejoining the course downstream of the mill. Biedermann's map also shows the location of the new lock which was constructed to the south of the Mill. The changes to the river at Oxnead are most clearly shown on the Ordnance Survey six-inch map of the 1880s. The mill stands across the course of the old river, with the straight new cut to the south.

Oxnead was only one of a handful of paper mills operating in Norfolk in the late eighteenth century. Paper was being made in Oxnead by 1716, and manufacture continued throughout the eighteenth century. Early in the century the demand for paper had risen rapidly, as printing presses became established outside London, with Norwich being an early centre. The woollen industry in Norfolk also helped to stimulate the demand for paper and board, both of which were used widely in pressing, finishing and

Ordnance Survey six-inch map, 1880s, showing Oxnead Mill and lock.

wrapping woollen cloth.[18] In 1758 the then master of the mill, John Pollings, retired, and the lease was advertised in the Norwich Mercury,

> Oxnead Mills are now to be let for any Term of Years not exceeding Fifty... being an old established and well accostomed Paperwork, commodiously situated on a constant regular stream. Nine miles from Norwich, five from North Walsham, three from Aylsham, and four from Coltishall, to which last Place, Junk and Materials may be brought up by water from Yarmouth; and Manufactured Goods carried down at the very least expense'[19]

In the years before the Navigation, Coltishall was the nearest navigable settlement but all materials arriving there would still have to be brought the four miles overland to the mill. In 1779 the mill was insured by Joseph and Daniel Armes and William Parkinson, when the mill was still being used for paper making.[20] The Navigation would, naturally, have had a large impact on the transportation of the raw materials used in papermaking, as well as the finished paper itself; all of which could now be loaded onto wherries direct from the mill. No tolls were charged on paper, or on rags, and the lack of documentary evidence for wherry cargoes means that it is difficult to know how much paper was carried along the Navigation in its early years. However, it is extremely unlikely that the papermakers of Oxnead would not have taken advantage of the opportunity on their doorstep.

---

18 Stoker, D. (1976) 'The Early History of Papermaking in Norfolk' in *Norfolk Archaeology*, vol. 36, p.241.

19 *Norwich Mercury*, 9th December 1758.

20 Stoker, D. (1976) 'The Early History of Papermaking in Norfolk', pp.244–5.

In the 1820s the mill was converted from a paper mill to a textile mill, specializing in the manufacture of Duffield blankets. This conversion was carried out by Robert and Page Bleakley, who continued to run the mill until 1850.[21] The Bleakleys were established textile manufacturers, and were first recorded in Norwich in 1802 when an 8 year old boy was killed in their mill after becoming caught in a mill-wheel.[22] White's Directory of 1845 notes that Robert and Page Bleakley employed over 100 hands at the mill, and also had premises in Norwich in St Mary's Alley and Coslany Street.[23] It seems likely that the Bleakleys would have used the Navigation to transport the raw materials needed for the manufacture of blankets, including wool and rags, as well as for transporting the finished product. As with paper, no tolls were charged for the carriage of any textile goods along the Navigation.

In 1850 Oxnead Mill was almost entirely rebuilt and refitted as a corn watermill by the millwright John Buttifant for Sir Edward Stracey, at a cost of over £900.[24] The 1871 census records that the miller was then Charles Browne, aged only 19, who employed two men to run the mill. Browne later acquired North Farm, and lived there with his family, employing various foremen and millers who lived in the Mill House itself.

Lammas

The small hamlet of Lammas lies on the eastern side of the river from Buxton. Despite being one of the smallest settlements along the Navigation, it was not immune from the effects of the venture. In the mid-nineteenth century a large gravel pit was opened in a meadow immediately adjacent to the Navigation, the earthworks of which are still clearly visible.

The Tithe Apportionment records the site of a limekiln close to the river on the land of Charles Barber who is described in White's Directory of 1836 as a farmer and lime burner.[25] The Apportionment also records the existence of a tiny brickyard on a small slip of land very close to Buxton Mill, in the occupation of Robert Mack.[26] Mack is listed in the 1836 edition of White's as a bricklayer and coal merchant, and he lived on Mill Street in Buxton, not far from the brickyard near the mill.[27] Little else is known about this brickyard, and nothing is shown on the 1880s Ordnance Survey map. However, the location right next to the mill and the Navigation must have meant easy loading of bricks; a heavy and bulky commodity to move overland. In the 1880s the Ordnance Survey marked a malthouse on the river in Lammas, which did not appear on the Tithe Map of 1840, and which has since been demolished and replaced with houses.

---

21   *Norfolk Chronicle*, 9 June 1849

22   NRO NCR Case 6a/14

23   White, W. (1845) *White's History, Gazetteer, and Directory of Norfolk*, p.183.

24   Neville, J. (2012) *Oxnead Mill*, http://www.norfolkmills.co.uk/Watermills/oxnead.html. Accessed 1st May 2012.

25   White, W. (1836) *White's History, Gazetteer, and Directory of Norfolk*, p.532.

26   NRO DN/TA 451.

27   White, W. (1836) *White's History, Gazetteer, and Directory of Norfolk*, p.532.

The earthworks of a nineteenth century gravel pit in Lammas, visible at the back of the field, next to the brick building.

Mill Street in Buxton

The mill and river lie at a distance from the village centre, but in the late eighteenth and early nineteenth centuries a number of houses were built on Mill Street, close to the Mill and to the Navigation itself. The 1809 enclosure map shows some of these buildings in existence, and by the time of the Tithe Award in 1842 more had been built.[28] Later in the nineteenth century a malthouse was built to the south of Mill Street, shown on the 1880s Ordnance Survey six-inch map. This cluster of nineteenth century residential and industrial development predates the railway line and can be strongly linked with the trade and employment opportunities offered by the Navigation.

The census data for Mill Street from the nineteenth century reveals that most of the occupants of these houses and cottages were employed in trades connected to the Navigation. Most obviously, some residents were recorded as millers and journeyman millers working in Buxton Mill. Others were carpenters, corn merchants, carriers and maltsters. From the 1860s onwards Samuel Helsdon, variously described as a waterman, boatman and wherryman, lived on Mill Street; by 1901 he was a resident of the workhouse in Aylsham. In 1901 the wherryman George Strike was recorded as living on Mill Street with his uncle William Rivett, also a wherryman. Strike was born in Burgh and was first recorded as a waterman or wherryman on the 1881 census, aged 14, living and working with his uncle on the Navigation. In 1871 Charles Franklin was listed as an apprentice miller at Buxton Mill, aged 17, but by 1881 he had moved on to work at Costessey Mill.

Mill Street is a good example of the economic and physical impact of the Navigation, which here prompted the development of a small additional area of settlement in Buxton, which appears to have been closely linked to the Navigation. This is typical of the impact of canals and navigable waterways across the country, and this trend is also found in Norfolk, albeit on a small scale.[29]

---

28 NRO DN/TA 612.

29 Porteous, J.D. (1977) *Canal Ports: The Urban Achievement of the Canal Age.*

6. Brampton to Burgh next Aylsham

A watercolour of Burgh Mill by Bruce Rushin.

The section of the Bure from Oxnead Bridge to Burgh Bridge is one of the shortest to be considered here, but is also one of the sections which saw the largest new cut constructed in the 1770s.

Construction

Biedermann's map shows the proposed two new cuts along this stretch of the Navigation, designed to cut off complex loops of the natural river in order to create a straighter and more direct route. The first came off the river north of the present Burgh Bridge and continued south until rejoining the river near St Mary's Church. The second cut led from a new lock, positioned near Burgh Mill, to a point further south, thus cutting off the millpool and the subsequent section of the old river. The canal above the mill was cut under Biedermann's direction in the second half of 1774, the back drains commissioned in March 1775 and work on excavating the canal below the mill was done by James Allen in the summer of 1775.[1]

---

1   ATCA, Commissioners' Accounts, 1795.

Several small parcels of land, totalling just over three acres, were purchased in Burgh for the construction of new cuts for the Navigation:

July 1774	Rev. Bartholomew Dye	2 roods 17 perches	£10 18s
July 1773	Edmund Burr	1 rood 30 perches	£12 6s, reduced to £9
July 1774	Robert Marsham for leasee Miles Branthwayte	2 roods 28 perches	£14
July 1773	Rev. Mr Wright, formerly Rev. Mr Villiers	1 acre, 2 roods and 17 perches, altered to 1 acre and 34 perches.	£30

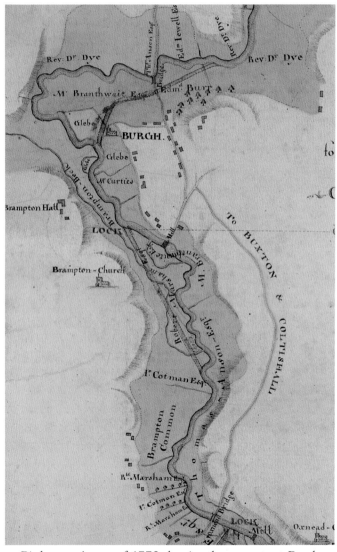

Biedermann's map of 1772 showing the new cuts at Burgh.

One of the tenants of Reverend Dye, John Coman, objected to the Navigation as it would cut off his access to ten acres of meadow that would be left isolated. The Commissioners agreed to provide Coman with a bridge in order to access the meadow. Biedermann accordingly designed a wooden bridge for the conveyance of carts and wagons over the canal in Burgh Hall Meadow, to the north of the road bridge at Burgh. This bridge came to be known as Woolsey Bridge, and is clearly marked on the Ordnance Survey six-inch map of 1886. The tenant, John Coman, was allowed £4 for making the short link road that would need one hundred loads of gravel.[2]

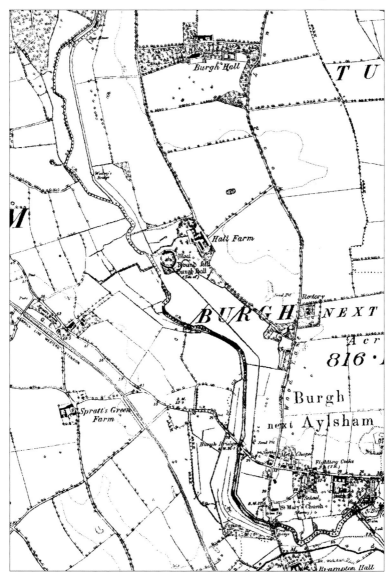

The Ordnance Survey six-inch map of the 1880s, showing Woolsey Bridge to the north of Hall Farm, on the new cut between Burgh and Aylsham.

2   ATCA, Commissioners' Minutes, December 1772 and January 1773.

 The lock near Burgh Mill was the only original lock that was to be built of brick, as stipulated by the Commissioners in November 1773. An undated plan of the lock survives in the archives, and shows the dimensions, cladding and position of the gates.[3] The plan shows that the base of the lock was covered in wood cladding. The present lock is topped with a modern sluice and the gates have been removed. The edges of the lock are capped with modern concrete, but earlier brickwork is visible below this which may be of late eighteenth century date. No major rebuilding or structural repair of the lock walls is recorded after 1783, although the re-hanging of the lock gates in the 1900s may have necessitated some repairs to the brickwork which went unrecorded.

In the summer of 1774 Thomas Harvey, the Aylsham millwright, and William Gill, an Aylsham carpenter, built the new wooden road bridge over the proposed canal at Burgh, quite close to the old river bridge but raised to allow passage of wherries. The pillars (or wings) were built of brick and then the superstructure built in wood. They estimated £81 9s 9d for the work, paid in September, but claimed another £54 6s 2d for extra work in

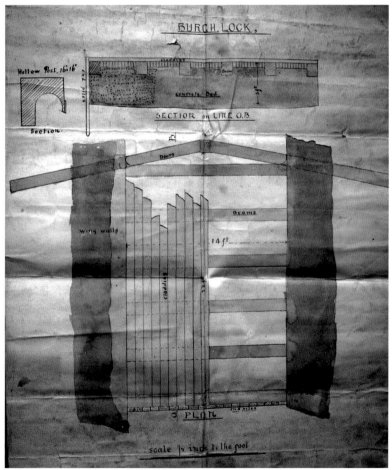

Plan of Burgh Lock, reproduced with permission of Aylsham Town Council.

3   ATCA, undated plan of Burgh lock.

November.[4] The Aylsham workers were able to offer comparable prices to those charged by James Frost of Norwich for the bridge at Mayton. In June 1775 Robert Marsham, who leased Burgh mill and the adjoining meadows to Miles Branthwayte, agreed with the Commissioners that they would provide a 'cart passage' for his tenant through the millpool at Burgh. Marsham also insisted on the construction of a bridge over the river near St Mary's Church – this is the genesis of the Cradle Bridge which now spans the river.[5] This bridge was built in March 1775 and was at first called the 'Church Bridge'. By 1837 it was known as the 'Cradle Bridge' and remained the joint responsibility of the two parishes (Burgh and Brampton) and the Commissioners. By September 1775, however, funds for the construction of the Navigation had run out and all work was stopped, with bills not or only partially paid, until February 1776 when £200 credit was raised by Thomas Durrant on wood stored at Buxton. Thomas Harvey and William Gill then submitted bills for wood and work totalling £43 and this may have been for the work on Woolsey Bridge.

The Enclosure map of 1814 clearly shows Burgh Bridge and the Cradle Bridge in place across the Navigation, as well as the course of the 'old river', which appears as a narrow channel winding through the meadows belonging to Viscount Anson on the south side of the new cut between Burgh Bridge and the Cradle Bridge.[6] This channel still survives on the ground, although now overgrown and with little to distinguish it from the other drainage channels in the nearby meadows.

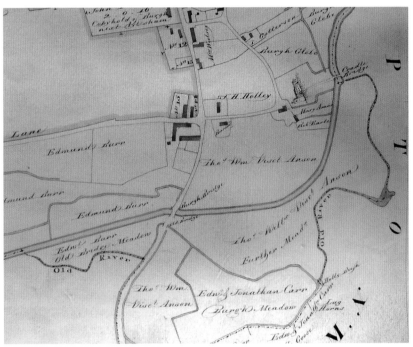

Burgh next Aylsham Enclosure Map, 1814, reproduced with permission of Norfolk Record Office.

---

4 ATCA, Commissioners' Minutes, September and November 1774.
5 Ibid., June 1775.
6 NRO C/Sca/261.

Operation and Maintenance

As on the other sections of the Navigation, repairs and maintenance were ongoing from the late eighteenth century onwards. In February 1783 John Berry, bricklayer, was to be paid £7 19s 6d for 'repairing the Navigation Bridge in Popes Meadow Lengthening the Wing Wall of the said Bridge & repairing Aylsham Lock Burrough Hall [Woolsey] Bridge and Burrough Lock.'[7] The lock gates were removed and rehung in 1804 at a cost of £60, but the lock then needed no major work until the late nineteenth century, perhaps because it had been built of brick rather than wood. Between 1892 and 1903 there were constant problems with the lock gates, culminating in 1903 when the Commissioners decided the Navigation would have to be closed for three weeks whilst the gates and mounting of Burgh Lock were repaired by Mr Watts for £78.[8] The closure of the Navigation appears to be a drastic measure, and the Commissioners had either been unaware of the deterioration or had decided to wait until repairs became absolutely necessary.

Burgh Lock in March 2011, showing the modern bridge and sluice.

---

7   ATCA, Commissioners' Accounts, 1783.

8   ATCA, Commissioners' Minutes, February 1903.

By 1791 the road bridge had fallen into decay, so Harvey and Gill rebuilt it for £81 in the following year. A reference in the minutes in 1860 mentions the new bridge at Burgh, perhaps suggesting another substantial rebuild which necessitated the road being built up to create a gentler slope.[9] In 1865 an iron replacement for the wooden Cradle Bridge had been proposed, but the Commissioners and the parish authorities could not agree on the expense. The wooden bridge was repaired in the 1880s when the woodwork of the main beam was found to be decayed and needed replacing.[10] Photographs from the mid-twentieth century show the Cradle Bridge standing some 12 feet above the water, held up by timber 'A' frames , each side resting on four concrete piles in the river, but this has now been replaced by a modern footbridge.

The Cradle Bridge, photographed by William C. Nobbs c1946.
Reproduced with permission of Geoffrey Nobbs.

In December 1808 the Commissioners were obliged to remind the inhabitants of Brampton that they should keep the banks of the Navigation clear along Brampton Common, where weeds and sedge had grown up. In the end, the commoners agreed to pay the Commissioners an annual sum of 10 shillings to keep the banks clear of weeds.[11] Vessels passing along the Navigation caused damage to the banks in Brampton and Burgh, which had to be repaired and consolidated in 1816.[12]

---

9 Ibid., August 1860.
10 Ibid., August 1883 and August 1885.
11 Ibid., December 1806.
12 Ibid., August 1816.

Next to the road bridge in Burgh was a small staithe where wherries could load and unload goods. The land belonged to the Burr family, who may have created the staithe in the middle of the nineteenth century. No staithe, or buildings, are shown on the Enclosure map (1814) or the Tithe map (1839), but are clearly shown on the Ordnance Survey maps from the 1880s onwards. An undated photograph shows a wherry being loaded or unloaded at this staithe, with a rectangular building in the background which was probably used for storing goods. There are no references to this staithe in the Commissioners' minutes, so little is known of its history.

An undated photograph showing a wherry at the staithe near Burgh Bridge. Private Collection.

Burgh Mill

The present mill dates to the late-eighteenth century, and although no longer working, retains much of the machinery put in place since the opening of the Navigation. In 1783 the mill, then leased by John Miller, was put up for sale; its position 'upon the New Navigation from Aylsham to Yarmouth' one of the key selling points.[13] When sold again in 1828, the mill's location was again an important factor,

> The Mill is situated on a fine Stream of Water, which is navigable to Yarmouth, and by means of which a large business, may be carried on without keeping any horses, and the Machinery of the Mill is entirely new.[14]

---

13 *Norfolk Chronicle*, 19th April 1783.
14 *Norfolk Chronicle*, 1828.

The suggestion here that the miller could run a profitable business based on trade along the Navigation alone is an interesting one, and although probably an exaggeration made by the solicitors selling the mill, is a reminder of how vital the Navigation was considered to be by the millers and tradesmen living north of Coltishall.

The mill is now slightly offset from the course of the Navigation due to the new cut created to the south-west and excavated in 1775, bypassing the mill and the sinuous course of the old river. This cut was necessary to allow access for river traffic past the mill, and created a shorter route between Brampton and Burgh.

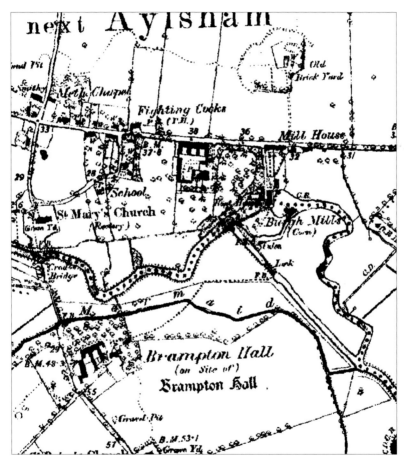

Burgh Mill on the Ordnance Survey six-inch map, 1890s.

During the nineteenth century Burgh Mill was owned by the Browne family, who employed several men from the village, some of whom worked at the Mill for several years. James Faulkes is recorded as a journeyman miller in 1851 aged 27. In 1861 his son, James William Faulkes, joined the mill as an apprentice. Faulkes remained at the mill throughout the 1860s and 1870s, but was recorded on the 1881 census as a 'gate keeper' on the East Norfolk railway.

Year	Name	Occupation
1851	William Browne	Miller employing 5 labourers
	John Spratt	Journeyman Miller
	Henry Spratt	Journeyman Miller
	James Faulkes	Journeyman Miller
	George Edwards	Miller's Carter
	Robert Postle	Retired Miller
1861	William Browne	Miller employing 2 men and 2 boys.
	John Taylor	Journeyman Miller
	James Faulkes	Journeyman Miller
	William Delph	Journeyman Miller
	James William Faulkes	Miller's Apprentice
	Thomas Jeremiah	Miller's Labourer
1871	William Browne	Miller
	James Faulkes	Miller
	James Key	Journeyman Miller
	George Kendall	Apprentice Miller
	John Taylor	Miller's Labourer
	William Bloyce	Miller's Carter and Primitive Methodist Preacher
1881	William Browne	Master Miller
	James Key	Journeyman Miller
	George Hinsley	Journeyman Miller
1891	George Hinsley	Miller
1901	James Thomas Brett	Miller's Labourer
	William John Brett	Miller's Labourer
	George Butterfield	Miller's Carter

Census information for Burgh relating to the Mill.

Burgh was a parish that was dominated by arable farming, and most men living in the parish during the nineteenth century were recorded on the census as 'agricultural labourer'. The majority of the land was concentrated into three large farms, which in the 1840s belonged to James Hunt Holley, Mary Burr and Stephen Barber.[15] Burgh Mill was well placed to serve the farmers in Burgh, as well as the surrounding parishes of Brampton and Oxnead (particularly as Oxnead Mill was a paper and textile mill, rather than a corn mill).

Brickmaking

Across the river from Brampton Common is the site of a brick yard, kiln and marl pit close to Lime Kiln Farm. The earliest map to show the brick yard is Faden's map of 1797 and the site is clearly shown on the Tithe map of 1839.[16] It is possible that, given the advantageous site next to the Navigation which would allow the easy loading and unloading of goods and materials, that the brick yard was established in the early years of the Navigation. The site was owned by Sir Thomas Anson, and it seems likely, therefore, that the brick yard may have been placed here with a clear view to the possibilities of trade. By the 1830s the site was owned by Sir Edward Stracey but occupied by Robert Bleakley, the textile manufacturer who also leased Oxnead Mill. The brick yard and kiln were still in operation in the 1880s, but by 1902 the Ordnance Survey marked the site as 'Old Kiln'. The location right on the course of the Navigation would have been an advantageous one for the owner, with the ability to load and unload goods and materials right next to the works.

The 1880s Ordnance Survey six-inch map shows an 'old brick yard' to the north of Burgh Mill, suggesting that it had perhaps been in use for some time. The Tithe Map, however, made in 1839, shows the sites as arable fields, one of which contained a marl pit.[17] It is this marl pit which was later enlarged and converted into a brickyard. No brickmakers were living in the parish on the 1851 census, but in 1861 John and Samuel Bulley were recorded as 'brick and tile makers', suggesting that the brickworks began operating at some point during the 1850s. Brick and tile makers continued to be noted in the census returns for Burgh until 1901, but the brickworks did not survive into the later twentieth century. The site of the brickworks is now visible in the field to the north of Mill Street, marked by a roughly circular line of trees which define the edge of the extraction pit.

Boathouse

In the 1880s the Ordnance Survey six-inch map shows a boathouse on a small island in the bend of the river near the mill. No building is shown on the Tithe surveys for Brampton or Oxnead, and it is unclear when the boathouse was

---

15 NRO DN/TA 223.
16 NRO DN/TA 284.
17 NRO DN/TA 223.

constructed. There is certainly now no trace of such a building on the site of the island (although the Ordnance Survey marked its location until the 1950s) and the bend in the river has also silted up.

7. Aylsham

Aylsham Basin, with the wherry Zulu, as it may have appeared in the nineteenth century, by Karen Rowlands. Reproduced with permission of Alan Rowlands.

1770–1790: Establishment

Aylsham is the most significant settlement in the story of the Navigation. The sponsors were largely from the Aylsham area, the Commissioners conducted their business here, it was the destination for many of the wherries using the Navigation, it was situated in a very fertile agricultural area, and indeed the town gave its name to the Navigation. In the 1770s most of the properties were huddled around the church on the rising ground south of the River Bure. The population in 1706 has been estimated at around 1,000 rising to 2,300 in 1831.[1] There were scattered buildings around the watermill in Millgate and only a few isolated dwellings north of the river, more evidently along Drabblegate than Dunkirk as shown on Biedermann's survey map. The properties, apart from the watermill, were all leasehold from one of the several manors, the Manor of Aylsham Lancaster south of the river and the much smaller Manor of Aylsham Wood to the north.

---

1   Mollard, T. (1990) 'Aylsham in 1706' in *Aylsham Local History Society Journal*, vol. 2, pp.326–332. The Bishop's returns for 1706 list 570 communicants and dissenters over 16, estimated as 60% of the population; Eve (1995), *The poor in Aylsham 1700–1836* estimates at 1,300 and gives 2,334 for 1831. Most of this section is based on Mollard & Gale (1993), Millgate, and the Minutes and Accounts of the Aylsham Navigation.

The watermill dates back to Domesday and was acquired by Robert Parmeter in 1771 following the death of Thomas Spurrell in 1770.[2] When Thomas Spurrell inherited it from his father in 1743 he was already a farmer, miller and maltster and seems to have kept the business well. When Robert Parmeter first appears as a ratepayer in 1763 he is listed as a leaseholder of the mill, indicating that Thomas Spurrell, now 53, was already handing over the management.[3] Parmeter was about thirty six and his first child was born in 1764, suggesting that he came to Aylsham as a newly married entrepreneur. He seems to have come from a family in Norwich and Sloley, but a record of his baptism has not been found. In 1768 he is probably responsible for building Bure House, the fine three-storey house in the angle of Millgate and Mill Row on land purchased from John Woolsey. This is usually posed with a query as the house bears on its south gable-end an inscription of T.R., but this is in all probability a builder's mark. The house is notable for 15 windows to the rear facing the mill, ten of them blank, no doubt to be opened once the window tax was withdrawn. He acquired the two former licensed 'Malting Offices' and built the new Maltings in 1771. Also from the estate of Thomas Spurrell he acquired the pair of fine houses at the bridge which he converted to the Anchor Inn in 1781, once the Navigation promised a trade. These were built in around 1700 with a gable in Flemish style that would impress visitors on the King's Highway from the north. Behind was Pond Meadow which he acquired in 1772 with its extensive fish-ponds and perhaps even then a smoke-house. This came from the Francis family into which his son Robert would later marry and in 1773 he acquired further pieces of land from them.

Mary Hammond, housekeeper, and Thomas Harvey, millwright, were Thomas Spurrell's executors and acquired property from his estate. Thomas Harvey took up residence in the Mill House and also bought the property a little south of Mill Row on the east side, where he eventually retired. The Belt, just behind the mill, was built in 1741.[4] It was occupied by the Wickes family, formerly tanners in Blickling. A new workhouse was built at the top end of Millgate just west of the fork now known as New Road in 1776. The annual expenditure on the poor had risen from £160 in 1700 to £600 in 1770, aggravated by the Seven Years War 1756–1763, that curtailed continental trade, and adversely affecting the textile trade in particular.[5] There were a few houses with gardens along Millgate, including that of John Power, the barber-surgeon/farmer, and small cottages clustered by the bridge and along Mill Row. The White Horse, near the workhouse, provided a beer house.[6] From the Millgate papers it is evident that in the early to mid-eighteenth century tradesmen and yeomen were busily acquiring diverse pieces of land and property as they became available for lease. They were beginning to exert an influence on economic and social life despite the pre-eminence of local aristocrats, solicitors and clerics. With the coming of the nineteenth century the

---

2 Rye, W. (1885) *A History of Norfolk.*

3 ATCA, Aylsham Poor Rate Books.

4 Norfolk Historic Environment Record, NHER 45977.

5 Eve, J. (1995) *The Poor in Aylsham 1700–1836.*

6 Gale, E. (2001) *Aylsham Inns and Public Houses, a History.*

Bure House, 1768, and The Maltings, 1771, in Millgate, built by Robert Parmeter.

documents seem to indicate a change with a tendency for land to be concentrated in the hands of the fewer, relatively wealthy families.

Henry Biedermann's survey was completed in October 1772. A major decision taken at the public meeting in November was to terminate the Navigation at Aylsham. His map depicts the Navigation as originally proposed, continuing to Ingworth with considerable excavation to bypass the turns of the river above Aylsham Bridge. We have no evidence of the prior discussions. Robert Parmeter, now well-established in town, might well have had some influence with John Adey, the administrator, Lord Walpole, Robert Marsham, father and son, who together seem to have had the main role in formulating the proposal for Parliament early in the next year. Biedermann's drawing of a 'bubble' for a basin at Aylsham was soon to become a lot more refined, as shown on the following maps.

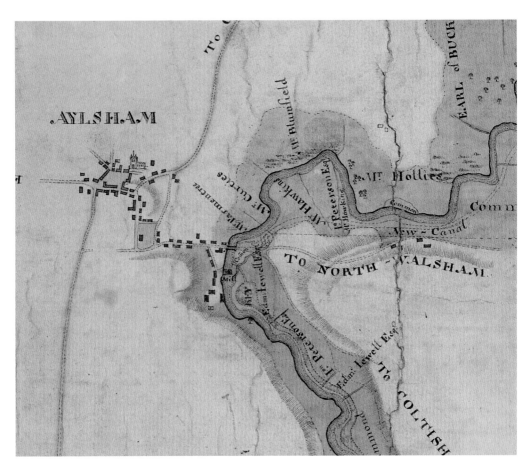

Aylsham on Biedermann's map of 1772.

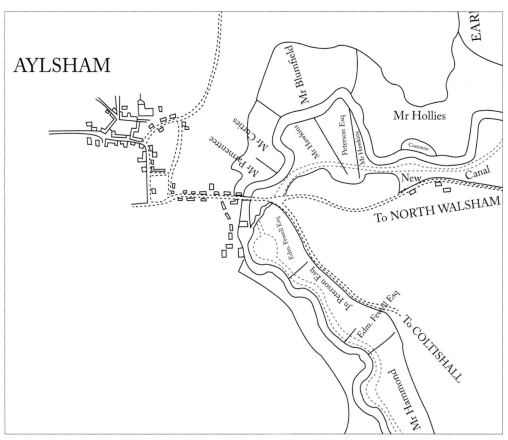

A tracing of Biedermann's map of 1772, showing the proposed line of the Navigation with a blue dotted line.

The Act of Parliament was passed in the summer of 1773. In the autumn Biedermann was instructed to stake out the land for the canals and in January 1774 the Commissioners were ordered to make an inspection with a view to land purchases. In March Mary Hammond was to be offered £52 13s 9d for 1 acre 3 roods and 10 perches near the Aylsham basin and John Peterson thirty years lease for the current rent for which his Meadow was let. As the construction of the Navigation began at Horstead, there was little urgency to buy land upriver. The conveyance for John Peterson, who held the Manor of Aylsham Wood at this time, was not made until September 1785 and the agreement with Mary Hammond was not completed until September 1787. She was to be paid £17 11s for 13 years rent, the first annual instalment of £1 7s due at Michaelmas. There is some discrepancy between the Millgate documents and the minutes of the Navigation Commissioners. Mary Hammond and Thomas Harvey were both executors for the sale of Thomas Spurrell's estate in 1771, and acquired property from him. It is not clear how they divided the land in Dunkirk.

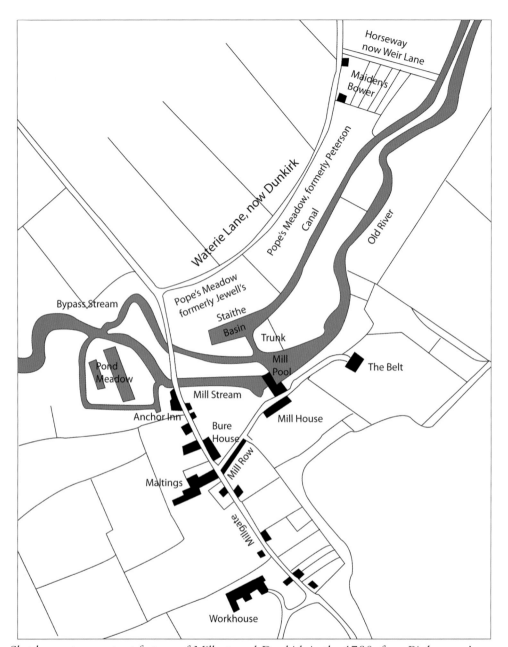

Sketch map to reconstruct features of Millgate and Dunkirk in the 1780s from Biedermann's map, contemporary documents and the Tithe Map of 1840.

The Court Books of the Manor of Aylsham Wood or Sexton's attribute to Thomas Harvey the 'close of arable land called Maiden's Bower… next to a horseway, leading to a meadow of the said Manor, on the part of the east, and a meadow called Pope's Meadow, on the part of the west, and abutting the King's Highway leading from Aylsham aforesaid to Tuttington towards the North, and upon the lands of the Lord of the said Manor towards the south, containing by estimation 1 acre and 1 rood more or less'.

Thomas Harvey was able to leave these lands in 1798 to his wife Ann and it is not clear how this relates to the Commissioners' dealings with Mary Hammond a decade before. The Maiden's Bower is of interest because it was rebuilt in 1843 as the Royal Oak public house.[7] It is easy to envisage that it had this informal status as a beerhouse in the eighteenth century. Pope's Meadow features prominently in the Commissioners' acquisitions and the horseway to the river still exists as Weir Lane. Dunkirk was formerly known as Waterie Lane, and the name Dunkirk seems to be of relatively recent origin. The most credible explanation is a derivation from Kirkmere along Waterie Lane mentioned in a seventeenth-century will, also a note by Mason in his *History of Norfolk* (1885) that Dunkirk was close to a field described in the Court Books of Sexton's Manor as Kirkfield and suggests the probability of a church or chapel having been thereabouts in early times.[8]

Robert Parmeter, now acknowledged as a gentleman, was admitted as a Commissioner in December 1773, joining several other Aylsham dignitaries: Peter Elvin junior, son of a former sheriff of Norwich, George Hunt Holley, the solicitor-landowner, partner and son-in-law of the notable solicitor Edmund Jewell senior who died in 1770, Edward Piggon junior, surgeon, James Curties, farmer and grocer, and Joseph Hammond. Parmeter can be credited with much of the Aylsham planning and supervision. In November 1774 it was decided to move the Aylsham (or Burrough Hall) Lock upstream from Burgh Hall Meadow to the Alder Carr belonging to Burgh Hall Farm. In the Spring of 1775 Biedermann was ordered to make a temporary canal across the land of Edmund Jewell and the Rev. William Jewell in the occupation of Stephen Cook, i.e. across Pope's Meadow. He was also instructed to put in some of the back drains to collect water from the adjacent meadows into the canal, one of which was in Burgh Hall Meadow. John Ives was paid £53 12s 9d for the canal, Thomas Emmerson £14 3s 4d and James Allen £12 4s 1d for making the back drains.

A general order was made in May 1775 for fence rails to be placed between properties along the canal to stop cattle straying. By September 1775, however, funds had run out and all work was stopped, with bills not or only partially paid, until February 1776 when £200 credit was raised by Thomas Durrant on wood stored at Buxton. Thomas Harvey and William Gill then submitted bills for wood and work totalling £43 and this may have been for the work on Woolsey Bridge to connect Burgh Hall farm with the island created by the canal below Aylsham Lock.

It seems likely that no further work was done until the new contract was signed with John Smith in the spring of 1778, but presumably the canal and Aylsham Lock were built over the next two seasons for the official opening in October 1779. Only in July 1779 did the Commissioners view the intended Aylsham quay and agree that Smith should build a wall on the north side. In November Robert Parmeter was allowed to order '14 oak poles to be driven into the foreside of the Quay to prevent the boats from injuring

---

7   Ibid.
8   Mollard, T. (1998) 'Mason's History of Norfolk' in *Aylsham Local History Society Journal*, vol. 5, pp.85–95, 148–158, 234–251.

the Wall'. In May 1780 £12 19s 8d was paid for iron-work to guard the walls of the basin and £2 19s 8d to level the quay.

Although in August 1779 John Ives was to be paid 15s for 'gathering up the utensils belonging to the Navigation' it was evident from an inspection in November that much work still needed to be done. The bank between the canal and the river in Pope's Meadow in the occupation of Stephen Cook needed to be made 20 feet wide and 18 inches above its current height. A shoal from Aylsham Lock to where the river joined needed to be taken out to give 3 feet of water. There were also four more shoals further down in Woolsey's Meadow to be removed. In May 1780 Robert Parmeter arranged for John Bell and Robert Rose of Burgh to keep the channels clean from end to end for £30 a year, which they did for many years.

In February 1780 Stephen Cook was castigated for removing earth from the bank between the river and the canal to the extent that the 'Navigation is greatly injured being now overflowed in time of Flood'. He was told to make good the damage immediately or he would be prosecuted.

The millpool at Aylsham, with the bypass stream coming in and the original trunk to the Basin to the right.

The rear of Maiden's Bower with seepage line to the canal and Weir Lane behind trees to left.[9]

His actions may have been inadvertent or wilful but anyway provided a pretext for the Commissioners to acquire valuable land. In April 1780 they arranged for James North to make a survey of the lands of 'Mr Jewell on which the Canal ends and which Lands are bounded by the River on the West, the Coltishall Road on the East & North and by Mr Petersons Lands on the South'. In May they ordered Stephen Cook to fence off 1 acre 3 roods and 27 perches including the basin at the top of Pope's Meadow where the staithe would be developed. The Commissioners immediately started to negotiate the purchase from Edmund Jewell and the Rev. William Jewell, extending the area to 4 acres 2 roods and 19 perches and completed it in March 1781 for £88 18s. A small part of this, comprising 1 rood and 11 perches, was then leased out to Robert Parmeter for 99 years so that he 'should at his own expense make a Quay or Staithe on the South side of the Basin…and keep the same in repair' (clearly shown on the sale map of 1855, below). This was next to the 'trunk' canal that joined the mill-pool to the basin and created Staithe Island. In October 1780 he was also given a lease for land between the river and the canal down to the lock at 5s a year for 40 years on condition that he 'keep the banks on both sides of the said pieces of land in repair and to annually cut the woods halfway of the said Canal and Old River and not to plant the said pieces of land with oziers or otherwise'. It is interesting that the Tithe Map of 1840 shows that sizeable fields east of Pope's Meadow a little back

---

9   Access for photo courtesy of John Broughton.

from the canal were held by Canfor Ellis the basket-maker in Red Lion Street; Staithe Meadow itself was leased by the next generation of Parmeters.[10]

More improvements and repairs are recorded during the 1780s. In the autumn of 1780 a cut was made by John Ives 137 feet long and 20 feet wide from the canal by Aylsham Lock into the old river, flanked by two dams, to keep the water level in the two channels. Earth and gravel dug out of the basin and canal were used for roads. The wings of Burgh and Woolsey Bridge needed attention in 1783, as did the staithe road. The wooden Navigation bridge (over the mill bypass stream, not the main brick bridge over the millstream) 'lately blown up by a late Inundation' had to be rebuilt in April 1784 for a sum not exceeding £50, and numerous small repairs to bridges and locks were needed in 1785 and 1786. In 1789 Burgh Bridge had become 'too dangerous for carriages to pass over' and the trunk joining the mill-pool to the basin needed repair, the latter partly done with 'shipwreck' wood. Robert Parmeter was often asked to supervise this work and from 1781 he and George Hunt Holley were allowed to inspect the Navigation and pay any sum not exceeding £2 at any one time for repairs 'without the approbation of seven or more Commissioners'. Thomas Harvey, William Gill and the bricklayer John Berry received most of the contracts, but by the end of the decade Francis Moy, carpenter, William Robins for bricks, Robert Cooke for bricks and wood, and Charles Porritt, blacksmith, begin to feature.

In 1792 158 boats were dispatched from Aylsham, rising to 383 a year by the turn of the century.

1790 to 1850: Consolidation

Aylsham Mill in 1840, painted by the Rev. James Bulwer. This is perhaps romanticised, but does indicate the rural appearance of Drabblegate. Reproduced with permission of Norwich Castle Museum.

10 NRO DN/TA 303.

Robert Parmeter died in 1791. Aylsham Mill passed to his second son William, a young man of 24, who was already working there, and who had been appointed wharfinger at the common staithe to supervise the dispatch of boats and collection of tolls. Unfortunately he died the next year in 1792, and his slightly older brother Robert inherited the business. Robert was now 28, married to Sarah Francis, and with a young family in Ingworth. He had been managing the mill his father acquired there in 1786 and seems to have been able, shrewd and energetic.[11] He was described by Arthur Young in his travels as 'a good farmer, and a very intelligible man'.[12] His younger brother John became the miller at Burgh and George Parmeter took the position at Ingworth.

Parmeter's staithe, on the south side of the Basin, was 75 feet long and in 1795 was said to have a large warehouse lately 'built upon it, brick and tiles with double floor'. This came to be known as the Granary, as shown on the 1855 sale map, and is the only building that survives from the eighteenth century on the basin. Parmeter bought more property near the river that year and in 1796 he acquired the Millhouse properties from Thomas Harvey. In 1798 he rebuilt Aylsham mill in its present form. Within a few years, however, he moved his growing family to Burgh – one of the terms of his father's will allowed his mother to continue to live in whichever rooms in Bure House she wished and Burgh might now have seemed more salubrious than Millgate.

Robert Parmeter junior took on his father's role of supervising repairs of the basin and canal. In 1795 the quay was raised four courses of bricks, the front backfilled with tarras (earth), the posts on the front of the wall repaired and proper ties used for securing the planks. In 1797 he was allowed £30 to repair damage between the canal and the mill pool. After he moved to Burgh it was more convenient to contract work through John Fielde. Fielde was born about 1762, probably in Saxthorpe, and was employed regularly on the Navigation as a millwright from 1803 (by 1805 described as an engineer) to 1830 and in that period was paid something in the order of £600. From this, other work and perhaps including his favourable marriage into the Hase family of Saxthorpe, he bought at least six properties along Millgate from the Parmeter, Francis and Rackham families. After 1830 he was steadily buying copyhold north of the river. When he died in 1837 he left a very considerable estate to his wife and daughter, the latter married to a Norwich surgeon, Matthias Phillippo. In 1833 the main contracts for maintenance passed out of Aylsham to Benjamin and then John Johnson.

Sir Thomas Durrant died in 1790. The post of Treasurer stayed in the Francis-Parmeter families almost to the end of this period: Clement Francis, formerly a surgeon in the East India Company (died 1792), then Robert Francis, draper and father-in-law of Robert Parmeter (died 1807), then Robert Parmeter himself (died 1831), and then his son Samuel until he resigned in 1846. John Adey continued as clerk until 1809, with

---

11 NRO AYL 407.
12 Young, A. (1813). *A General View of the Agriculture of the County of Norfolk.*

Aylsham Mill, rebuilt by Robert Parmeter in 1798. Part of the warehouses on the basin are visible in the background. Reproduced with permission of Aylsham Town Council Archive.

his nephew and partner William Repton, the son of Humphry Repton, starting to take minutes from 1806. The meticulous record continues in perfect copperplate, only the curlicues change a little. In time the work began to be devolved to Repton's partner William Henry Scott, both signing the minutes in the 1840s, after which it is more evidently an office job rather than a personal commitment.

The officers of the Navigation took an active part in other civic duties. The Loyal Aylsham Light Infantry was raised in 1803 in response to the serious threat of invasion from France.[13] The two captains were Robert Parmeter and William Repton, responsible for regular drill and exercise days. William's expenses and notes on parade drill manoeuvres have been neatly preserved, the conscientious record of a young man of 20, probably still articled to his uncle. Only a relatively small number of mostly poor men were called up to serve in the militia, but high food prices and low wages caused much hardship. The decline in work for hand-loom weavers hit Aylsham and the surrounding villages hard and increasingly so throughout the period.[14] The population of

13 Eve, J. (1995) *The Loyal Aylsham Light Infantry Volunteers.*
14 Fiske, R.C. (1995) 'The Plight of the Marsham and Hevingham hand-loom weavers' in *Aylsham Local History Society Journal*, vol. 4, pp.124–127.

Aylsham almost doubled from 1,667 in 1801 to 2,741 in 1851. In 1821 370 people lived in Millgate, about a fifth of the Aylsham population.

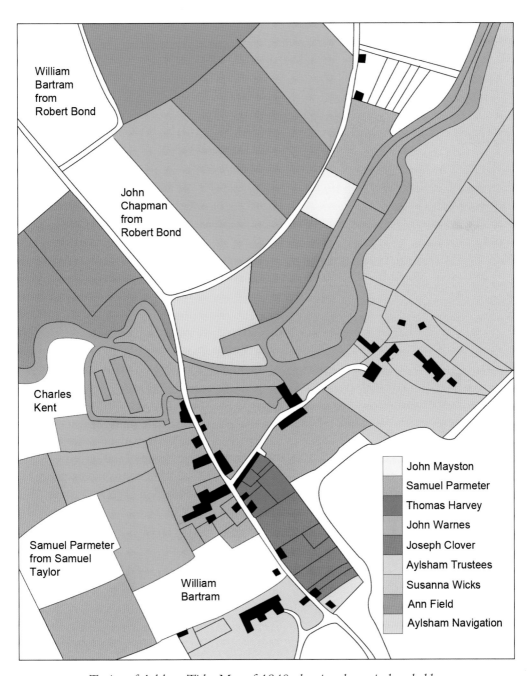

William
Bartram
from
Robert Bond

John
Chapman
from
Robert Bond

Charles
Kent

Samuel Parmeter
from Samuel
Taylor

William
Bartram

John Mayston
Samuel Parmeter
Thomas Harvey
John Warnes
Joseph Clover
Aylsham Trustees
Susanna Wicks
Ann Field
Aylsham Navigation

Tracing of Aylsham Tithe Map of 1840, showing the main leaseholders.

The Anchor Inn in 1831 by Francis Stone. Thomas Wright, the boatbuilder, was landlord in the latter part of his life between 1868 and 1872.

This is not to gainsay activity on the staithe itself. As early as 1791, when William Parmeter was wharfinger a byelaw was passed to forbid 'timber, bricks, tiles and like heavy articles' being laid within 15 yards of the basin. In 1835 Thomas Wright, the boat builder, was appointed wharfinger at Aylsham and Burgh with instructions to enforce new rules for tolls and fines for goods left on the quay. Robert Lemon remonstrated at the annual general meeting of the Commissioners in 1841 for one such fine for abandoned timber that was referred to legal counsel. The case rumbled on to 1848, with the decision going against the Commissioners, who still tried to reclaim legal expenses. In 1847 it was reported that 'in consequence of goods being suffered to remain there for a long time (in some cases up to six years) there was no room upon the Staithe for the deposit of Timber and other Goods intended to be immediately sent down the Navigation and that a very large quantity of the Timber brought onto the Staithe was removed by land carriage and consequently paid no toll whatsoever'. In consequence further byelaws were devised and in 1848 Thomas Wright was engaged to measure all timbers brought on or carried off the staithe and keep a proper account. He was paid an extra 3d for measuring up the timber on each dispatch. New warehouses were also built and let out in 1848.

The wherries were mostly owned by the millers and coal merchants. Wherrymen were paid by the voyage. They got 35 shillings for the round trip to Yarmouth and back and had to provide a mate. The voyage of some 40 miles took a week on average if the winds were fair. The trade directories record that in 1822 R. Parmeter & Sons provided a service to Yarmouth each week and by 1846 this was daily.[15] By 1842 several other merchants owned their own

---

15   Gale, G. & Mollard, T. (2004) *Aylsham Directories 1793–1937.*

wherries. Frederick Copeman, a farmer and miller of Itteringham, bought the Brick Tower Windmill south of Mill Lane, and was in partnership with his brother-in-law, James Brown, a tanner at Itteringham.[16] Frederick Copeman also had a share in the windmill on Cawston Road owned by the farmer Henry Soame. White's Directory of 1845 lists Copeman & Soame as corn, oil-cake, etc. merchants in the canal basin and provider of a wherry service. There were five coal merchants listed, including Copeman & Soame and John Mayston. They soon had a further outlet at the works to provide gas lighting built in 1850 at the top of Millgate. The shareholders included Samuel and Robert William Parmeter, William Repton, William Henry Scott, George Soame, John Warnes and many others.

REFERENCE — MAP OF AN ESTATE in AYLSHAM, NORFOLK.

	Nos	Description					
F	1	Water Mill, Build.gs & Yards				1	5
C	2	House Build.gs Yard & Garden			1 2	2	
C	3	House and Garden					24
C	4	House and Garden					10
C	5	House Build.gs & Garden			2	30	
C	6	Cottages and Gardens			1	19	
F	7	Malt House, Stable &c			1	37	
C	8	Pond Meadow	1 2 11				
C	9	Cascade Meadow	2 5				
F	10	Dam Meadow	2 14				
L	11	Granary and Staithe			1	6	
C	12	Cinder Oven and Yard			1	6	
C	13	Pool Meadow	1 3 16				
C	14	Cottages and Gardens					21
C	15	Warehouses and Staithe	1 2 37				
			6 1 9	4			
		Pasture			6 1	9	
		Total			10 1	9	

C Y.e Ladder Room adjoining
number 7 and included in
the measurement thereof

Scale
3 CHAINS TO AN INCH

Map that accompanied sale of Samuel Parmeter's Millgate estate in 1855. The Granary (no. 11 on the map) is the only warehouse to survive from this period.

Thomas Wright is listed as boatbuilder at the Staithe in 1842. On the Tithe Map of 1840 he is shown to live in the house and garden in Dunkirk at the north-east corner of John Warnes' holding on the Staithe and no doubt worked from his warehouse on the inlet from the Basin. In 1848 Mr Warnes' warehouse was replaced and let to Mr Barham at £7 per year. John Mayston, a coal merchant, had the smaller more distant wharf in 1840 and this was let to William Mash in 1848.

The roads had been improved a little by the Norwich to Cromer Turnpike. An Act to develop the section from Norwich to Aylsham was passed in 1794 and a second one to extend the road to Cromer in 1811.[17] In 1821 John Warnes of Bolwick Hall

---

16 Bailey, F. (2010) 'Frederick Copeman and his Aylsham Steam Mill' in *Aylsham Local History Society Journal*, vol. 9, pp.272–277.

17 Belton, V. (1992) 'Aylsham and the Norwich to Cromer turnpike' in *Aylsham Local History Society Journal*, vol. 3, pp.230–233.

proposed an 'Improvement in the Road from Aylsham Bridge to North Walsham if the Commissioners would consent that the road should pass over part of the Navigation Staithe', but this is not very evident on the maps of 1840 and 1855. The Norwich to Yarmouth railway, the first in Norfolk, was opened in 1844. In 1846 the Parmeter family was split over the proposal for a railway from Norwich to Aylsham. Samuel Parmeter was a promoter. Robert William Parmeter, Samuel's older brother, solicitor and Justice of the Peace, chaired a Meeting of Shareholders of the Aylsham Navigation on 7 March 1846 at the Royal Hotel, Norwich. Subscribers to £3,064 of the original £5,000 invested in the project were present. The following motion was passed unanimously, 'Resolved that it is expedient that the Shareholders should join the opposition now organising against the North Norfolk Railway it being considered that such a project will be very prejudicial to their interests'. A sum of £200 was set aside to oppose the plan, to be co-ordinated by James Hunt Holley, William Repton and Robert William Parmeter.

In August Samuel Parmeter resigned as Treasurer, the 'duties being incompatible with his interest in a projected Railway to the Town of Aylsham promoted by him'. The well known banking family the Gurneys of Norwich were appointed as Treasurers in his stead. The railway scheme came to nought and Samuel Parmeter continued as a Commissioner for some years. There was another proposal for a Norwich, Aylsham & Cromer Railway in 1859.[18] The line would have come to Aylsham via Coltishall, with a branch from Brampton to North Walsham, and from Aylsham to Cromer via Ingworth. It would have provided a more satisfactory route than the two lines eventually built by different companies with their main interests outside Norfolk.

Returning to 1846, a committee was set up to consider suggestions for the improvement of the Navigation. It was suggested that there should be a single Superintendent to act as Clerk of Works and also supervise the collection of tolls. He would have his house at Horstead Lock and be paid a reasonable salary of £30 per year and 5% of the tolls. In December 1847, the threat of the railway now passed, John Mace was appointed as Superintendent. It was one of his first recommendations, cited above, that the Staithe should be cleared of clutter.

So in the middle of the nineteenth century a new era began. The small group of gentry and merchants that had run the business for eighty years with much personal attention and considerable profit were replaced by professional bankers, a solicitors' firm and a salaried manager. The business was now to be overseen by small committees, each with prescribed responsibilities.

1850 to 1912: Industrial Development and Decline

In the early 1850s Samuel Parmeter went into business with John Thornton Bullock and his brother Stanley Bullock and sold out to them in 1856 (the map for the sale is shown above). The Bullock brothers almost immediately mortgaged for £5,000 (with interest at 5% p.a.) the freehold property of the water mills, mill dam, mill pool, dam meadow,

---

18 Mollard, T. (1996) 'Norwich, Aylsham & Cromer Railway' in *Aylsham Local History Society Journal*, vol. 4, pp.365–370.

Aylsham Steam Mill c.1903. Reproduced with permission of Aylsham Town Council Archive.

the maltings and some other land, and the extensive copyhold properties including the Mill House, cottage and counting house and Bure House. Later on they were allowed a further £2,000 mortgage on the properties. Stanley was the active partner, becoming a Commissioner in 1867 and taking an active role on the committees to within a few months of the end of his life in 1914. It seems that John Thornton's inefficiencies were the main cause of their financial difficulties. Stanley took on the whole business, with all debts repaid, in 1893. The brothers resided conveniently in Mill House and Bure House across the road.

On the other side of the Basin the enterprising Copeman family from Itteringham expanded their business. As indicated above Frederick Copeman, in partnership with Henry Soame, had interests in both windmills in Aylsham town and ran a wherry service. James Lee Case, his cousin, assisted him as book keeper in Aylsham. By 1850 he had taken up residence in Millgate as an accountant and farmer and it seems likely that the family took up land in Dunkirk shown on the Tithe Map of 1840 occupied by John Warnes, who died that year. James Brown, Frederick Copeman's brother-in-law, was listed as a timber merchant in 1850. In 1853 he renewed the lease of a warehouse on the staithe and in 1854 he was listed as a corn and coal merchant with a wherry.

In 1856 Frederick Copeman built the Steam Mill on the Staithe. Benjamin (Ben) Cook, who was to buy the business in 1878, made a note in his Memorandum Book about the contract for the machinery.[19] Ransomes & Sims of Ipswich (forerunners of Ransomes, Sims & Jeffries, iron founders and lawnmower manufacturers) installed a Ten Horse Power High Pressure Fixed Steam Engine with machinery for sawing and milling. The contract is dated 6 November 1855 and the bill for £1,140 9s 5d was paid in July 1856. By modern standards this was a very small machine for that purpose.

---

19 ATCA, Memorandum Book, B. Cook.

In 1857 land to the east became available. George Copeman had inherited the land held by his father Robert, shown on the Tithe Map, that had been leased to the coal merchant John Mayston. In 1855 George and Thomas Copeman had sold their Aylsham banking business, Copeman & Company, to Gurney & Company. George was now moving to Dunham. The Commissioners purchased 2 roods and 12 perches of the 1 acre and 2 perches for £182 and leased it to James Brown. In 1858 James Brown closed his tannery in Itteringham and developed the Aylsham site as a tan yard and sawmill. In time the warehouse became known as the Bone Mill and used to produce a variety of manure products. At one time waste products were brought up from the herring industry in Yarmouth to be incorporated. As noted in the chapter below on trade, timber was an important product for regional use and in the second half of the nineteenth century, for the north of England. In addition the smaller branches of oak trees were valued as billet to smoke herring in Yarmouth.

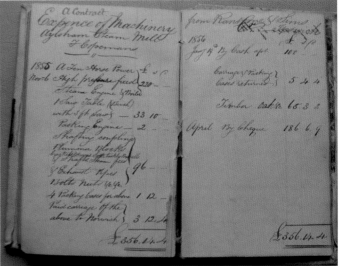

Ben Cook and his Memorandum Book with details of the steam engine bought by Frederick Copeman in 1856. Reproduced with permission of Aylsham Town Council Archive.

Frederick Copeman built a fine double-fronted two-storey house, the Miller's House, across the road from the steam mill in 1860. It is not clear who lived in the other half, but over the next few years the business moved on to the next generation. In 1864 Frederick Copeman moved to Long Stratton to be near his wife's family.

Their only son William Utting Copeman continued in Dunkirk for only a few years before moving to Yarmouth. In 1867 James Brown retired to Itteringham. His elder son, Edward Copeman, formerly a seaman in Australia, came to Aylsham in 1868 to assist principally with the sawmill. In 1869 he was joined by his younger brothers, Frederick, a farmer from Cawston, and John. Frederick, listed as a tanner in Aylsham, soon returned to Cawston. Edward also left the business to run the Royal Oak public house, just down

Miller's House, Dunkirk, built in 1860 by Frederick Copeman.

the road, from 1872 to 1875. He suffered from a lung complaint, no doubt exacerbated by the mill. In 1883 he returned to Australia, where he died within five weeks. John continued the business until 1878, when the mill was put up for sale.

The steam mill was bought in 1878 by Ben Cook. He had considerable experience as a miller, having previously acquired the mills at Itteringham and Blickling from Frederick Copeman. His memorandum book in the Aylsham Town Archives contains detailed notes about the condition and improvements that had been made to them. He soon set about renovating the Dunkirk premises. The mill had four pairs of millstones. In 1886 he installed a four sack/hour roller mill plant – the first in the district. In fact the first exhibition of roller milling in England had taken place in London as recently as 1869, indicating Ben Cook was at the forefront of modern technology. In 1881 he built new offices, seed granary and stabling beside the road, the yard enclosed with the bone mill on the fourth side. James Vince lived in the Miller's House and carried on the trade in bone meal, meat meal and other associated products until at least 1896. In 1894 Ben Cook added wheat washing and drying machines and carried out other changes. He finally retired in 1907, selling the mills by auction. He was a Commissioner from about 1882 to 1911, attending meetings regularly and often assigned to committees and negotiations. He lived at the Belt and worshipped at St Michael's Church and in 1890 commissioned a mission room to be built adjacent to the churchyard at a cost of £400, which is now the Heritage Centre. He married a much younger woman quite late in life and died in 1913, but Mrs Cook lived until 1970, when she died aged 89.

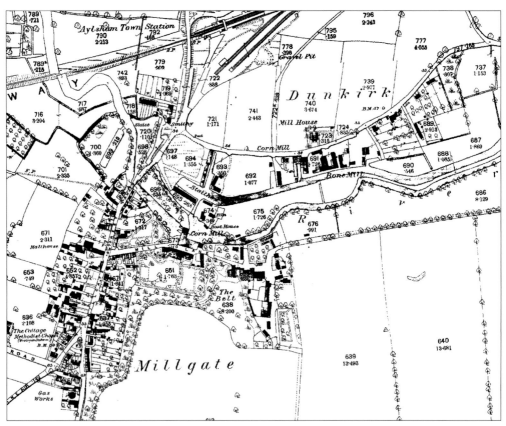

The Ordnance Survey 25-inch map of 1886 showing Millgate and the Navigation in Aylsham. Note the development of buildings along the canal compared to the map of 1855 above.

Barclay Pallett & Company, with their headquarters in North Walsham, purchased the Dunkirk mill from the auction in 1907 and improved the milling plant further in 1910. They also bought the water mills after Stanley Bullock died in 1914. Robert Rust managed both mills for the next 50 years. Barclay Pallett had wherries in use until 1912. Several other traders leased warehouses from the Commissioners. Stanley Bullock had his premise on the common staithe as well as loading facilities behind the water mill on the Millpool. Thomas Shreeve took on the mill at Bolwick Hall and rented the warehouse previously used by John Warnes from some time before 1882 when the 99-year lease was renewed. By the turn of the century he had milling interests also in Cawston, Burgh and Buxton. In 1883 he is listed in the Trade Directories as corn, cake, coal, herring, scale, salt, flour and pollard merchant. He also ran wherries and soon had a warehouse at the railway station. He continued trading until 1896, the business passing to Henry Shreeve. George Bircham, coal merchant and wherry owner, leased a warehouse from around 1875 to 1888. Both he and Thomas Shreeve were reprimanded several times in later years for late payment of rent and tolls. James Lee Case and John Goulder, trading as Case & Goulder, also had one of the Commissioners' warehouses in the 1880s. James Lee Case was admitted as a Commissioner in 1881 and took an active part in the administration until the end of his life in 1893. By that time he was living at Valley Farm on the Heydon Road and his property was taken over by John Goulder.

Thomas Wright was employed as the Aylsham wharfinger until 1862. The Commissioners then considered that in consequence of his age a new man should be employed and in January 1863 Thomas Wright the younger was taken on. Thomas Wright the elder was also the water bailiff and from 1868 to 1877 ran the Anchor public house. Thomas Wright the younger died in 1883 and his place was taken by Elijah Wright. Robert Wright had been the main boat builder in the 1840s and 1850s and his youngest son Elijah became the principal craftsman in the second half of the century. They not only built and repaired wherries but also built pleasure boats for the more affluent.

The Anchor Inn was the base for the early regattas held on the river above the inn, and Walter Mileham commemorated the 1850 regatta in a painting. The Aylsham Aquatic Club was launched in 1851 'to promote sailing and rowing matches between members'.[20] Its first president was Samuel Parmeter and the Commodore was Dr Frederick Smith.

Aylsham Regatta in 1850, painted by Walter Mileham. Reproduced with permission of Aylsham Town Council Archive.

---

20 Aylsham Local History Society (1998) 'The Aylsham Regatta and Rowing Club' in *A Backwards Glance.*

Subsequent regattas were held on the canal between the staithe and Aylsham lock. In 1871 the club was re-formed as the Aylsham and Buxton Rowing Club. Regattas were held at Aylsham each month in May, June, July and August. In September, at least in 1872, there was a big regatta at Lammas with 'sailing matches, rowing matches and canoe racing, also running matches and steeplechases in the water'. The club was disbanded after four years because some younger members spoilt the boats. In 1885 the Parish Magazine records the Annual Treat in August. The children, 155 boys, 151 girls and 70 infants, piled into three wherries lent by the Bullock brothers and Thomas Shreeve and proceeded through Aylsham Lock to Mr William Case's meadow.

> Mr. Stanley Bullock had set up a number of swings, roundabouts, see-saws etc. on which the children disported themselves. These amusements, with races, throwing for sweets, scrambling etc. filled up the time till tea was ready, when the children sat down, mostly on sail cloths spread on the grass, and did ample justice to the fare provided. After tea, the games were resumed, some joined in a dance, and others watched the sending off of balloons till the bugle sounded for the return at 7.30. The wherries were soon filled and moved amidst hearty cheers for Mr. & Mrs. Case. Coloured fires were burnt, and Roman Candles let off on each wherry. The staithe was safely reached at 8.30, and a crowd of parents and friends were ready to receive the returning children.[21]

Dr William Wynne, son of Frederick Smith mentioned above, born in Aylsham in 1835, kept a diary that gives further indication of private boating on the Navigation. He and his father had a series of wherries and yachts mostly built by Robert Wright. He visited Aylsham in 1877 after a long absence. He and his mate had to bow haul from Oxnead to Aylsham, which took most of the day. They received hospitality from the Bullock brothers but 'saw no old friends, and the place looked dull and strange'.[22] In later years he would meet Stanley Bullock and others using their wherries for pleasure on the broads. The chapter on wherries recounts more on these vessels including the story of the *Gipsy,* built in Aylsham in 1875 by Elijah Wright. She traded for about ten years until Henry Montagu Doughty turned her into a pleasure craft and in 1888 crossed the North Sea and cruised extensively in the Netherlands and beyond.

In 1891 Thomas Shreeve offered a hire service consisting of 'two wherries fitted with every convenience for the enjoyment of parties wishing to visit the Broads and rivers of Norfolk. Two men are provided by the owners to look after and sail the yachts, and are under the direction of the party hiring the boat....a jolly boat is with each yacht'.[23]

---

21 Nobbs, G. (2003) 'The Annual School Treat' in *Aylsham Local History Society Journal*, vol. 7, pp.31–32.

22 Nobbs, G. (1992) 'Aylsham river in the last century' in *Aylsham Local History Society Journal*, vol. 3, pp.173–178.

23 Ibid.

Wherry Palmerston loading at the Aylsham Watermill in around 1910. Reproduced with permission of Aylsham Town Council Archive.

During the winter the cabins would be removed and the craft returned to more mundane commercial duties. The Commissioners never relented on their intention to restrict the Navigation to traders apart from the wherry owners and the privileged few who held land along the river and their friends.

As indicated above John Mace was appointed Superintendent in 1848 and was responsible for the upkeep of the Navigation and collection of tolls from the Lock House at Coltishall. John Mace resigned in 1861 and was replaced by his son William in 1862. By 1869 the Commissioners were dissatisfied with his work and he was replaced by Elijah Bircham of Norwich. A delegated group of Commissioners made an annual inspection of the Navigation, generally in July. They had their own lighter and usually breakfasted at the White Horse in Coltishall and took luncheon on board. In 1884 they used Ben Cook's steam launch.

The years between 1850 and 1880 were the most profitable for the Navigation with a great range of products moving up and down the river. The trade declined sharply from 1880 onwards when the East Norfolk Railway reached Aylsham and provided a link to Norwich. In 1883 the station of what was to become the Eastern and Midland Railway was built just north of the staithe. This line provided access not only to Yarmouth but also a direct link to the Midlands. William Forster, reporting on the Navigation survey in 1889 noted that 'the Navigation was considered to be in good order especially with so small an amount of traffic'. In 1900 it was reported that 'the decrease in the amount of tolls makes it necessary to curtail the expenses if it can be done without being

Aylsham Basin in 1928. Courtesy of Norfolk County Council Library and Information Service.

detrimental to the Navigation'. The Navigation bank account was down to £42 6s 7d and an assessment showed that the total amount of tolls for 1899 was down to £315 12s 6d and for 1900 £287 2s 9d. Of these about two-thirds (£219 in 1899 and £198 in 1900) came from Stanley Bullock and Ben Cook in nearly equal parts.

It was decided that 'the men employed on the Navigation be informed that their services would probably have to be dispensed with after the October meeting and if required next Spring it was proposed to give them an advance of 2s per week'. The Commissioners also raised the toll on all marl, gravel, stone, macadam, etc. going downstream to 2s from 1s 6d. By 1902 the balance was down to £11 3s 8d. In 1908 all staff were paid off including Parsons who had been in charge of the Commissioners' boat It was also agreed to compound the tolls – Stanley Bullock to pay £45 p.a., Ben Cook £45, Barclay & Pallett £60, Cross & Co. £40, Ling £35 and Browne £22 10s. This was considered the minimum to keep the Navigation open. Negotiations were opened with the County Council for them to take on the upkeep of the bridges. Elijah Bircham was dismissed, but allowed to keep his cottage on condition he did much of the work for which he has been previously paid. A modicum of dydling was allowed as well as minimal repairs.

On 4 September 1912, ten days after the deluge on 25th to 26th August, a Committee was appointed 'to confer with the owners of Buxton and Oxnead Mills, the Road Authority (the Aylsham R.D.C.) and see what steps can be taken to put the River in order and repair the damage….it being understood that the appointment of such a Committee is in no way an admission of liability'. Ironically in February 1912 the Commissioners had received a letter from C.F. Rump, Clerk to the North Walsham and Dilham Canal, asking whether the Commissioners 'would be prepared to sell the Navigation'. After some discussion they decided to write and enquire about a possible purchase price, but no reply was ever recorded.

8. The People of Millgate and Dunkirk 1841 to 1901

The Staithe in Aylsham.

Much of the history of the Navigation is centred on, and derived from, the land-owners, solicitors and businessmen who initiated, funded, and presided over the Navigation. These are the people who wrote our history. It is not until detailed census material becomes available from 1841 onwards that we can get some picture of life for most ordinary people who lived and worked in the area.

The ability to move goods more quickly and easily at a time of slow road transport was a great asset, and the surrounding area prospered accordingly. Millgate is a story of industrialisation and development that is tiny in relation to Manchester or Birmingham, but for the time and the location it was remarkable. For local people, and for many who came to Aylsham seeking work, it was an important opportunity.

Where did they live?

Faden's map of 1797 shows 'Millgate Street' as the focus for buildings, and this was obviously centred around the water mill. At that time there were many small cottages between the bridge and the mill. In addition there were a few significant buildings such as the mill, Bridge House (c1700), Bure House (1768), The Belt (1741), and 15–17 Millgate (early eighteenth century).[1] In these properties lived the wealthy and, apart from these few buildings, the area presented a pastoral scene. There were farms and smallholdings not only to the north of the river, but on Millgate even in 1840, as evidenced on the Tithe map.[2] The immediate area was fertile farmland, and the dominant occupation was that of farm labourer. Successive censuses show that farm labourers continued to live in this area throughout the nineteenth century (see table below). However, whilst the percentage of the national population involved in agriculture was falling in the nineteenth century, the actual numbers stayed much the same because the population was growing at the same time. This, however, was not the case in Millgate where the numbers of agricultural labourers fell markedly.

There is a remarkable concentration of houses built, or re-built in the late eighteenth and early nineteenth centuries; the early years of the navigation. These houses, some 28 addresses within about 13 listed buildings, make up the bulk of the Millgate conservation area. Most are built of local brick, pantiles, and flint, and contribute to a street of great charm and character. William Mash had properties built in around the middle of the century at Mash's Row (1845 and 1848) and at the top of Millgate (numbers 2,4,6 built in 1845). These, together with properties to the north of the river at Drabblegate (numbers 44 and 46, built in 1860), were extending the built area probably because there was no room left on Millgate. They may also mark a watershed in architectural style as they are probably some of the last built in the vernacular, or local, style and with local materials, particularly flint. The next houses built around New Road at the top of Millgate such as Garner's Cottages (1869) and Sycamore Place (1875) effectively joined Millgate to Bure Way (formerly Commercial Road and Workhouse Road). Other contemporary buildings are the Old

2 to 6 Millgate, built in the mid 1840s.

1   Estimated dates for building construction throughout this section are taken from Norfolk Heritage Explorer, Norfolk Museums and Archaeology Service.

2   NRO BR/276/1/1069/1.

Stonemason's and Victoria Place (1851). Apart from the style of building, these buildings were clearly intended for those working in the immediate area.

Further building from this period extends into Bure Way. These are clearly not cottages, but red brick houses with Victorian style windows. The School House and School Room in Drabblegate were built in 1857 and almost certainly reflect the growth in population and the need for education in the area. Mr Frederick Copeman, who had the steam mill built at Dunkirk in 1856, also built himself a house opposite the mill. Both the school house and room, and Copeman's house are built in the Victorian gothic revival style with slate roofs. The slate is an early example of building materials brought in to the area; a trend which would accelerate with the coming of the railways from the 1880s onwards.

The mid nineteenth-century school house and school room on Drabblegate.

Employment and Trade

The Navigation provided opportunities for all sections of society. Labourers, artisans and craftsmen, businessmen and investors were primary 'trades'. But these people themselves needed boots, shoes, clothes, tools, food and drink, baskets, servants, laundresses, buildings and furniture; secondary trades included hauliers and carters, harness-makers, basket-makers and blacksmiths. This is reflected in the population growth and varied occupations of nineteenth century Millgate as seen in the censuses. There was a great need for women as servants, laundresses and dressmakers. More than half of the women living on Millgate were not born in Aylsham; a far higher proportion than for the men.[3]

Occupation	1841	1851	1861	1871	1881	1891	1901
Bricklayer	4	0	0	3	3	6	9
Carpenter / joiner	2	11	7	6	12	11	8
Miller / granary man / apprentice	4	5	9	9	5	16	17
Dressmaker / apprentice	2	6	8	5	10	14	12
Gardener	0	5	4	3	6	6	7
Agricultural labourer	51	36	71	54	45	38	22
Launderess / washerwoman / charwoman	0	1	5	3	6	5	1
Grocer	1	1	2	3	1	1	4
Stonemason	1	7	4	1	1	1	2
In receipt of parish relief / inmate / pauper	4	18	0	0	2	12	0
Coal porter / carter / merchant	2	3	2	2	6	2	4
Shoe/boot maker	4	4	2	1	9	3	1
Basket maker	1	5	6	3	1	1	1
Innkeeper / publican	0	2	2	4	2	4	1
Teacher / governess	0	1	1	1	3	2	1
Blacksmith / apprentice	1	0	3	1	4	2	5
Draper	0	2	1	0	0	2	3
Housekeeper / assistant	0	2	7	6	7	5	5
Baker	2	4	1	1	1	1	0
Railway worker	0	0	0	0	0	11	11
Butcher	1	1	1	1	4	5	2
Servant	8	19	19	19	23	13	14

---

3   Aylsham Local History Society (2006) *Millgate*.

Boat builder / boatwright	2	2	5	4	2	2	3
Waterman / wherryman	2	5	19	20	14	13	5
Chapel minister / curate	0	0	1	1	3	0	0
Coach builder / coachman	2	0	3	3	4	2	1
Harness maker	0	0	0	3	2	0	1
Labourer / general labourer	1	25*	2	5	8	5	6
Farmer	2	5	3	8	2	1	1
Tailor	1	6	2	1	1	0	0
Sawyer	2	5	8	1	2	0	0

Occupations recorded in censuses 1841 – 1901 for the Millgate and Dunkirk area of Aylsham. Occupations listed where there are 3 or more entries for any one census.

★ *The term 'labourer' has probably been used to cover many agricultural labourers in the 1851 census.*

Trade directories record the various businesses at the staithe, or the basin as it was known to contemporaries.[4] William Boorne and later James Brown were timber merchants. Robert Hudson, John Mayston, Thomas Peachman and John Warnes were coal merchants, Frederick Copemen and then James Brown and Benjamin Cook ran the steam, saw and corn mills.

James Martin and then his sons were blacksmiths next to Mash's Row. They had a small blacksmith's forge which has been re–built as a double garage. Thomas, Robert and Elijah Wright were three generations of boatwrights and watermen. They were well known for their skills, and one wherry in particular, the pleasure wherry 'Gypsy', was much admired. At least three generations of Wrights were wharfingers at Aylsham staithe. The Bullock brothers and later Thomas Shreeve were corn millers, and Frederick Brown a tanner. Henry Smith and James Vince manufactured manure, and George and Edmund Bircham were coal and coke dealers. D and J Wells were tanners, millers, corn, cake, seed, coal, timber and manure merchants. All of these businesses would have been employers, and depended on secondary trades and suppliers.

So many primary and secondary trades created a demand for a service sector. This existed for the most part in the main town centre of Aylsham. However, by the mid nineteenth century there were four public houses in the Millgate area; The Stonemason's Arms, The Anchor, and The White Horse on Millgate, and The Royal Oak (at some time also known as The Butcher's Arm's, Maidens Bower and The Watermen's Arms).[5]

---

4   ATCA, Aylsham Trade Directories.

5   Gale, E. (2001) *Aylsham Inns and Public Houses: a History.*

The former Royal Oak public house.

There were once shops on Millgate. Some originated in the public houses such as the butcher at the White Horse, fish at The Anchor, and another butcher at The Stonemason's Arms. Evidence of shop fronts can still be seen, and the last one (no. 34) still retains the shop window.

With such a development in the area, it is not surprising that, in addition to the public houses and shops, other services grew, particularly between the Navigation and the town. A schoolroom and curate's house were built at Drabblegate in 1857. Later in the nineteenth century the school was used as a mission church for the Drabblegate area until 1892. These buildings are now private dwellings. A parish workhouse was built at the top of Millgate in 1776. The Aylsham gas works was established also at the top of Millgate (Gas House Hill) in 1849. No doubt access to coal from the staithe must have been a critical factor. A chapel (Wesleyan Reform) was built in New Road in 1868, and is now a dwelling with 'Tabernacle' clearly on the front.

The opening of the Great Eastern Railway station at Aylsham (South) in 1880, and the Eastern and Midlands station at Aylsham (North) in 1883 meant that some businesses were transferred from the staithe to the new stations. Kelly's Directory of 1912 lists no businesses at the staithe for the first time since the first Directory in 1822.[6] The event of August 1912

---

6   *Kelly's Directory of Norfolk* (1912).

hastened the end of an already declining waterway, and the basin was later largely filled in. However, the industrial legacy of Dunkirk was established, and today the old steam mill buildings are dwarfed by the thriving Dunkirk Industrial Estate. The layout of Millgate has changed little since the Ordnance Survey map of 1880, and Millgate itself is a charming road of interesting and desirable properties.

Wherry Loke – a sign of Millgate and Dunkirk's former history surviving in modern street names.

9. Trade on the Navigation

The petition to Parliament in January 1773 for an act authorising the construction of the Navigation included the statement,

> That the making and extending the Navigation of the said River by and from Coltishall to a bridge near the Town of Aylsham, called Aylsham Bridge, will be of very great benefit and advantage to your petitioners and to all persons having estates in that Neighbourhood and will tend to the *Improvement of Trade and Commerce*, and be of public Utility.[1]

Trade and commerce, then, were to be the lifeblood of the Navigation and its raison d'être. The Act itself made provision for the levy of tolls, which would provide the Commissioners with one of their main sources of income. The locks would only be opened upon the payment of the toll, and the cargoes carried by wherries were supposed to be strictly policed. Any boat found to have given a 'false account' of their goods would be fined £5 on top of the toll charges. If a dispute arose then the Collector of the Tolls was allowed to detain and search vessels, weighing or counting their cargo if necessary.[2]

Tolls

The first toll collector was the Buxton miller William Pepper, who, as discussed above, was pursued by the Commissioners for outstanding toll payments for several years after he was removed from his office. Pepper was replaced by another miller in August 1777, John Colls of Horstead Mill, who was to collect the toll payments at Horstead Lock, which marked the beginning of the Navigation. In July 1780 the Commissioners debated whether a second toll collector was needed between Aylsham and Horstead, but nothing ever seems to have been resolved. Colls was ordered not to let any vessel pass through the lock at Horstead without a written declaration of goods signed by the owners of the vessel or by the bargemen. In October 1836 John Field of Coltishall was appointed toll collector at Horstead Lock for 3 years, drawing a salary of 9d in every pound for all the tolls he collected.

The Act of 1773 listed the goods which were to be charged a toll for passage along the Navigation,

> For every Ton Weight of Coals, Cinders, Bricks, Pavements, Tiles, Lime, and Terras, the Sum of One Shilling; and for every Ton Weight of Corn, Grain, Meal, Flour, Timber, Goods, wares, Merchandizes, or Commodities whatever… the Sum of One Shilling and Six Pence, and so in Proportion for any greater or lesser Weight than a Ton.

---

1   ATCA, Commissioners' Minutes, 12th January 1773.
2   ATCA, Act for the Improvement of the River Bure, 1773, p.13.

1775-1777	William Pepper, Buxton
1777-1806	John Colls, Horstead.
1807-1836	Mary Gant, Hautbois.
1836-1847	John Field, Coltishall.
1848-1862	John Mace, Superintendant at Horstead Lock
1862-1869	William Mace
1869-1912	Elijah Bircham
1912-1920	Frederick Stevenson

Toll Collectors on the Aylsham Navigation between 1775 and 1920.

The tolls were to be reduced to two-thirds for goods transported to and from Skeyton Beck, just upstream from Buxton Mill, and which would therefore pass through the locks at Buxton and Horstead only. No toll was to be charged on 'Straw, Muck, Marle, Clay, or other Materials to be used in the improving or manuring of Lands only, nor for any such Boat, Barge or other Vessel laden with any materials for the Repair of any Mill or Mills upon the said River'.

In 1791 a toll table for the Navigation was published, probably one of many editions which have not survived. The cheapest rates were charged for tiles and bricks; a heavy and bulky load but one in which the unit value of each brick and tile was relatively low. Coal was also a bulky load with a relatively low value, and this was charged at 1 shilling per chaldron (a standard unit of measurement for coal which equates to 36 bushels). Oak and fir timber and most agricultural produce were charged tolls of 1 shilling and six pence, apart from barley and oats which were charged slightly less. This higher toll reflects the higher value of these products, and the number of different types of grain listed shows how closely the Navigation was linked to the local agrarian economy.

During the nineteenth century the tolls were amended periodically. In February 1836, for example, the toll on coal was to be 10 pence a ton, but only two thirds of this would be charged if the coal was landed at Buxton. In July 1857 there was a more comprehensive review, and tolls were reduced on certain items. The tolls were charged either to Skeyton Beck or to Aylsham. Skeyton Beck was an important cut off point for tolls throughout the life of the Navigation. Located between the locks at Buxton and Oxnead, it was a convenient halfway point along

Cargo	Toll per ton
Wheat	1s 5d
Barley	1s 3d
White Bricks	1s
Red Bricks	9d
Malt	1s 6d
Buck	1s 6d
Oats	1s 5d
Peas and Tares	1s 6d
12 inch Pavement (tiles)	9d
9 inch Pavement (tiles)	9d
Red Pantiles	9d
Roof Pantiles	9d
Rye	1s 6d
Flour and Meal	1s 6d
Oak Timber	1s 6d
Fir Timber	1s 6d
Blue Holland Tiles	1s
Roof Tiles	1s
10 inch Kiln Tiles	1s
Coal	1s per chaldron

Details of tolls from the 1791 toll table.

the Navigation which meant that vessels which were not going all the way to Aylsham were not charged the full toll.

	Wheat	Flour	Barley	Timber	Oilcake
To Aylsham	1s 3d	1s 3d	1s	6d	1s
To Skeyton	10d	10d	8d	4d	8d

1857 reduction in tolls on certain goods.

The accounts of the Navigation do not record the individual tolls made on each cargo, nor have the day books survived for the eighteenth and nineteenth centuries. However, the accounts do show how much the Commissioners received in toll payments in total (after the toll collectors took their cut of 5%), which gives an overview of the total amount of tolls charged.

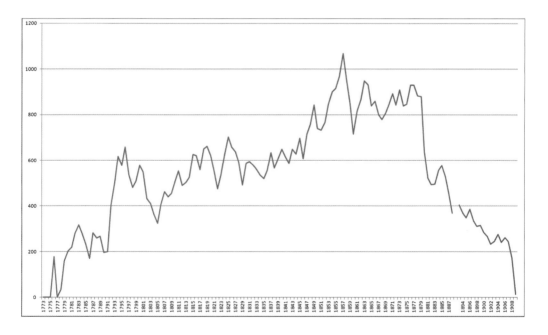

Graph showing the income in £ from tolls between 1773 and 1909.

The total amount of tolls received can be interpreted in two ways; the amount reflects the number of vessels passing along the Navigation and the value of the goods carried by each wherry. There is almost a full run of toll figures for the whole life of the Navigation, from 1773 to 1909. On average the Commissioners received £538 a year from tolls, but this varied hugely on a yearly basis. In 1790 there was a significant drop in tolls when £196 was taken, compared to £266 in the previous year. After this, the amount of tolls begins to rise significantly, with £658 received in 1796. The rapid growth in the amount of tolls taken during the 1790s could perhaps be attributed to the fact that the Navigation was now fully finished and that a number of warehouses had been constructed on the staithe at Aylsham; after what appears to have been a relatively slow start, the 1790s appear to have been the decade when the Navigation began to be more heavily used. Thereafter the amount received from tolls declines, dipping to £364 in 1804. Without more detailed records it is difficult to be certain about the reasons behind these fluctuations. In general terms the picture up until the 1790s was one of growing prosperity, perhaps as the Navigation became more widely used in the first twenty years after its completion. The decline in the amount of tolls received after the late 1790s is not surprising given the general political and economic situation. Apart from a few months of peace after the Treaty of Amiens in 1802, the war against France continued. In particular, international and coastal trading routes were disrupted due to naval hostilities, and it was not until after the Battle of Trafalgar in 1805 that the British Navy effectively dominated the seas. For this period, therefore, there must have been a significant amount of disruption with the Yarmouth trading routes, and there was perhaps a decline in the number of wherries bringing cargoes from the coast upstream to Aylsham. In addition, a series of failed harvests in the years after 1800 may have meant that less agricultural produce was being taken downstream from Aylsham.

However, the toll payments recovered during the later 1810s and 1820s, and generally continued to rise into the middle of the nineteenth century. In 1849 the amount being received in yearly tolls was significantly higher at £842, compared to £364 in 1804. Generally the Navigation was doing far better in the late 1840s than at any earlier point in its existence. It was by now a well established part of the local trading landscape, and a vital part of the transportation network. The middle years of the nineteenth century also saw a burst of activity on the staithe in Aylsham itself, including the construction of the steam mill by Frederick Copeman in 1856, and the development of a tannery and sawmill in the 1860s. In the early 1850s there was a slight drop in the tolls, but this was quickly recovered to a peak in 1857 when £1067 was collected. This was the year in which the decision was taken to reduce the tolls on wheat, flour, barley, timber and oilcake, and in the years following the amount taken in tolls falls relatively quickly. In 1860 £716 was collected; a drop of just over 30% in three years. The following year, in 1861, the toll on timber was raised again, to 1 shilling per ton, and the Commissioners recognised that the previous toll of 4 pence or 6 pence was far too low.

During the late 1860s and the 1870s the income from tolls remained relatively stable, with a few fluctuations up and down, but never dropping below £750 per year. In the 1880s the tolls began to nosedive, for reasons which will be discussed later in this chapter.

Wharfingers and Dispatches

A wharfinger was an officer appointed by the Commissioners, who was responsible for overseeing the dispatch of vessels from the quay, or wharf. In 1791 the first wharfingers were appointed, William Parmeter at Aylsham, Thomas Pearson at Buxton and William Pratt at Yarmouth. Pearson did not last long, and was replaced a month after his appointment by Thomas Welch. William Parmeter died in 1792 but the position of wharfinger at Aylsham remained with the Parmeter family until 1836 when Thomas Wright, the boatbuilder, was appointed as the temporary wharfinger from Aylsham to Burgh Mills. The millers at Burgh, Buxton and Horstead generally acted as wharfingers for their respective staithes. In September 1846 the position of wharfinger at Great Yarmouth was abandoned, and the Commissioners noted in the minutes that it was a cause of 'great expense but without any corresponding advantage'. At the same time a committee of the Commissioners recommended a reorganisation of responsibilities, with a salaried Superintendent based at Horstead Lock taking responsibility for maintenance, the collection of tolls and the administration of the staithes. John Mace was appointed to the position and the post of clerk of works and collector of tolls remained bundled together for the rest of the Navigation's history.

The importance of the wharfinger lies in the fact that he was responsible for charging six pence for every boat dispatched along the Navigation. The tickets issued by the wharfingers have not survived, but the total amounts charged by them are recorded in the accounts of the Commissioners. This means that it is possible to reconstruct the number of boats dispatched along the Navigation from 1793 to 1847. In total, just over 48,000 vessels are recorded as being dispatched during this period from Aylsham, Burgh, Buxton and Yarmouth. Of course, some vessels may have travelled along the Navigation without a dispatch ticket, or without the ticket being recorded, so we must treat these figures with some caution, but in general terms they do show the volume of trade, and the relative importance of each staithe.

More vessels were recorded as being dispatched from Yarmouth than any other point on the Navigation, although Aylsham was the other key dispatch point. Both Burgh and Buxton maintained a steady number of dispatches throughout the period. In 1793, when the records begin, 890 vessels were dispatched, and £504 was collected in tolls. Traffic peaked in 1796 when 1,222 vessels were recorded. The number of vessels decreased sharply in the first decade of the nineteenth century, with the inevitable effect on the amount of tolls received. As discussed above, the economic situation created by the wars with France, and a series of poor harvests almost certainly accounts for this dip in trade. In general terms the 1820s were a time of economic crisis across the whole country, caused by a slump in prices and an agricultural depression brought about by the end of the war in 1815. However, the Navigation appears to have bucked this trend to some extent, and the 1820s was actually a period of recovery rather than crisis, after the tolls record an apparent slump in trade in the very late 1790s and early 1800s.

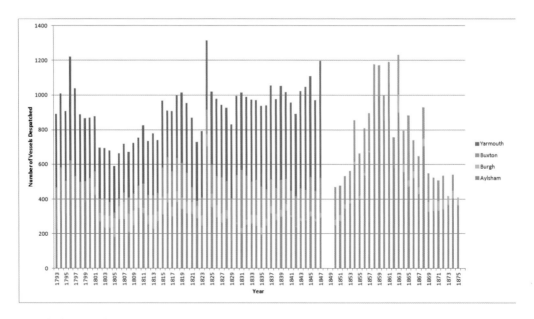

Graph showing the total number of vessels dispatched from Yarmouth, Buxton, Burgh and Aylsham between 1793 and 1847. The apparent growth in the number of dispatches from Aylsham in the late nineteenth century may relate to the fact that tickets were no longer being issued at Yarmouth from 1847 onwards.

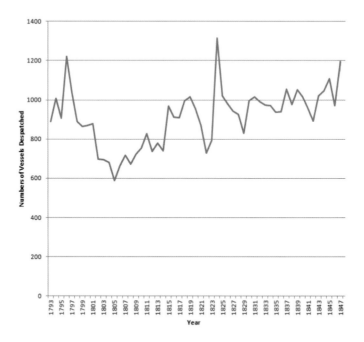

Graph showing the total number of vessels dispatched per year in total (regardless of location).

Agricultural Produce

One of the main cargoes carried on the Navigation was agricultural produce, hardly surprising for an area where the main focus was on arable farming. The 1791 toll table shows that the Commissioners clearly expected wheat, barley, oats and rye to be carried along the Navigation. The lack of documentary evidence about the exact cargoes of the wherries means that it is impossible to know in what proportions each of these crops was carried in the eighteenth and nineteenth centuries. The only surviving day book which describes the cargoes of each wherry is from 1907/8, at the end of the Navigation's life. These books record the constant passage of wheat, barley, maize, oats and millet along the Navigation, loaded onto wherries in Aylsham and Buxton and sent downstream to Yarmouth. Between February 1907 and January 1908 over 800 tons of wheat were carried on the Navigation, much of which went on the *Zulu* which was owned by Ben Cook, the miller at Aylsham, and then by Barclay and Pallett, who operated on the staithe at Aylsham. Flour was also a more minor cargo, presumably ground at the mills along the Navigation itself from wheat produced by local farmers.

Barley was also one of the biggest cargoes taken along the Navigation in 1907/8, see p 135, and had probably been one of the most important crops from the outset. In 1813 Arthur Young remarked that Norfolk was 'the greatest barley county in the kingdom, this grain forming the chief dependence of most of the farmers'.[3] In East Norfolk, he noted that the seed barley was planted 'when the buds of the oak are breaking, a few days before the expansion of the leaves'.[4] Young discussed the barley crops of Mr Parmeter of Aylsham, and of Mr Repton at Oxnead. Repton shared the detailed results of his barley yields between 1773 and 1800 with Young. In 1773 he harvested 1 bushel of barley from 113 acres, and by 1800 was taking 3.5 bushels from 94 acres.[5] The productivity of Repton's land was generally increasing over this period, no doubt due to improved methods of drainage, sowing and fertilizing that were common among late eighteenth-century landowners, and advocated by Young. The barley crop, therefore, was important to the Navigation from the late eighteenth century onwards.

The main use to which the barley carried on the Navigation would have been put was the production of malt for brewing. As discussed above, most of the villages along the Navigation had at least one malthouse in the nineteenth century. Malthouses were located alongside the Navigation in Aylsham, Lammas, Buxton, and in Coltishall in particular there were significant numbers of malthouses by the late nineteenth century. In Yarmouth, there were also large numbers of maltings; in 1836 White's Directory listed 23 separate maltsters, and the Ordnance Survey maps of the 1880s show maltings all along the Yarmouth quayside.[6]

---

3   Young, A. (1813) *General View of the Agriculture of the County of Norfolk*, p.239.
4   Ibid., p.243.
5   Ibid., p.253.
6   White, W. (1836) *History, Gazetteer and Dictionary of Norfolk*, pp.289; 298.

The other most significant agricultural cargo on the Navigation, after the crops themselves, were the various fertilisers used during this period, which were exempt from tolls. The two most important of these were lime and marl. Marl is a calcareous chalky subsoil, found throughout Norfolk, and extracted in large quantities to apply to the soil as a fertiliser. The chemical properties of marl help to neutralise the acidity of sandy soils which, along with a package of other measures, meant that yields were likely to increase. Such sandy soils were a particular feature of the area between Norwich and the north Norfolk coast, and in the late eighteenth century a large tract of open heathland survived in the area to the south and west of the Navigation, around Marsham and Stratton Strawless, which were being improved and reclaimed for arable use with the application of marl and other fertilisers. Huge amounts of marl were needed to bring the poorest soils into good condition. It was not unheard of for 100 barrow loads of marl to be applied per acre in some parts of west Norfolk.[7] Young was quite clear that the best way to transport marl was by water, and mentions various farmers who purchased marl 'from the staithe', including a Mr Cubit at Catfield in the Broads, who bought marl at Horstead and carried it by water down the Bure.[8] However, Young does also suggest that some marl was carted overland, and mentions Mr Margateson of North Walsham who 'brings it five miles from Oxnead and Lammas', a journey which must have been made overland, even if the marl was collected from the staithes on the river.[9]

Lime was used to the same effect, but was more efficient and concentrated than marl. Lime was produced in specialist lime kilns, where limestone was burnt at a high temperature in order to produce a powder, known as quicklime which could be applied to the soil, as well as being used for lime mortar for the building trade. The agricultural revolution of the late eighteenth century and the expansion of towns and cities prompted a huge demand for lime from both the agricultural and building sectors, prompting the construction of well built limekilns across the country, many of which survive (earlier limekilns were often temporary structures).[10] As limekilns required a constant supply of limestone, they were often built near the coast, a navigable river or a canal. However, in East Anglia limestone does not occur naturally, so chalk was more commonly burnt to produce lime. Lime itself is vulnerable to damage by rain and moisture, so the main role of the Navigation may have been to transport the chalk to burn to produce lime, as well carrying the finished product itself.[11] In October 1786 George Anson of Oxnead 'was desirous' of making a limekiln on his estate at Oxnead, to be linked to the Navigation by a short new cut 'for the convenience of water carriage'.[12] The Commissioners agreed in principal, as long as the Anson estate agreed to take responsibility for the new cut and to keep it in good repair. However, no new cut appears to have been constructed, perhaps because Anson was not prepared to maintain it. The limekiln was located on the site of what is now Limekiln Farm, on the same site as the brickyard which was shown on Faden's map of Norfolk of 1797. In Lammas a field near the Navigation was recorded as 'Limekiln Pightle' on

7   Young, A. (1813) *General View*, p.406.

8   Ibid., p.408.

9   Ibid.

10 Williams, R. (1989) *Limekilns and Limeburning*.

11 Jones, J. and Manning, M. (1993) 'Limeburning and Extractive Industries' in P. Wade Martins ed., *An Historical Atlas of Norfolk*, p.162.

12 ATCA, Commissioners' Minutes, October 1786.

the Tithe Apportionment of 1841, but there is no kiln shown on the Ordnance Survey map of 1880, and the site was subsequently built over. Two more limekilns were located in Coltishall, both of which were substantial brick built structures and which have both survived. The kiln on Station Road is one of the best surviving examples in Norfolk, and is now a Grade II listed structure.[13]

Oil cake was used as both a fertiliser and an animal feed, and was particularly recommended as a fertiliser for turnips. Oil cake took various forms, but in general it was a solid cake made up of seeds, nuts or other produce which had been pressed to remove their oils. The remaining husks were compressed into a cake which could be used as a fertiliser or as animal feed. Mr Syble, of South Walsham, told Young that he found the muck from cattle fed on oil cake was one of the best manures.[14] Cake remained important into the nineteenth century, when it became a particular feature of so-called 'High Farming' between the 1840s and 1870s, a period when farmers were increasingly reliant on purchased fertilisers, rather than those produced on the farm. The 1907/8 day books record the passage of cake on the Navigation regularly, see p 135, but it had been important since the late eighteenth century, when it was often imported from Ireland and Holland as well as produced in England. Imported cake from Holland would have landed in Yarmouth, and then was perhaps transported along the Navigation, and by the 1830s there were five cake merchants in Yarmouth.[15]

As well as the more obvious fertilisers, farmers in this period were also applying more experimental fertilisers. Young records the efforts of one farmer,

> Mr Palgrave, at Coltishall, uses much sea-mud, scraped up by the bear from the bottom of Yarmouth Haven: he lays on 40 loads per acres, and has thus manured 70 acres; the improvement very great.[16]

This 'sea mud' must have been brought by wherry from Yarmouth to Coltishall, although not on the locked part of the Navigation itself. Palgrave also tried scooping mud from the bottom of the riverbed at Coltishall, which he mixed with both lime and marl before spreading it over his fields, only to discover that it caused 'a profusion of weeds' to grow.[17] Other farmers elsewhere in the county experimented with applying seaweed and river weeds to their land, although Young does not mention any examples from the area of the Navigation. Ashes, night soil and even sticklebacks were applied to the soil in the quest for improvement.[18] Later in the nineteenth century, bone meal and other general fertilisers were being produced in Aylsham at the bone mill on the staithe, which included the use of imported herring offal.

Marl and lime both left their mark in the landscape in the form of kilns and extraction pits. The map below shows the distribution of extraction pits, lime kilns and brick kilns in the nineteenth

---

13 Norfolk Historic Environment Record 16680, accessed at www.heritage.norfolk.gov.uk.

14 Young, A. (1813) *General View*, p.420.

15 White, W. (1836) *History, Gazetteer and Dictionary of Norfolk*.

16 Young, A. (1813) *General View*, p.414.

17 Ibid., p.433.

18 Ibid., p.417.

century. There were no such features along the Navigation in the stretch leading into Aylsham itself, but from Burgh to Coltishall the landscape was full of pits and kilns of all types. Brick and tile making is discussed in more detail below, but in terms of the fertilisers carried along the Navigation, this map shows the location of 16 marl pits and 5 lime kilns. Some of the marl extracted from these pits would have been used by the local farmers themselves on their own fields, but some may also have been supplied for the construction of the Navigation itself, and of course it was free to move marl and lime along the Navigation as they were exempt from tolls. There are also 16 gravel pits shown on the map, as well as 13 unspecified extraction pits, most likely sand, gravel, marl or clay. Gravel was used widely in the eighteenth and nineteenth centuries for repairing roads, and each parish throughout the county maintained a number of gravel pits. In 1907 the *Zulu* did carry gravel along the Navigation, and there are several pits very close to the river, but it is difficult to assess how significant gravel was as a cargo; much of that extracted may have been for parish use. The other extraction pits may have included sand or clay pits, which were a common feature of the Norfolk landscape. Sand and clay was used for building, brick making and were also sometimes applied to the soil itself.

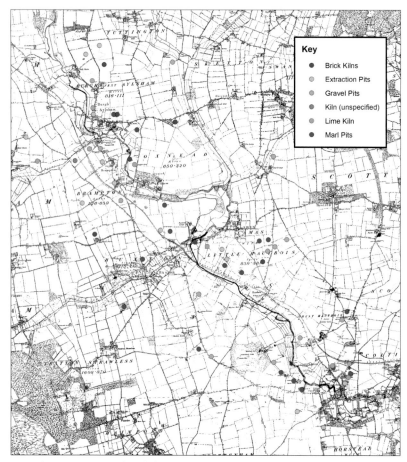

The location of extraction pits, limekilns and brick kilns along the Navigation in the nineteenth century, shown on the Ordnance Survey six-inch map of 1880. Compiled from field names in the Tithe apportionments (c1840) and locations shown on the Ordnance Survey six-inch map.

Bricks and Tiles

Brickmaking was a key regional industry in Norfolk in the nineteenth century. By the middle of the eighteenth century brick had replaced timber as one of the main building materials in the east of England, and many parishes supported a brick kiln which was owned by a local landowner or large farmer who could operate the kiln with the help of their own agricultural labourers. The industry developed in a small-scale disparate way, with a large number of small brickyards spread across the whole county, rather than a small number of very large brickyards. Roof and floor tiles, drainage pipes and pots could also be manufactured in local brickyards and often fired in the same kiln. The production of locally made bricks and tiles was an important industry along the Navigation, and a key cargo on wherries. Bricks were a heavy and bulky cargo with a low unit cost, and it was much cheaper and easier to move them around using water transport. The 1791 toll table lists a variety of different bricks and tiles; red and white bricks, different types of floor tiles, pantiles and other roof tiles. All of these were charged a toll of either 1 shilling or 9 pence, the cheapest rates on the Navigation. A total of 7 different brick kilns are shown on the map above, most of which appear to have been relatively small yards, owned and operated by local farmers. The exception to this was Anson's brickyard in Oxnead, discussed in more detail in the chapter above.

In most rural yards the clay was extracted during the autumn and winter, the bricks moulded and dried over winter and early spring, before being fired from late spring into the following autumn.[19] After moulding the bricks had to be dried for up to a month before being fired. The photograph below shows an unidentified brickyard along the Bure in the late nineteenth or early twentieth century. The newly moulded bricks are being loaded onto a barrow, and would then be stacked in 'hacks' and covered with straw and timber to protect the bricks from the weather. The neat row of straw bundles in the background of the photograph is probably concealing stacks of drying bricks waiting to be fired.

An undated photograph of a brickyard on the River Bure by Dr P.H. Emerson. The exact location is unknown.

19   Lucas, R. (1993) 'Brickmaking' in P. Wade Martins ed., *An Historical Atlas of Norfolk*, p.154.

In 1784 the government introduced a tax on bricks and tiles, which was payable by the brickmakers themselves. Bricks were charged at 2 shillings and 6 pence per thousand, and tiles at 3 shillings per thousand. In 1794 and 1803 the taxes were raised to a high of 5 shillings per thousand for bricks, and 4 shillings and 10 pence for tiles. This had the effect of raising the cost of both bricks and tiles significantly. Although there has been no detailed examination of the figures for Norfolk, research in Bedfordshire suggested that this had an adverse effect on the brick and tile trade. The Duke of Bedford's estate office worked out the cost of bricks carefully in the first half of the nineteenth century, including the transport costs. A load of a thousand bricks cost 34 shillings, and it cost 9 pence to move the bricks over a mile; 2% of the total cost. As the mileage increased, the costs rose dramatically, and a distance of 5 miles cost 14 shillings, thus adding over 40% to the total bill.[20] This emphasises the importance of local brickyards in the nineteenth century economy, and in the case of the Navigation, the critical importance of water transport to the brick trade.

The repeal of the brick tax in 1850 opened up the brick trade to huge expansion across the country. In 1861 there were 114 brickyards in Norfolk, the fourth highest in the country.[21] The rising population and demand for new housing in both urban and rural areas prompted an upsurge in brickmaking, as did agrarian developments, such as the widespread introduction of tile drainage on heavy soils from the 1840s onwards.[22] The arrival of the railways stimulated demand for bricks in the construction of stations, bridges and other features. However, the railways also meant that bricks could be imported from outside the county, from the huge brickyards in Bedfordshire and Northamptonshire. In the 1880s there were only 24 brickyards left in Norfolk, due partly to this flooding of the market.[23] Along the Navigation, many of the smaller brickyards had disappeared by the 1880s. The only active one was that in Oxnead, shown on the 1880s Ordnance Survey map, but this too had disappeared by the time the 1906 edition was published.

Textiles

In the 1770s when the Navigation was being constructed, the textile industry was on the brink of change, but would still have been broadly recognisable to a weaver from the sixteenth or seventeenth centuries. Most spinning and weaving was still being carried out in the home, albeit often for large-scale producers based in urban areas like Norwich. Mechanisation had arrived in the parts of the north and the Midlands, but most areas had not yet adopted the shuttle or the spinning jenny, and still relied on hand looms and spinning. Norfolk was well known for being a key centre in worsted production, and the trade continued to expand in the eighteenth century, albeit at a slower rate than other areas. In 1772 Arthur Young valued the Norwich textile trade at £1.2 million, but in the same year the Yorkshire trade was valued at £3.3 million.[24] It has been estimated that about half of the cloth produced in England in

---

20 Cox, A. (1979) *Brickmaking: a history and gazetteer*, p.31.
21 Lucas, R. (1993) 'Brickmaking', p.154.
22 Cox, A. (1979) *Brickmaking*, p.35.
23 Lucas, R. (1993) 'Brickmaking', p.154.
24 Jenkins, D. and Ponting, K. (1982) *The British Wool Textile Industry 1770-1914*, p.1.

the 1770s was being exported, mostly to Europe but also to North America and the East Indies.[25] The Norfolk textile industry and trade was a complex one; a master weaver would 'put out' the work of spinning yarn, weaving cloth, dying and finishing to workers all over the county before sending the finished article to London, or other major markets. This type of disparate, decentralised system was effective, but not necessarily conducive to factory-style organisation which came to dominate the North.

In the 1820s the woollen industry in national terms began to recover from the interruption of trade caused by the Napoleonic Wars. Although there were some sharp falls during the 1820s, overall the pattern was one of growth, stimulated by the demand for exports from the United States and South America.[26] In particular, the production of blankets for the American market was a key export in the first half of the nineteenth century. In 1827 1.2 million yards of blankets were shipped to the United States, and in 1852 the trade peaked at 6.7 million yards.[27] In the 1820s the mill at Oxnead was converted into a textile mill producing Duffield blankets by Robert and Page Bleakley. No archival documentation about the details of their trade has survived in public archives, but they also maintained a strong presence in Norwich, with its strong links to the London and European textile trades, it is not unreasonable to suggest that the Bleakley's blankets may have ended up on the international market.

Although the mill at Oxnead appears to have prospered during the early nineteenth century, on a national scale the production of woollen textiles was falling due to the huge increase in cotton production. At the turn of the eighteenth century the export market was significantly disrupted by the wars with France, and briefly against America. In 1800 the value of woollen exports was £8 million, but had dropped to £5 million by 1808, a 30% drop in the value of exports. In the same period, the value of cotton exports doubled.[28] The woollen textile industry had already been in decline, but the Napoleonic Wars certainly accelerated the decay. However, this decline in exports was not mirrored in the domestic market, which actually increased during the late eighteenth and early nineteenth centuries. Many English manufacturers began producing higher quality textiles during this period, and Norwich became well known for it calimancoes and bombazines, as well as blended cotton and wool textiles.

At the end of the eighteenth century the textile industry was still to some extent dominated by small-scale producers, although large-scale manufacturers employing large numbers of people were becoming more typical. The process was also becoming more geographically restricted, particularly to urban areas like Norwich and other towns and villages, where the population was rising quickly.[29] In areas which specialized in worsted

---

25 Ibid., p.7.

26 Ibid., p.68.

27 Glover, F. (1961) 'Philadelphia Merchants and the Yorkshire Blanket Trade' in *Pennsylvania History*, vol. 28, no. 2, p.130.

28 Seward, D. (1972) 'The Wool Textile Industry 1750−1960' in J. Geraint Jenkins ed. *The Wool Textile Industry in Great Britain*, p. 36.

29 Ibid., p.40.

cloths, like East Anglia, new technologies were not considered to be appropriate, and were not adopted in Norwich until the 1820s. The adoption of machinery did not necessarily equate to factory production, however, as they could be hand operated and could be small enough for domestic–scale use.[30] The use of power looms for both weaving and spinning meant that more women and children could become involved in processes which had previously been dominated by men, and who could be paid a cheaper rate. The census returns for this period show that the Bleakleys were using both female and child labour in the mill at Oxnead during the first half of the nineteenth century.

With respect to the Navigation itself, it is unclear how the venture was affected by the slow decline of the textile industry in Norfolk, and in East Anglia more widely. The lack of surviving records about early wherry cargoes means we cannot know how many were related to the production of textiles. However, it seems extremely unlikely that the Bleakleys would not have made full use of the Navigation when producing blankets at Oxnead Mill, both for shipping the finished product to Yarmouth or Norwich, or for receiving the raw materials needed for blanket-making; wool, shoddy and other rags were widely used.

Coal

Crops, marl, lime, bricks and possibly textiles; these were the goods moved up and down the Navigation that were being produced, and often used, relatively locally. However, one of the biggest and most important cargos that was carried into the area was coal. For the majority of the eighteenth century coal was mainly used for domestic purposes, as well as for limited industrial use in iron smelting, lime burning, brick making and malting (all of which were also carried out using wood and other fuels, such as gorse or heather).[31] Most power was still generated by water, and occasionally by wind. However, the eighteenth century was also the period in which coal consumption began to change, and by 1830 it was widely used in industry and to power steam engines.[32] Like other bulky commodities, coal had a relatively low unit price, but was costly to transport over land. Again, water transport was critical in the coal trade as it meant that more coal could be transported for a cheaper price than it could by being taken overland.[33]

Most of the coal consumed in London and in East Anglia came from the coalfields in the north-east, in Northumberland and County Durham. Despite the long journey by sea to the ports of Kings Lynn and Yarmouth, there were no other coalfields which could have supplied the eastern region without a long journey overland.[34] In 1749 21% of the coal shipped from Newcastle ended up in Yarmouth, compared to just 8% which was taken all the way to London.[35] By 1829 Norfolk's share in the coal trade had diminished to just

---

30   Ibid., p.43.
31   Flinn, M.W. (1984) *The History of the British Coal Industry, vol. 2: 1700-1830 The Industrial Revolution*, p.1.
32   Ibid., p.2.
33   Ibid., p.3.
34   Ibid., p.19.
35   Ibid., p.220.

9% of the total carried from Newcastle, but was still second only to London (52%).[36] The north-eastern coalfields saw sustained and rapid expansion in the period after 1780, and they remained the country's most significant producer of coal throughout the nineteenth century. In 1775 the north-east produced 2,990,000 tons of coal, and by 1830 this had increased to 6,915,000 tons; a reflection of both increasing output as mining technology improved and a growing number of collieries.[37]

However, the fact that coal was simply not economically viable to transport overland in large quantities meant that many communities were cut off from easy access to coal, unless they were situated upon a navigable waterway. It was this need which prompted the construction of many river navigations and artificial canals during the eighteenth and early nineteenth centuries. One of the most famous early canals, the Bridgewater Canal, was constructed purely for the purpose of moving coal from the Duke of Bridgewater's mine at Worsley into Manchester. This was a distance of only 6 miles, but the economic incentive was such that the financial outlay in constructing the canal would be amply repaid. Before the construction of the canal coal was selling in Manchester for 7 pence per hundredweight and after the canal opened the price dropped to 4 pence, but the amount of coal which could now be moved cheaply and easily outweighed the drop in price.[38] The north-eastern coalfields, which supplied the east of England with coal, jealously guarded their monopoly over the trade to the extent that the owners of collieries prevented other canals and navigations from carrying coal to London. In 1769 the Oxford Canal linked the coalfields of the Midlands to London along the Thames, but the act of Parliament prohibited the carriage of coal beyond Oxford, a clause inserted at the behest of northern coal suppliers.[39]

In terms of the Navigation itself, coal is rarely mentioned in either the Commissioners' minutes or the account books. Evidence for the importance of coal to the history of the Navigation must therefore be drawn from other sources. One of few references to coal in the minutes comes from December 1790, when George Gott, a farmer from Oulton, leased a small piece of land near the head of the Navigation in Aylsham to build a warehouse and coal yard.[40] By 1845 five coal merchants were listed on the staithe in Aylsham, as well as a number of others along the course of the whole Navigation, as detailed below.[41] In 1849 the Aylsham Gas Works opened, the £1,500 cost of which was raised by local shareholders, followed in 1854 by a steam mill on the staithe in Aylsham. Both of these were powered by coal which at this date would have been transported on the Navigation, rather than by rail.

It is very difficult to quantify the importance of coal to the Navigation and to the immediate area, as the exact cargoes of wherries are not recorded for the majority of the

---

36 Ibid., p.221.
37 Ibid., p.26.
38 Ibid., p.182.
39 Ibid., p.186.
40 ATCA, Commissioners' Minutes, December 1790.
41 White, W. (1845) *History, Gazetteer and Dictionary of Norfolk.*

Parish	Name
Aylsham	Copeman and Soame
	Matthew Howes
	Robert Margetson Junior
	John Mayston
	Joseph Sexton
Brampton	George Bircham, coal merchant
Lammas	James Daniels, coal merchant
	James Kerrison, coal merchant
Buxton	Robert Mack, coal dealer
Horstead	James Wright, coal and timber merchant
Coltishall	Samuel Buck, coal merchant and brewer
	Mealing and Mills, corn merchants of Norwich
	Robert Watts, carpenter and coal dealer
	Thomas Wright, coal and timber merchant
	George Ives, butcher, brewer, coal merchant and proprietor of the White Lion.

Coal merchants listed in White's Directory, 1845.

Navigation's life. However, in general terms, the Navigation opened up the rural area between Coltishall and Aylsham to a much cheaper and more accessible supply of coal, which became something that was now within the financial and physical reach of a much larger number of people than ever before.

Water transport was one of the critical factors in the expansion of coal consumption in the eighteenth century, but the arrival of widespread railway transport in the nineteenth century revolutionised the trade. Huge amounts of coal were eaten up by the heavy industries developing in the Midlands and the north, as well as by the railways themselves. In 1851 the Great Northern Railway Company began carrying coal to London, and the trade in coal shipped by rail began to expand rapidly, particularly to areas well outside the main coal producing regions, including East Anglia.[42] In 1830 the coastal trade in coal accounted for 20% of the trade, but by the 1880s this had fallen to just 8%.[43] However, the coastal trade staged a huge recovery in the 1890s and 1900s, due

---

42 Church, R. (1986) *The History of the British Coal Industry, vol. 3: 1830-1913 Victorian Pre-eminence*, p.20.

43 Ibid.

partly to the increasing size and efficiency of vessels, and the links between the north-eastern coalfields, the east coast ports and London remained strong.[44] In the 1850s a rare reference to coal in the Commissioners minutes notes that the limekilns at Oxnead were powered by coal, and in the 1907 day books the *Zulu* carried several loads of coal.[45]

Timber

Timber was another important cargo carried along the Navigation. It was heavy, bulky but with a high value, unlike many of the other goods discussed above. As the Navigation was being constructed, timber was moved by water along the completed sections to be used for building the locks. Some timber, however had to be moved overland. In 1775, for example, the Commissioners employed teams of horses to move oak and deal timber being stored in fields in Coltishall to the site of Buxton Lock.[46] The Commissioners continued to purchase large amounts of timber for repairs during the eighteenth and nineteenth centuries, and the minute books contain numerous notes about purchasing timber to repair the locks, bridges, buildings and fences alongside the Navigation. As timber was unloaded at the staithe in Aylsham each load was measured and recorded by the wharfinger, but unfortunately these records have not survived.[47] In December 1847 there were complaints about timber which was stacked on the staithe at Aylsham, some of which had been there for 6 years, and which was now blocking access to parts of the staithe. The Commissioners came up with a new by-law, which stated that any timber remaining on the staithe for over a year was charged a fine of 1 shilling per load, and the wharfinger also had the right to remove the timber. There was also a 10 shilling penalty if the timber was removed by road, instead of by water.[48] This suggests that timber was stored on the staithe until needed; it was bulky and was not consumed or used as quickly as coal or bricks may have been. The tolls on timber had been reduced to 6 pence in 1857, but in 1861 there was anxiety about income after the 'Great Frost' of that year and the failure of the barley, so the 'low rate of tolls' on timber was raised in 1862 to 1 shilling per ton. In 1863 it was reported that 'persons using the Navigation especially in the conveyance of Timber are accustomed to overload the wherries and that thereby the Navigation and its water have been materially affected'.[49] In August 1874 Commissioners passed a by-law which banned the floating of timber down the Navigation, a 'practice injurious to the Staithes, Locks, Banks and other works of the said Navigation'. The by-law stated that all timber had to be carried on wherries, at the risk of forfeiture of the timber and a hefty £5 fine.[50] This is an intriguing note, which conjures up images of timber bobbing about in the water as it was floated along the river. It is difficult to be sure whether this actually took place, but for the Commissioners to pass a new by-law and impose a large fine suggests that it may well have happened.

---

44 Ibid., p.21.
45 ATCA, Commissioners' Minutes 1854; Wherry Day Book, 1907/8.
46 Ibid., June 1775.
47 Ibid., December 1848 which includes payments to the wharfinger for measuring loads of timber.
48 Ibid., December 1847.
49 Ibid., February 1863.
50 Ibid., August 1874.

William Frederick Starling discussed the timber trade along the Navigation in the 1860s in his memoirs.

> Agents for the great Yorkshire wood firms go to the estates round the town and buy up the very large oak trees for ship building. There would be gangs of Yorkshire working men lodging with the cottage people in Millgate. These great trees were all taken down to Yarmouth by wherry, then by ship to the north of England, and if you went down any time of day, you would see gangs of men working on these trees – some loading them into the wherries, some cutting them, so they would pass through the locks in the river. And possibly, if you waited a little time, you would see one of the large timber drugs with four horses, bringing in a load of timber. And again if you looked at the quay, you would find a wherry unloading coal; one loading goods for the tradesmen in the town, and one loading up grain to go to Yarmouth. So you can see what a busy little place it used to be.[51]

Timber was an important product in the late eighteenth and nineteenth centuries, used extensively for building, for fuel, for making fences and tools, carts and a myriad of other uses. The main producers of timber in this period were landed estates, like Blickling, Felbrigg, Stratton Strawless or Gunton. Most landowners took the opportunity to plant extensively during this period, prices were high and timber represented a good, long-term investment. It was also a way of getting a high return from relatively poor land which would not have produced a significant yield of grain. The newly enclosed heaths and commons in north Norfolk were a prime location for new plantations of fir, oak and other trees. In 1813 Arthur Young noted that 'the modern spirit of planting took place in Norfolk as early as in other parts of the kingdom, and in some cases, upon a considerable scale'.[52] On the Holkham estate over 2 million trees were planted between 1780 and 1801, and other estates followed a similar pattern, albeit on a smaller scale.[53] Fir and pine timber was also imported from the Baltic in this period, and could have been brought along the Navigation from Yarmouth. The minutes and accounts do not usually specify the source of the timber used and transported along the Navigation, but it would seem likely that wherries were bringing cheap fir and pine timber in from Yarmouth, and taking deciduous timber grown on local estates down from Aylsham.

Staithes

Once a wherry had reached its destination, it was loaded or unloaded at one of the staithes constructed along the Navigation. The first staithe to be built was at Aylsham in 1779, as discussed in detail above. Another staithe was built near Mayton Bridge, and in September 1780 the Commissioners ordered a locked gate to be placed there for 'the better collecting the money to paid for the use of the said staithe'. Any wherries unloading at Mayton were charged 1 shilling, with a penalty if the goods were not removed by 6pm on the same

---

51 Peabody, R. (2000) *Memories of Aylsham: The memoirs of William Frederick Starling 1851–1937.*
52 Young, A. (1813) *General View*, p.381.
53 Ibid.

evening. John Bell of Little Hautbois was appointed as the staithekeeper, with a salary of 5% of his takings. Loading and unloading of wherries also seems to have taken place at all the mills along the Navigation, and possibly at a number of other points, such as the brickyard in Oxnead, but these were not owned by the Commissioners.

During the nineteenth century there were various complaints about the condition of the staithes, and the impact that this might have on trade. In December 1843 Mr James Ladbrooke, a farmer in Hautbois, complained to the Commissioners that Mr James Royall had contracted the area of the staithe at Mayton Bridge by erecting a hedge and fence. Sir Henry Durrant authorised Ladbrooke to remove the obstruction to enable full use to be made of the staithe.[54] In 1847, as mentioned above, John Mace reported complaints about the amount of goods which had been left upon the staithe at Aylsham, including some which had been there for six years. This meant that there was no room on the staithe for goods to be sent down the Navigation 'and that a very large quantity of the timber brought onto the staithe was removed by land carriage and consequently paid no toll'. Commissioners introduced a new bye-law which fined owners, who left marl and muck on the staithe for more than 6 days, a penny per ton, and 1 shilling for 14 days. After 14 days the wharfinger could remove the goods and charge the costs to the owner. Stone, bricks, tiles and slates were all charged at 1 shilling per ton if left for over a month. Timber, however, could be left for up to a year without a fine.

In the middle of the nineteenth century the Commissioners explored the option of creating new staithes. In February 1853 they approached landowners in Oxnead and Buxton to investigate the possibility of making new staithes. In the summer of the same year it was noted that the stakes that had been put down for a new staithe at Coltishall were to be taken up, as no new staithe was deemed necessary. The Commissioners also wrote to Henry Stracey of Oxnead about the possibility of renting the staithe at Oxnead Mill, which was in the possession of Cooke and Gambling, and of creating another staithe between Oxnead and Buxton Mill. Nothing ever seems to have come of the plans for new staithes, and in March 1854 Cooke and Gambling leased the staithe at Oxnead to the Commissioners.

The Coming of the Railways

The advent of the railways, inevitably, had a profound and adverse impact on the Navigation. By the time of the flood in 1912, trade on the Navigation had almost ground to a halt due to the competition offered by the railways.

In 1843 concern over the threat posed by the railways appears in the Minutes for the first time, when the Commissioners expressed concern over a proposal to build a railway bridge over the River Bure in Yarmouth by which 'their interests are likely to be prejudiced'.[55] Early in 1844 they agreed to put a petition to Parliament against the proposed bridge over the Bure, although the bridge was built regardless. At a meeting of the shareholders in Norwich in

---

54 ATCA, Commissioners' Minutes, December 1843.
55 Ibid.

March 1845 it was agreed to join the opposition to the proposed North Norfolk Railway 'it being considered that such a project will be very prejudicial to their interests'. The committee appointed to head up the opposition campaign consisted of James Hunt Holley, William Repton and Robert William Parmeter. A year later, in summer 1846, Samuel Parmeter resigned as Treasurer of the Navigation, 'the duties of that office being incompatible with his interest in a projected Railway to the Town of Aylsham promoted by him'.[56]

1846 was a key year in the history of the Navigation. James Hunt Holley put forward a number of suggestions to the Commissioners for the improvement of the Navigation, and which were designed to put the venture on a more commercial footing, perhaps with the aim of making it more viable in the face of potential competition from the railways in the future. Horstead, rather than Aylsham, became the centre of the operation, and a paid Superintendent was to be employed at a salary of £30 per year, plus 5% of the tolls. He was to live in a newly built house next to the lock at Horstead, and would manage the collection of tolls, the maintenance of the waterway and the management of the staithes. Rather than appointing another Treasurer, the finances of the Navigation were placed under the care of Gurneys Bank in Norwich. The quay and wharfinger at Yarmouth were also dispensed with following these changes.

In 1847 another railway scheme, the North Norfolk Railway, appeared to threaten the Navigation. In January the engineer Mr Phipps attended the Commissioners' meeting and 'submitted to the Commissioners a rough sketch of the proposed terminus of the railway near the Commissioners' staithe, to which the Commissioners made no objection.'[57] The name of the staithe is not recorded, but it seems most likely to have been Aylsham. In the same year the North Norfolk Railway bill was withdrawn, and the Commissioners wrote to the shareholders to update them on various improvements, including the construction of the lock cottage at Horstead, which they felt safe to proceed with now that the threat of the railway appeared to have passed.

It was not until the 1880s that the railways finally reached Aylsham. In February 1879 a letter was received from John Wilson, the engineer of the Aylsham Extension to the East Norfolk Railway, which requested the Commissioners consent about the proposed railway bridge across the river at Buxton.[58] This time there was no question of objecting, merely trying to get the best position of the brick piers for the bridge in the course of the waterway. In January 1880 the station at Aylsham South opened, connecting the town with Norwich. Three years later, in 1883, a station was opened at Aylsham North, which provided services between Great Yarmouth, Melton Constable and the Midlands. Merchants in Aylsham and the surrounding area were quick to react; Thomas Shreeve had opened a milling and coal transport business at Aylsham South by 1883, and his son Henry Shreeve later transferred the business to Aylsham North. Cross and Company, who were corn, cake, coal and seed merchants were established at Aylsham North by 1904.[59]

---

56   Ibid., August 1846.
57   Ibid., January 1847.
58   Ibid., February 1879.
59   ATCA, Aylsham Trade Directories (various).

The 1891 census also sheds some light on the impact of railways on local employment. 34 men were listed as being employed on the railways in the parishes alongside the Navigation, 21 of whom were living in Aylsham. Their occupation included station masters, porters, signalmen, clerks, engine drivers and railway gatekeepers.

The Beginning of the End

The arrival of the railways in Aylsham marked the beginning of the decline of the Navigation. In 1880, the year that Aylsham South Station opened, the tolls fell to £639, a decrease of over £200. Tolls continued to fall throughout the 1880s and 1890s, dipping to £370 in 1888 and £315 in 1899. As well as the declining tolls, the minute book also sheds some light on the problems faced by the Navigation during this period. In 1889 the Commissioners ordered that 'an old wherry belonging to Mr George Bircham of Brampton, lying in the Limekiln Reach' should be broken up and removed from the river; such an obstacle would probably not have remained in situ in years when traffic along the Navigation was at its peak. In the same year the Commissioners summed up the situation succinctly in their annual review, 'the Navigation was considered to be in good order especially with so small an amount of traffic'.[60] In February 1893 the Clerk of the Navigation issued a circular to the shareholders apologising for the lack of dividends in the past year 'owing to the depressed state of trade and falling off of tonnage dues'.[61]

The situation did not improve in the first decade of the twentieth century. In August 1900 the Commissioners noted that 'the decrease in the amount of tolls makes it necessary to curtail the expenses if it can be done without being detrimental to the Navigation'.[62] In the summer of 1901 the men employed as labourers on the Navigation were informed that their services were to be dispensed with in the autumn, and they might not have work again until the following spring. The Commissioners also attempted to charge tonnage on marl and gravel for the first time, presumably as a way of increasing their revenue, but a note in red ink in the minutes noted that this was contrary to the Act and had to be stopped.[63]

In February 1903 it was reported that animals were straying onto the staithe at Aylsham and grazing. The Commissioners decided to let the staithe as grazing for 5 shillings per year. In 1905 Mr Mayes, who leased the grazing, complained that cattle and other animals were being brought to the staithe to graze so a noticeboard was erected stating that the grazing belonged to the Commissioners of the Navigation and that animals were not to be turned onto the grass. This situation does not conjure up images of a bustling quayside in Aylsham at this point. In 1905 just £240 was collected in tolls. This is also the first year in which pleasure craft using the Navigation were first mentioned in the minutes. A vessel had passed upstream through Coltishall Lock, but no one had noted the names of the craft, or the dates, and no tolls had been taken. In August 1906 Mr Ling of Buxton

---

60 ATCA, Commissioners' Minutes, February 1889.
61 Ibid., February 1893.
62 Ibid., August 1900.
63 Ibid., August 1901.

Mill wrote to the Commissioners complaining that Mr Starling of Aylsham had been passing through the locks on pleasure boats. The Clerk replied to Ling to say that Starling owned property next to the Navigation and was therefore entitled to use pleasure boats. In August 1909 the Commissioners received a letter from a Mr Hartridge asking for permission to pass through the lock at Coltishall, but they decided against letting pleasure boats onto the Navigation.

In 1908 the tolls collected amounted to just £172. Desperate to raise funds for maintenance and repairs, the Commissioners asked wherry owners using the Navigation if they would be prepared to compound their tolls into one payment, and to pay the amount direct to the Clerk. It was proposed to charge Barclay and Pallett £60, Cross and Co. £40, Ling £35 and Browne £22 'in discharge of all tolls and to point out that this involved no increase all round and that the Commissioners considered these were the minimum amounts required to keep the Navigation open in its present state'.[64] At two special meetings in September 1908 Barclay and Pallett offered £50 a year in tolls, and Browne refused to pay more than £17. Lord Orford suggested that the present rate of tolls should be continued until the start of 1909, after which point the Commissioners would accept the offers on the table. Mr Browne and other wherry owners would be allowed to continue the practice of paying tolls which were collected on each voyage. The lock-keeper at Horstead, Bircham, was allowed to stay in the cottage rent free, provided that he collect the tolls from Browne and other wherrymen, and prevented 'strange craft' from entering the Navigation. As a result of the compounding of tolls, only £14 were collected in other tolls in 1909; illustrating how reliant the Navigation was on a handful of regular businesses.

In February 1912 the Commissioners received a letter from the North Walsham and Dilham Canal Company asking if they would be interested in selling the Navigation. After some discussion, they wrote back asking what price the North Walsham and Dilham Company had in mind. However, nothing more ever came of this proposal, due to the events of August 1912.

---

64   Ibid., August 1908.

10. Wherries

The earliest illustration of a clearly drawn Norfolk wherry appears on a horn cup in Norwich Castle Museum, dated 1789.[1] Reproduced with permission of Norfolk Museums Service.

---

1   Malster, R. (1971) *Wherries and Waterways.*

It is clear that by the time the Aylsham Navigation was started in the 1770s wherries were not only providing a service for passengers and light goods from Norwich to Yarmouth, but also taking a greater part of the cargo otherwise carried by the larger keels that had their mast amidships and a large square sail.[2] The essential features of a Norfolk wherry relate principally to the hull and rig. The great carrying capacity, on a shallow draught, was achieved by the relatively broad midship sections and some flare of the bow and stern. There is a single mast to the fore of the hold and a single loose–footed sail with a gaff.

The Navigation was dug to allow for just 3 feet of water and was not intended to take wherries of more than 20 tons burden. In 1904 Bradshaw states that the Navigation was suitable for vessels of a length not exceeding 54 feet and a width of 12 feet 8 inches.[3] The *Albion* is 58 feet long, 15 feet wide and carries 44 tons, so the maximum tonnage of wherries would have been around 30 to 34 tons, with perhaps a maximum of 36 tons.[4] Wherries using the upper reaches of the River Bure and the North Walsham and Dilham canal were built with a detachable slipping keel. For the Navigation these could be unbolted and left in the water at Horstead. The hull was clinker-built, that is with overlapping strakes of oak 2 inches thick, usually 14 on each side of the keel, and tarred.

The hull was divided into three sections, with the large transverse beams separating the fore section with the mast and the stern section with the cabin and tiller. The beams were strongly held by knee supports. In the bows was the 'tabernacle', the double post holding the 40 feet mast on a pin (or pintle) with a lead balance weight at the foot so that the mast could be lowered with ease, even when under way with sail up. Hence wherrymen could 'shoot' some bridges by careful approach under sail and at a nicely judged moment lower the mast while still moving forward and on getting through heave up the mast and sail with very little loss of progress. The mast was traditionally of larch, but in later periods Baltic pine was favoured. The sail was hoisted on a gaff by hand in the eighteenth century, but by a winch forward of the mast when the gaff became longer. In later models the sail would be some 1,200 square feet and always dressed with a mixture of coal tar, herring oil (or neatsfoot oil) and lamp-black. The side decks or plankways were usually made of single broad planks. The decking was surrounded by a 4 foot wide wooden strip, the planksheer (plancea or plancher as the wherrymen prounounced it) that was always painted white so as to show up at night. There was then a protective iron rim known as the binns.

When the wind was contrary or lacking the wherryman had to quant. The quant was a 22 to 24 foot pole with a knob or 'bott' at its head and a wooden heel and iron toe at the base. The man walked to the bows, pushed the quant into the riverbed, put the bott to his shoulder and walked the plankway towards the stern. He then twisted the

---

2   Clark, R. (1961) *Black Sailed Traders: The Keels and Wherries of Norfolk and Suffolk.*

3   Bradshaw, G. (1904) *Bradshaw's Canals and Navigable Rivers of England and Wales.*

4   M. Sparkes, personal communication.

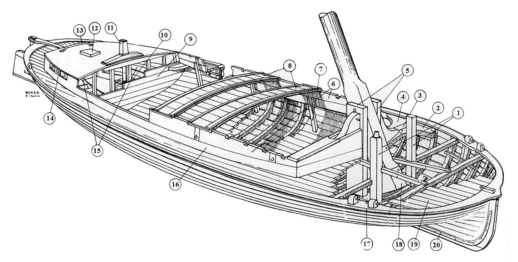

Construction of a Norfolk Wherry drawn by Roger Finch, and reproduced from Malster (1971). 1 Winch stanchions; 2 lodging knees; 3 mainbeam; 4 knees; 5 tabernacle cheeks; 6 shifting right-ups; 7 stanchions; 8 hatch covers; 9 after bulkhead; 10 cabin stove; 11 removable chimney; 12 cabin hatch; 13 main horse; 14 cabin lights; 15 cabin bunks; 16 standing right-ups; 17 iron rubbing band; 18 mast counter weight; 19 deck planking; 20 slipping keel irons.

quant from the mud and returned to repeat the action at the bow. It was heavy labour and accounts of pleasure craft voyaging up to Aylsham in the late nineteenth century indicate that the upper reaches of the Bure often needed quanting or bow-hauling.[5] The hollow bow built up a wedge of water between the vessel and the river bank that held the vessel off the lee shore. The wherryman would approach a headed reach by sailing hard, sheeting in the sail for more speed, and as the bow cut across the corner and started going up to wind the mate would use the quant against the bank to keep the wherry moving forward. Crucially the speed and weight of the wherry would take over 'making way', giving the impression of heading very close to the wind, a technique known as 'lee shoring'.[6]

The hold between the main transverse beams had a surround about 1 foot high known as the standing right-ups. On top of these were the removable shifting right-ups on which were the hatch covers. These were made in 15 to 16 two-foot sections stretching across the width of the hold, cambered so that they shed water, and slotted at their ends into the right-ups. They provided a watertight cover to the hold, but were often covered with a tarpaulin if the cargo was sensitive to water damage.

The stern section of the wherry had the cabin, known as the 'cuddy', with a detachable chimney to the stove, that accommodated the wherryman and his mate – sometimes his wife or even a boy. Further cramped sleeping accommodation was available in the forepeak if necessary. The wherryman stood at the tiller just outside the cabin door and in normal weather steered not so much with his hands as his back. With a high load of hay the mate

---

5   Emerson, P.H. (1893) *On English Lagoons.*

6   Ibid.

might have to guide him from the top of the pile. The name boards flanking the tabernacle bore the name of the wherry, the owner and the place from which she hailed.

Wherries and their Cargo

On the Navigation the Commissioners also insisted that the vessels should display their tonnage, presumably by a mark at water level when laden. In July 1791 the Commissioners ordered that 'whereas the Owners of Boats and Barges using the said Navigation have not been able to mark their Boats and get them gaged so as to ascertaine the Tonnage by the exact Draught of Water pursuant to a Notice of the Commissioners dated the 10th day of June last directing the said Boats and Barges to be marked and gaged previous to this day or that they should not be allowed to pass the Locks of the said Navigation'.[7] They were ordered to comply before 3rd August and a wharfinger was appointed at Yarmouth to monitor their despatch. The records of tonnage recorded for the *Zulu* in 1907/1908, referred to below, were all for a 15 ton load, a part load of 9 ton or a mixed load of 9 ton plus 6 ton, suggesting that she had two marks.

Wherrymen had to deal with a wide variety of cargoes and keep the hold in suitable condition. Agricultural products and timber formed the bulk of material going downstream with coal, and manufactured goods making up the return load. For a load of timber about two-thirds of the load would be carried in the hold, and then planks were stacked along the plankways until they were level, and interlocked with, the timber in the hold. Then the whole width of the craft was used to build up a solid stack two or three feet high. The Aylsham to Yarmouth voyage of about 40 miles normally took one to two days, though the return to Wroxham could be done in five hours. The majority of vessels seen on the Navigation would have been dealing with the cargoes mentioned above and mainly owned by the millers and coal merchants living in the communities along the river.

The transport of other goods may have been brought up to Aylsham from Coltishall or Yarmouth by wherrymen without access to warehouses. The transport of marl and fertilisers, carried free of tolls, was a significant business but the wherry owners were charged groundage, as ordered by the Commissioners in 1791: 'We do hereby order and constitute a bye-Law that every Owner of a Boat or Barge or Boatman belonging to the same on payment of 6d for every Boat or Barge Load upon the Quay or Staith at Aylsham aforesaid belonging to the said Commissioners as a Groundage for keeping the said Quay and Staith in repair Provided the same as laid under the direction of the said Wharfinger not within less than 13 yards from the side and end of the Bason or Canal joining the said Staith.'[8] There was to be a fine of 20 shillings for failure to pay and a threat to seize the cargo if the fine was not paid. They also ordered that 'all Timber Bricks Tiles and such like heavy Articles as shall be brought and laid upon the said Quay

---

7   ATCA, Commissioners' Minute, July 1791.
8   Ibid.

or Staith shall not be laid within 15 yards of the Side or End of the said Bason or Canal but shall be laid on such part of the said Quay or Staith as the said Wharfinger shall appoint or removed by the order of the said Wharfinger to such part as he shall think proper'.[9] By the middle of the nineteenth century the staithe at Aylsham was built up to a greater extent with warehouses and businesses around the steam mill, clearly shown on Ordnance Survey maps from the 1880s onwards. Aylsham merchants probably had much of the market for subsidiary goods as indicated by the entry by D. & J. Wells in the trade directory in 1875 which listed tanners, millers, corn, cake, seed, coal & timber merchants & agents for Odam's chemical manures. Providers of marl from Horstead, bricks from kilns along the river, thatching reeds from the Broads and others would still have had access to the common staithe.

Peter Henry Emerson, a pioneer 'naturalistic' photographer visited Aylsham in his wherry *Maid of the Mist* in February 1891.[10] He was rather dismissive of the town, but noted that a woman carrying a hungry-looking, peevish baby, asked his skipper if he would take them to Newcastle. This is the only written record of vessels being used to hitch a ride, though it may have been a common practice. There is no evidence that the wherries ever provided a regular passenger service on the Navigation.

The census returns and trade directories for Aylsham show the marked increase in activity from 1840 to 1885, as shown in the table below, where the number of wherrymen jumped from 5 to 19 in the decade between 1851 and 1861. The Commissioners tended to discourage pleasure craft from using the Navigation and it seems that only the millers found it convenient and economic to carry on the old trade with the wherries they owned right up to the floods in 1912.

Occupation	1841	1851	1861	1871	1881	1891	1901
Boatbuilder / boatwright	2	2	5	4	2	2	3
Waterman / wherryman	2	5	19	20	14	13	5

Watermen and boatbuilders recorded in the census returns 1841–1901 for the Millgate, Drabblegate and Dunkirk areas of Aylsham.

The *Zulu* is the best known of the wherries trading out of Aylsham. She was probably built in Coltishall at John Allen's boatyard in the 1870s. The 1881 census for vessels docked at Acle records that she was sailed by John Money from Coltishall and his young son from Aylsham. The first known image of her was taken in the 1890s when moored by Acle Bridge, when her name boards then indicated that she was owned by Ben Cook, the miller at Aylsham. She remained with the Aylsham mills until 1912. The *Zulu* is mentioned in 1889 when Harry Brittain, a Norwich bank manager, took a pleasure trip up to Aylsham.

---

9   Ibid.

10 Emerson, P.H. (1893) *On English Lagoons.*

The Zulu being hauled out at Buxton in June 1913 to be taken down to Allen's boatyard in Coltishall for overhaul. Photograph reproduced with the permission of Henry Catchpole.

In the reach which runs straight for Aylsham Lock we overtook a wherry, but as we were in no particular hurry we gave up our turn, and worked them through, much to their delight. It seemed that they had left Yarmouth the previous day at six o'clock in the evening, and sailed on till midnight, when they stopped at Wroxham Bridge. By six next morning they were again under way, and it will be easily believed that they were becoming a bit fagged, although I am bound to admit they did not appear so when we saw them "cleaned up", two hours later, in the town. In due course we, too, passed through the lock, but did not again overtake the *Zulu*, as the wherry was called.[11]

The Zulu at Acle Bridge c.1880. Reproduced with permission of the Finch collection.

11 Brittain, H. (1889) *Notes on the Broads and Rivers of Norfolk and Suffolk.*

In the year from April 1907 to March 1908 the *Zulu* made 101 voyages to Yarmouth, an average of twice a week.[12] She carried 15 tons laden, quite often took mixed loads, and sometimes only part loads. In all she took down a total of 1048 tons, made up as indicated below. On 14 occasions she went down light, probably to pick up coal. She also took down one load of malt from Buxton in March 1908. Allowance should be made for the fact that the Navigation business was now much reduced and only the millers found it convenient to continue using wherries rather than the railway or road. The timber trade had now, for example, ceased to use the river. Nevertheless it does give some idea of the standard work load of an Aylsham wherry. Best noted that trade was seasonal, with higher incomes from the tolls in September, October and November associated with the harvest.[13] This was also a good time to bring up coal on the return journey in preparation for the winter. The summer months were quieter and wherries could be hauled out of the water to be retarred, painted and generally overhauled.

Cargo	Full Loads	Part Loads
Wheat	25	14
Flour	14	9
Barley	9	9
Cake (cattle feed)	5	7
Maize	0	7
Oats	1	0
Salt	2	0
Pollard (bran)	1	3
Wool	1	0
Gravel	1	0
Coals	0	4
Billet (small branches used in herring smoking)	0	1
Beans	0	1

Produce carried from Aylsham to Yarmouth by the Zulu for the year from April 1907 to March 1908.[14]

12 ATCA, Wherry Day Book 1907/8.
13 Best, D. (1976) *The Aylsham Navigation*.
14 ATCA, Wherry Day Book 1907/8.

Boat Building on the Navigation

Allen's yard at Anchor Street, Coltishall. Photograph reproduced with permission of R. Malster.

There was a boatyard at Aylsham and several at Coltishall. Wright's yard in Coltishall was active in the 1770s and the family name is associated with building and repairing boats, skippering wherries and acting as wharfingers and water bailiffs. Robert and Thomas Wright were the main boat builders in Aylsham between the 1840s and 1860s. The Tithe Map of 1840 records Thomas Wright as occupying the cottage in the meadow next to the Maiden's Bower and it is reasonable to suppose that the boatyard was on the inlet from the canal near there. Robert Wright lived in one of Samuel Parmeter's cottages near the maltings. Later it seems that more activity was focussed around the basin, where one of the doorposts on the granary on the south side of the basin, dismantled in the 1970s, had boatmen's graffiti.[15] The boathouse on Staithe Island near the millpool, marked on the Ordnance Survey map of the 1880s, was probably for the use of the miller, but David Wright is said to have worked there and it has also been suggested that some boatbuilding took place in Millgate near the Stonemason's Arms.[16] Thomas Wright, born in Horning like some of the Wright family of Coltishall, was also the Aylsham wharfinger up to 1862 and from 1868 to 1877 ran the Anchor Inn. He had two sons, Thomas and James, who both became watermen. Thomas the younger took his father's place as wharfinger until he died in 1883.

Robert Wright had three sons, David, James and Elijah, who all became boatwrights and lived with their families in Millgate. Elijah became the principal boatbuilder in the second half of the century and was appointed wharfinger in 1883 when Thomas the younger died. He built the *Gipsy* in 1875 for Henry Montague Doughty of Therberton in Suffolk. It is renowned as the only wherry that was towed to the continent and toured extensively around the low countries.[17] Bartlett Wright was another waterman in Aylsham in 1861 but had died by 1871. William, a younger son, and Frederick, a

---

15 Tom Bishop, personal communication.

16 Tom Bishop and Alan Rowlands, personal communication.

17 Doughty, H.M. (1891) *Our Wherry in Wendish Lands.*

grandson by his eldest son Bartlett, were both wherrymen, the latter serving on the *Kate*. By 1901 only Elijah and James were still associated with river trades.

In 1841 three families named Wright lived in Horstead. In Coltishall Francis Wright, aged 80, is recorded as a boatbuilder, as was Thomas Wright. Stephen Wright and Edward Wright were watermen who lived with their families in Watermen's Row, Anchor Street and Kings Head Street. Horning was an important base for the family and Francis's son Thomas was born there, and he became a coal and general merchant in Coltishall, as did James Wright. Three further generations of Thomas Wright were boatbuilders and moved to Norwich St Clement, where their grandson was described as a boatbuilder of 14 in 1861. In 1871, the descendants of the Thomas Wrights were living in Surlingham, and were still described as boatbuilders. In 1881 and 1891, they had moved to Staithe Road in Bungay. Their skills as boatbuilders may have encouraged the mobility of these families. However by 1901 the third Thomas Wright had died. His wife, Catherine, moved back to Norwich, with two of her nine children. Her only son, Albert, had found work with a different form of transport as a railway bookstall clerk.

Allen's boatyard in Anchor Street Coltishall was established in 1864, the premises bought for £400, and continued long after the end of the Navigation. Edward and Samuel Press and John Kerrison were also boatbuilders in Anchor Street in the mid-nineteenth century. Allen's yard not only reconditioned the *Zulu* after the flood, but also repaired the *Hilda*, owned by Cross & Co, that had been brought from Aylsham just ten days before the floods of August 1912. The work was completed on 27th September 1912 for £22 7s 5d, the work including some 450 hours of boatbuilders' time.[18]

It could take up to a year to build a wherry, which was done on a riverside yard without elaborate cranes, gantries or slipways. The oak timber needed to be seasoned for two years and the craftsmen would select the trees they needed for the job, including gnarled specimens from which to hew knees and supports, by eye without drawings or plans. Malster mentions that the woods around Aylsham were one of the principal places for supplying timber in the 1880s.[19]

Jigs were made first for the stem and stern posts. These were cut from oak and affixed to the hog, the broadly T-shaped frame above the keel, the whole mounted on blocks on the slipway. Once supported, jigs or moulds were put in to take the shape of the sides and stringers of wood run round the edges and down the middle from stem to stern.[20] At Allen's yard in Coltishall the strakes were assembled using three moulds until the turn of the bilge was reached, and at that point the frames were inserted; planking of the topsides then proceeded. When fixing the strakes, that had been cut on a pit saw and shaped by eye, they would be heated to make them pliable. The boards were first soaked in the river and then heated with burning reeds before putting them on. The ironwork was done by the local blacksmith, but the mast, gaff, blocks and sail were bought from tradesmen in

---

18 Geoffrey Nobbs was kindly granted the privilege of access to John Allen's repair accounts.
19 Malster, R. (1971) *Wherries and Waterways*.
20 Fuller, M. (undated) *How to Build a Wherry*.

Yarmouth. The sail was allowed to stretch for a month or two, before it was dressed with a mixture of coal tar, herring oil (or neatsfoot oil) and lamp-black as mentioned above. The dressing was done at least once a year.

Wherrymen

Inn sign painted by John Crome the elder c.1790, entitled The Wherryman. Reproduced with permission of the Victoria & Albert Museum.

The inn sign by John Crome painted about 1790, entitled *The Wherryman,* gives an idea of a wherryman's garb that matches quite closely G. Colman Green's 'few personal allusions to my own "trading" services to the wherrymen' in the 1890s.[21] They typically wore cardigan jackets with long sleeves and two waistcoat pockets made of thick worsted and very heavy flannel shirts of cotton with large pink or blue checks. The skippers

---

21 Colman Green, G. (1944) *The Norfolk Wherry,* No. 1, 6 June 1944.

usually wore blue serge trousers of melton cloth with a slight 'spring' which was a more pronounced bell in those of the mate. The pea jackets were double breasted, thick melton, with flaps over the pockets. Waistcoats were used for 'Sunday going to meeting' and heavy Albert chains and Swiss Lever watches were common. Boots were well made of soft yielding black crome. Underclothing was of red merino, both vests and drawers. The Samson Brace was almost universally used, and the dickey, a polo collar with white lined front attached. Overcoats were rarely worn on wherries. A red bandanna handkerchief was tied round the neck, lying over the chest in the form of a sailor's knot. In winter a real or imitation sealskin cap was usually worn, with flaps over the ears, and fastened with a brown silk ribbon under the chin. Lastly there were the black silk squares or half squares passed round the neck, as was the bandanna, but passed through a gold ring and tucked into the cardigan.

> The selection of the Black Silk squares was always made with a nice distinction, which lent an air of ceremony to the transaction, and was the hallmark of a good wherryman. So careful was our firm to see that the men were properly served, in the eighties, only the Manager (Mr. Jimmy Edwards) and Miss Neave were allowed to touch this part of the trade.....It was a strange business – nearly every wherryman had a good cigar given to him before leaving the Rampant Horse Street Establishment.[22]

William Starling notes that in the late nineteenth century, when there were still about two dozen wherries sailing from Aylsham, the wherrymen were only given two days holiday on 29 May, the general day of feasting, parading and merrymaking known as Oakapple Day, and the day following.

> They used to come up two or three days before and get their wherries all ready for return, and then on the 29th. come out in all their glory – nice white duck trousers, blue cloth waistcoat and coat with bright golden buttons, blue cloth cap with patent peak, and a lot of smart fellows they were. And didn't they enjoy themselves! It was quite a treat to see them, some of the young men especially, dancing the old-fashioned country dances on the greens, but this as I say, has all passed away.[23]

Nat Bircham worked on wherries along the Bure in the 1920s, and his memories of life on the river were recorded in 1979.

> On leaving school in 1919 I joined my dad on the Wherry *Emily*. There were over a hundred wherries trading at this time and often twenty or more of these craft could be seen leaving Yarmouth on a flood tide. I well remember sailing from Yarmouth to Wroxham – a journey of approximately five-six hours. Leaving Yarmouth at night about 10.00 pm, moon shining, smart breeze from the east. As we approached each windmill (there were eleven between Yarmouth and Acle) the sound was wonderful. The wind shrieking through the sails, the water flying from

---

22 Ibid.
23 Peabody, R. (2000) *Memories of Aylsham: The memoirs of William Frederick Starling 1851–1937.*

the paddles and being churned to foam as they pumped water from the marshes. The millman with his hurricane lamp patiently tending the mill, calling out as we passed by. The wherries heaved to, bound in opposite directions, opened their doors and called out, "There you go, Jimmy, lovely night", "Plenty of wind". As we approached eel sets the mate would go forward and hail the eel catcher. Out he would come and wave a light letting us know his net was down. There were five sets on the Bure at Stokesby, Acle, South Walsham, Horning and Wroxham. As the sails of the wherry jibed water would wash from one plankway to another making noise indescribable. Those days are memories never to be forgotten.[24]

For their religious needs, the wherrymen first used makeshift chapels in existing buildings such as the sail loft on Fuller's Hill, Great Yarmouth, loaned to them by ship-owner and magistrate Richard Hammond.[25] However, the need for a chapel by the mid nineteenth century meant that the Bishop of Norwich granted a certificate to William Sapcoat on behalf of Benjamin Southcote in March 1844, which allowed the use of a cottage as a place of worship. The cottage was one of a group in Millgate Street immediately opposite the Anchor Inn. The cottage was occupied by Southgate and his wife Lucy but owned by Samuel Parmeter, a miller who may also have employed Southgate at the mill. Benjamin Southgate appears to have been the main force behind the religious use of the cottage, although it was small it provided the wherrymen with a place to worship which was close to the canal and river. The origins of this request for a dissenters chapel in Aylsham seem to have begun in Great Yarmouth where a church for the express use of wherrymen and mariners had been established in 1826. A similar chapel was then needed for the wherrymen at the end of their journey in Aylsham.

One of the cottages shown in this photograph served as the wherryman's chapel in Millgate (the exact building is unknown).

---

24 Bircham, N. (1979) *By the Last Wherryman*, unpublished notes.
25 Palmer, C.J. (1872) *The Perlustration of Great Yarmouth*, p.152.

In 1858 the Norwich Wherrymen's Mission was established by the Rev. G.I. Pellew.[26] It was served by a Scripture Reader, trained in Yarmouth, who visited the wherrymen on their boats and in their homes on three days each week. A mission boat, *Gabriel*, also plied the river. The Mission subsequently became the Norfolk Wherrymen's Mission and later the Norfolk and Suffolk Wherrymen's Mission. The Mission also helf a fortnightly meeting at St Julian's National School Room in Norwich.[27] The Navigation Company supported the Wherryman's Mission with a donation in November 1860 of £10, and during the same year they began a regular annual donation of £2 until 1882 when they made the last of these annual donations. In total the Commissioners' donated £52 over twenty-one years. In 1863 the Mission was costing £40 a year but subscriptions were only £16 and a further appeal was launched.[28]

The Rev. John Gott (Bishop of Truro 1891−1906) worked to establish a wherrymen's church in Great Yarmouth. He was supported by an appeal from the wherrymen themselves, and the foundation stone of St Andrew's was laid by the Mayor of Yarmouth in November 1859 on Bessie's Piece and was consecrated by Dr Pelham, Bishop of Norwich, on 9th October 1860. The St Andrew's Institute was also established nearby and contained a Reading Room, a library and a Penny Bank.

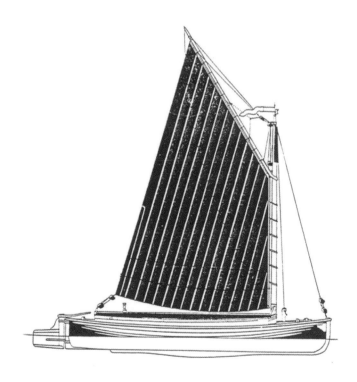

---

26 NRO MC 1866/27.
27 Bayne, A.D. (1873) *Royal Illustrated History of Eastern England, Volume One.*
28 NRO MC 1866/27.

11. Maintaining the Waterway

Within a couple of months of the official opening of the Aylsham Navigation in September 1779 it was ordered that 'proper Labourers or Workmen be immediately employed under the direction of Mr Smith the Surveyor to repair defects & to depthen and take out the following shoals reported as appears by a survey of the Navigation made the ninth day of November inst. by four of the Commissioners'.[1] There then follows a list of the places where work needed to be done, raising banks and removing shoals to the requisite three feet of water, with the proviso that 'the Labourers be employed as aforesaid weekly until the same be finished out of such money as now remains in the hands of the Treasurer'.[2] Almost as soon as the Navigation was completed, therefore, the long process of maintaining the waterway began. The income from tolls had to be shared between essential maintenance and the interest on loans from the subscribers. It was not until 1849 that the Commissioners were able to pay all the interest that was due in the same year.

A small number of Commissioners, usually between four and seven, were delegated to make an annual survey in the summer. This was usually preceded by breakfast in the White Horse next to the bridge at Coltishall. There is no charge mentioned for boat hire in the early years so it is likely that they rode or walked along the river up to Aylsham inspecting locks, bridges and banks as well as taking evidence from the contractors, lock-keepers and millers. In 1793 Thomas Bollum built a boat for the Navigation and from 1806 there is a record of a charge made for the Annual Survey of £1 5s, rising to £2 in the 1820s. There is one mention of extra cost for men to tow the survey boat. Much later in 1884 the Commissioners were able to use Ben Cook's steam launch and dined on board.

The essential task of 'didling the Navigation and keeping the same clean' was allocated to Joseph Bell and Robert Rose of Burgh for £30 a year, paid quarterly from 1780.[3] Didling, or dydling as it was more correctly called in Norfolk, was a term for removing the weeds and deposits in the channels for which a dydling tool was a prerequisite, tools that continued to be used until more recent times for ditching. A dydling tool was essentially a shovel with slots in the blade to let through the water, or in some cases just a robust rope net, with a long handle which could be used from the bank or a boat. The crome, a fork with prongs at right-angles to the long handle, was another tool used for clearing the banks. Rose and Bell's duties were specified more clearly in 1781 'to didle the filth dirt gravel out of the said Navigation mow the weeds draw the Hoves levell and repair the Banks, & keep the said Navigation clean from end to end'.[4] The hoves or

---

1   ATCA, Commissioners' Minutes, September 1779.
2   Ibid.
3   Ibid., September 1780.
4   Ibid., May 1781.

hovers were small floating islands of vegetable matter.[5] They worked together for 23 years until Joseph Bell either died or retired in 1803 and there is no evidence that their work was ever faulted. Robert Rose continued with John Digby for a few further years and also did other odd jobs.

Dydling tools and a crome.

Control of growth on the banks was assigned to the landowners where possible. In 1780 Robert Parmeter, the miller at Aylsham, leased land on the island between the canal and the old river above Aylsham Lock for 40 years at a yearly rate of 5 shillings 'covenanting to keep the Banks on both sides the said piece of Land in repair and to annually cut the weeds halfway of the said Canal and Old River and not to plant said piece of land with oziers or otherwise'.[6] The summer survey of 1802 provided the first intimation of problems to come:

---

5   Malster, R. (1999) *The Mardler's Companion: A Dictionary of East Anglian Dialect*, Malthouse Press, Holbrook.

6   ATCA, Commissioners' Minutes, September 1780.

'that several of the occupants of land next the River had suffered the weeds and sedges to grow on the sides of their respective lands to the great detriment of the boats passing on the said Navigation'.[7] Receiving no satisfaction from the rebukes issued, John Adey, the Clerk, was ordered in May 1803 to seek legal advice on who was responsible 'to repair Banks of such parts of the Navigation as were Old River before the passing of the Act of Parliament'.[8]

In December 1806 notices were to be immediately given to the 'several persons who have neglected to cut weeds and clear the Banks'. If they failed to do so within fourteen days notice, Bills of Indemnity were to be issued at the General Quarter Sessions.[9] This seemed to work for a time, but in August 1825 it was 'resolved that the Clerk lay before Mr Batchelor a Copy of the Case with Mr Wilson's opinion thereon taken by the Commissioners in 1803'. It was the opinion of the Commissioners that 'there is nothing in the Act of Parliament to relieve him and the other owners of Lands adjoining the old River from their liability to cut the weeds and clear away the hoves as formerly has been done by him as well as other owners'.[10] Thomas Horatio Batchelor attended the meeting of the Commissioners in October and it was 'agreed upon by both parties and resolved that the present nuisance complained of shall be removed at the equal expense of the Commissioners and the said Thomas Horatio Batchelor and that for the future repair of the River all weeds growing at the bottom shall be cut and cleared away by the said Thomas Horatio Batchelor at the expense of the said Commissioners and that all Weeds & Hoves growing against the Banks of the said River next the lands belonging to the said Thomas Horatio Batchelor shall be cut & cleared away by & at the expense of the said Thomas Horatio Batchelor or his Heirs annually'.[11]

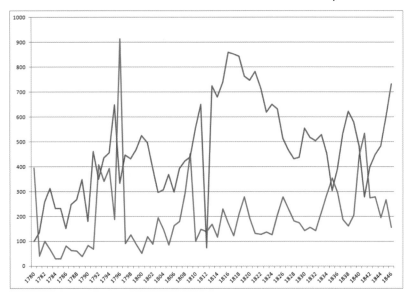

Expenditure in £ on maintenance (blue) and annual balance of revenue (red) between 1780 and 1846.

---

7   Ibid., November 1802.
8   Ibid., July 1803.
9   Ibid., December 1806.
10 Ibid., August 1825.
11 Ibid., October 1825.

In 1803 John Fielde, an enterprising millwright from Aylsham, began to take on the main contracts for the upkeep of the waterway and the dydling work was mostly assigned to the Platten family of Platten & Co. on a piecemeal basis. John Fielde died in 1831 and Benjamin Johnson, styled engineer and carpenter, began to supervise work on locks and bridges. He was formally assigned the contract for dydling at £60 per year in 1837.

The expenditure on maintenance along the Navigation steadily increased over the course of the late eighteenth and nineteenth centuries. It reached a peak in 1795, when around £900 was spent on repairs and maintenance, including the considerable expense of rebuilding the lock at Horstead, as well as repairs to the staithe wall in Aylsham and repairs on four bridges. For the most part, however, the costs of maintenance did not outstrip the balance of revenue. The exception to this was in 1841, when Mayton Bridge needed expensive repairs.

Later in the nineteenth century dydling continued to be critical along the course of the Navigation. In 1847 the Commissioners decided that dydlers were to be paid according to the weight of silt removed, rather than the number of days worked. In 1854 the possibility of a steam engine for dydling was considered, but no action ever seems to have been taken on the suggestion.[12] From the middle of the century the dydling was carried out by contract in two stretches; from Aylsham to Oxnead Bridge and from Oxnead to Horstead. The Commissioners provided the tools and a boat for the work. In 1862 the contract for dydling the whole course of the Navigation was awarded to James Ives, from Burgh at a cost of £120.[13] William Wickes, who lived in Millgate in Aylsham, was employed to keep the banks clear of weeds and branches. Although Ives' contract was renewed every year it was still often noted in the minutes that dydling was required on certain stretches, and in August 1870 it was recorded that there was an accumulation of weeds in the turns of the river near Oxnead.[14] In 1870 the finances of the Navigation were in a poor state, and it was decided to suspend all work on the Navigation except the criticial work of dydling, which was to be continued regardless – if the waterway became choked with silt and weeds, passage would become more and more difficult and the trade would be adversely affected.[15]

During the 1880s and early 1890s there were often complaints recorded in the minutes about weeds growing in the river and other blockages. In 1893 the Commissioners decided to investigate the possibility of a steam dredger,

> It was unanimously resolved that it was necessary to take steps for obtaining a Steam Dredger, the foulness of the weeds and mud in the Navigation whereby the water was held up in the tributary streams was a subject of complaint.[16]

---

12 Ibid., May 1854.
13 Ibid., January 1862.
14 Ibid., August 1870.
15 Ibid., August 1870.
16 Ibid., August 1893.

They received advice from the Port Authority at Great Yarmouth, who recommended the testing of a steam dredger before purchasing. Unfortunately, there is no record of when or where the test took place, but in 1894 the Commissioners duly purchased a steam dredger from Crabtree's engineering works in Great Yarmouth and advertised for an engineer to work it. However, by 1897 the dredger had still not been delivered to Coltishall, and despite the threat of legal action against Crabtree's the matter was dropped.[17] In autumn 1898 local men began dydling again in the quiet period after the harvest, and continued dydling by hand until the flood of August 1912. After the floods, the burden of the repairs needed and other maintenance issues would prove too much for the Navigation's finances to bear.

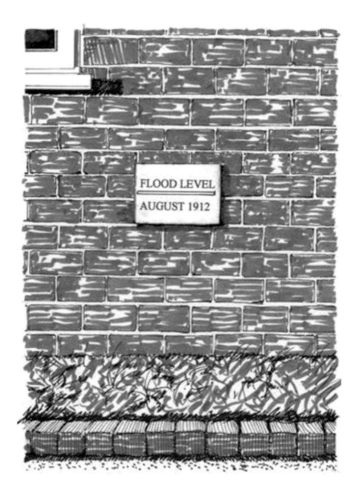

---

17 Ibid., February 1897.

12. Deluge and Demise

The catalyst for this book is the centenary of the 1912 deluge that prompted the demise of the Navigation. This chapter will focus on the events on and around the 26th August 1912. The story of how the flood affected Norwich is quite well documented but there is a lack of reliable witness testament and a deficit of reporting in rural areas, which means that there is speculation about how the flood progressed in the area along the Navigation. The damage caused was documented after the fact by many photographs and the long–winded process of trying to repair the damage, but some of the details about the actual events of the rain and flood are less well known.

A commonly held theory for the flooding above Coltishall is that it started at Thurning where the flooded Blackwater was held back by a tiny culvert on the railway bridge. When that bridge finally collapsed the water surged forward until it met the next bridge which obstructed its flow, backing up again until that bridge also collapsed. The Bure then continued tsunami-like downriver in a single surge taking out each obstruction as it reached it. This is probably only partially true. There are many flood plains between obstacles where the power of the water could have been dissipated and also many tributaries joining the Bure where collected flood waters from other parts of North Norfolk could add to the torrent, so there may actually have been several sites of separate inundation.

The Cause of the Flooding

The summer of 1911 was often called 'the perfect summer' with almost continuous sunshine and very high temperatures throughout July and August. Kings Lynn saw a local record of 92°F (33°C), local farmers brought in early harvests and day-trippers flocked to the seaside towns. Yarmouth's tarmac streets were melting, milk prices rose for the lack of pasture and there were heat-related deaths across the country. The heatwave also produced a drought and across central England only 1.7 inches (42.9mm) of rain fell throughout August.[1]

Such are the vagaries of the English weather that few were probably surprised when the summer of 1912 did not start off in the same way. June was particularly unsettled with frequent rainfall and several heavy thunderstorms. July improved with a couple of fine spells but otherwise dull, until the 23rd when it became wet and thundery – and didn't stop. On the 10th August 1912 the *Norfolk Chronicle* reported one farmer as saying:

> We are getting such a lot of rain that we are getting frightened as to the effect on the crop. They are getting knocked about badly.[2]

---

1   Hadley Centre Precipitation dataset, the Met Office. Accessed at www.metoffice.gov.uk/hadobs/hadukp.
2   *Norfolk Chronicle*, 10th August 1912.

August 1912 was noted for a procession of shallow depressions passing east from the Atlantic which the Meteorological Office noted were 'unusual, even for a winter month'.[3] On the 25th and 26th of August the southern part of the country was lying in a trough of low pressure that slowly tracked northwards before moving east over the North Sea. It brought with it heavy rain that began to fall in the south-east late in the evening of Sunday 25th August and then in Wales and the east of Ireland soon afterwards. The front moved across East Anglia at some 20mph but it was an irregular front hence whilst it started to rain in Norwich around 4am, it was after 5am before it started in parts of North Suffolk and South Norfolk. Once it started though, there was no holding it back and it rained continuously across the county for the next eighteen hours.[4] In August 1912 the total rainfall average across central England was 6.85 inches (174.1mm), about four times as much as in the summer of 1911.

Recent research by David Parker of the Meteorological Office has thrown new light on the dismal summer and suggested it might not have been solely due to the normal factors that seem to make British weather so random. In September 1912, W.N. Shaw of the Meteorological Office had noted a number of letters from weather enthusiasts who had observed 'a peculiar, persistent whitish haze which has covered the sky on even apparently cloudless days during the past summer'. It is now known that the haze was caused by the eruption of the volcano Mount Katmai in Alaska in early June. In the same way Eyjafjallajökull in Iceland threw plumes of smoke and ash into the atmosphere in 2010, Katmai had sent its fine ash into the stratosphere almost 100 years earlier. It may well be that this veil of ash was a significant contributor to the unprecedented weather that summer.[5]

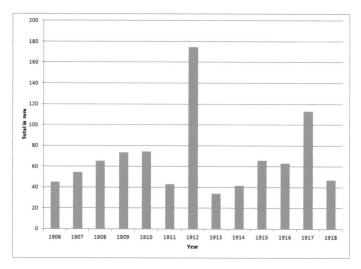

Average August rainfall in East Anglia 1906 to 1918.[6]

3   Kendon, M. and Prior, J. (2011) 'Two Remarkable British Summers – 'perfect' 1911 and 'calamitous' 1912' in *Weather*, vol. 66, no. 7, pp.179–184.

4   Robert Mill, H. (1912) 'The Great Rain Storm of August 25th to 26th, 1912' in *British Rainfall*.

5   Kendon, M. and Prior, J. (2011) 'Two Remarkable British Summers'.

6   Hadley Centre Precipitation dataset, the Met. Office. Accessed at www.metoffice.gov.uk/hadobs/hadukp.

The rainstorm of August 1912 was more severe than almost any other in living memory. East Anglia was no stranger to flooding but generally this was caused by exceptionally high tides and storms coinciding to drive the sea ashore, as would happen devastatingly in 1953. The last previous major flood in Norwich in November 1878 was caused by rainfall but was compounded by melting snow and tide-locking (where a high tide prevents the rivers from draining efficiently), and was restricted to the Yare and the Wensum. The 1912 downpour would not prove to be so geographically limited.

The amount of rainfall recorded varied across the county and the figures quoted in the press depended on what time they were recorded. The Times reported that 6 inches (152.4mm) fell on Norwich between 4am and 3.15pm on the 26th; another source quotes 7.3 inches (186mm) of rain at Norwich. At a more localised level one local weather enthusiast, Robert Cross of Worstead, noted that,

> We had a remarkable rainstorm here on the 26th August which yielded 5.89" in the 24 hours, by far the largest amount I have ever registered in one day during the last 25 years. The total for the month is 9.86", which is a record. The barometer fell to 28.95", which is also a record for August.[7]

Of the officially recognised weather stations listed in 'British Rainfall' the following stations are of particular interest; on Monday 26th August the station in Aylsham Millgate recorded 5.46 inches (138.7mm) and that at Coltishall 6.18 inches (172.7mm).[8] It is clear that there was heavy and consistent rainfall from the early hours of Monday morning through into Tuesday, following on from weeks of largely wet weather.

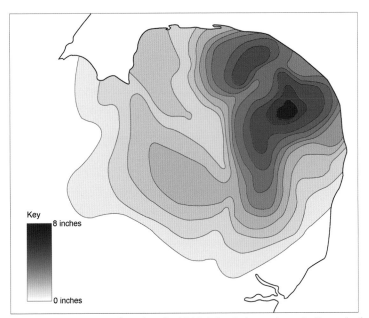

Rainfall in East Anglia on August 25th and 26th, 1912. The darkest colours indicate the heaviest rainfall.

---

7   *Eastern Daily Press, Norfolk Chronicle, Norwich Mercury,* 26th Aug 1912 to 29th Aug 1912.

8   Robert Mill, H. (1912) *British Rainfall.*

The Effects of the Rainfall in Norfolk

Nowhere in the UK totally escaped the unseasonal weather although the areas worst affected by rainfall lay in a broad band stretching diagonally across from the West Country to East Anglia. The River Exe at Tiverton in Devon was in flood; there was severe flooding of the Soar in Leicester and the Great Ouse burst its banks in Godmanchester flooding the town. Peterborough was also particularly badly affected. However, it was Norfolk where the effects were most dramatic. The effects were first noticed in Norwich throughout Monday as streets in the low lying areas began to flood with rainwater mainly due to debris being washed into gullies and blocking them. The council quickly cleared these and the waters receded, but the worst was yet to come. The streams and rivers began to swell beyond capacity and the further the water travelled downstream the greater the torrent grew, finally bursting the river banks.

As the only city in the county it was inevitable that the damage in Norwich would be the focus of the coming days' newspapers. Of course, as one of the few densely populated areas in the flood zone Norwich was hit hard. It was the Wensum that caused the most damage, breaking out of its narrow channel as it flowed into the city through the suburb of Heigham. The lowest lying parts of the city were inundated including City Station and the Bullard brewery at Coslany. Carrow and Trowse were also badly affected, as were parts of Lakenham. The Yare also spilled out and Thorpe Hall was amongst those places being drenched in flood water. There were just two deaths by drowning reported in the city. One, George Brodie, a 46 year old fish porter from Sawmills Yard was recorded a hero's death as he had spent six hours rescuing flood victims before perishing; the other was an infant, Edward Poll, accidentally dropped into the water by his mother whilst being passed into a rowing boat.[9]

The level of the Broads rose several feet but the peat diggings and the marshes that surrounded them held much of the water, preventing the Bure & Yare from causing quite so much devastation at Great Yarmouth. However Wayford Bridge, Stalham, Ludham and other places in Broadland were severely washed out, as shown in many contemporary photographs. In the south of the county the Waveney valley was another badly hit area with Loddon, sitting on the River Chet, particularly badly affected. Even towns such as Wymondham which were not normally associated with flooding were under water.

Damage to the infrastructure included the roads and bridges over the river, but this was far from the only damage caused by the heavy rain and floods. Norfolk was primarily an agricultural county and inevitably the farmers and smallholders were going to be affected. The wheat crop had been mostly harvested, although it was a poor crop because of the wet weather. However the barley and oats were mostly uncut and were battered down by the rain. Stooks that stood in the fields by the rivers were washed away and indeed compounded the problems by blocking the bridge culverts. Cattle and sheep were drowned and it was reported in the press that pigs and poultry were seen floating everywhere; both dead and dying.

---

9   *Eastern Daily Press,* 26th Aug 1912 to 29th Aug 1912.

Rain had fallen for days, seriously interfering with harvest operations and, indeed, where farmers had not gathered in their crops or thatched their stacks, promising something akin to ruin. Friday and Saturday were miserable days, rain falling continuously but Sunday showed some improvement, and there was some ground for belief that at least the worst was over.[10]

Although the main culprit of this natural disaster was the heavy rain, the high winds were also destructive. Trees were brought down all over the county including in Chapelfield Gardens in Norwich. The parks of North Norfolk such as Felbrigg and Gunton lost many great oaks and elms. The wind also whipped up the sea and it was reported that cliff erosion left the famous Garden of Sleep church tower at Sidestrand on the very edge of the cliff, and it would eventually fall in 1916. Lady Battersea's famous gardens at the Pleasaunce in Overstrand were badly flooded and damaged and had to be closed to the public.

The Flood and the Bure Valley

The Bure itself rises in the Sinks Plantation to the south of Melton Constable but the area is rich with springs and it is fed by numerous tributaries in a very small area. Most notable are the Craymere Beck which rises in the grounds of Melton Constable Hall, flowing eastwards south of Briston where it is joined by another feeder that rises at the top of Briston Common. Passing through and around Thurning Union Mill, the Beck joins another stream just east of Church Farm in Thurning. This third stream is known as the Blackwater River, although it has also been known as the Thurn or Thurne. It starts in the lake south of Thurning Hall although that lake is fed by other streams. The combined Blackwater and Craymere Beck then flow northwards to converge with the Bure in a plantation just west of Town Close.

However, in 1912 before the combined stream reached the Bure there was an obstruction to contend with. It was this obstacle that may have been one of the causes of the devastation downstream, and could nearly have been the site of a disaster. The impediment in question was a 20 feet high embankment and a brick built bridge that carried the Midland and Great Northern Joint Railway's Yarmouth to Melton railway line over the stream. Although most of the route was a single line, the section from Corpusty to Melton had been doubled in 1901 and with a siding near the bridge serving the gravel pit, it was a well used section of line.

The watercourse below the bridge was little more than a culvert and it was unable to cope with the rush of water coming down the Blackwater. The waters started to back up as far as the lake in the grounds of Thurning Hall. In mid-afternoon the 1.25pm Summer Express from Beach Station, Great Yarmouth pulled in at Melton Constable having passed over the bridge a few minutes earlier. The driver reported that he had spotted water building up against the embankment by the bridge. The signalman

---

10 *Norfolk Chronicle,* Saturday 31st August, 1912.

quickly put a stop on all movements on the line until the track could be investigated. In due course the pressure against the bridge reached tipping point and the bridge gave way leaving three lengths of track dangling over the gap like a rope bridge.[11] With the obstruction gone the Blackwater surged through joining with the Bure from Melton Constable just a few yards north of the bridge.

The rail bridge at Thurning, August 1912.

The next bridge after the Thurning rail bridge was across the lane at Little London. According to one report in the press the bridge was lifted wholly from where it stood and flung into a nearby meadow where it stood briefly in one piece before crumbling.[12]

A few hundred yards east of Little London is the double village of Saxthorpe and Corpusty, which was so neatly bisected by the river that grain entered the watermill in Saxthorpe and left as flour in Corpusty. The main river was crossed by a narrow bridge on the front of the mill although the public thoroughfare was through a deep ford on the main street between the two villages. As the mill stream comes across the meadow to the mill it curves in to the north-east corner of the building before passing under and turning the wheel. From the photographs taken shortly afterwards it seems the surge must have cut across the north-east end of the mill taking out a chunk of land at that end of the bridge across the mill.

The mill bypass stream reconnected with the river at this point so there may have been a small stream here already but in the photograph below this is a wide stream, and the people of Saxthorpe and Corpusty were quick to improvise a bridge using planks, and a line strung between the remainder of two branches impaled in the ground. The water would have then swirled back around the front of the mill and turned the ford into a torrent. It was at this site that one of the true tragedies of the Great Flood occurred. At some time on Monday a 52 year old mail carrier from Holt, James Starling, became one of the few human fatalities of the flood. He apparently attempted to cross the raging ford, possibly on horseback, but was swept away and drowned leaving a widow, Betsy, and several children.[13]

---

11 M&GN Society, *Circle.*
12 *Eastern Daily Press,* 26th Aug 1912 to 29th Aug 1912.
13 *Eastern Daily Press,* 26th Aug 1912 to 29th Aug 1912.

The damage at Corpusty Mill, August 1912.
Courtesy of Norfolk County Council Library and Information Service.

Leaving Corpusty, the raging torrent reached Saxthorpe Elmerdale bridge, near
Saxthorpe Hall, which was washed away. Then the river turned northwards to the marshy
lands to the west of Itteringham. As the surge reached the edge of the village it was once
again checked by the small bridge. The waters flooded out over the meadows to the
south and began to overrun the Walpole Arms public house. The landlord, Sidney Wilch,
his wife Edith and their customers were driven upstairs as the flood waters rose. It was
only when the bridge gave way and the water was free to rush on to Itteringham Mill
did the levels around the pub begin to fall.[14]

It was late afternoon on Monday 26th August when the problems began at Ingworth. The
river was joined by Scarrow Beck just above the village and since the Scarrow drained
a large section of the district up to Aylmerton and Gresham, it could be argued that
the Bure became an even greater torrent as it crashed through the tall wooden mill at
Ingworth, which stood on a stone bridge. The mill survived in reasonable working order
but stopped working around 1912 so it is possible that the floodwaters took their toll.
The 6pm mail cart from Aylsham to Cromer (via Calthorpe and Aldborough) was able to
pass through Ingworth, but it was to be the last to get through. By Tuesday morning the
water was up to the level of the hedgerows and Aylsham and Cromer were cut off from
one another.

From Ingworth the Bure drifts eastwards before turning south and heading down
Drabblegate into Aylsham between the site of the old Abbott's Hall and the existing hall.
It winds through the east of the Burebanks' estate and reaches the M&GN line again just
north of Millgate. This is the first major inhabited area on the path of the Bure, the site of
Aylsham North railway station, and of course, the head of the navigation. Inevitably the
impact of the floodwaters at Millgate/Dunkirk was relatively severe. A row of cottages,

---

14   Neville, J. (undated) 'Itteringham Mill', Norfolk Mills. Accessed at www.norfolkmills.co.uk.

Mash's Row, near the station were submerged to the level of the bedrooms, and the inhabitants had to be rescued by boat.

When the Midland and Great Northern Joint rail network ground to a halt late in the afternoon, the 2.45pm from Great Yarmouth's Beach Station was stopped at Aylsham North. On board was Arthur Dorer, Chief Clerk in M&GNs Traffic Manager's office at Kings Lynn. He was returning from Great Yarmouth on the train when it stood at Aylsham for an inordinate amount of time. Dorer went out to investigate and found the train standing in water nearly up to the platform, and seeking out the Station Master he found that a 'stop order' had been put on all trains in the vicinity. The MG&N staff learnt that the Blackwater Bridge ahead on the line was down and the embankment a mile or two behind them had been washed away. At Barningham, the Blackwater Beck (a continuation of the Bure tributary, Kings Beck) had washed away the railway bridge, which meant that the stretch of line from Barningham to Thurning siding was disconnected from the rest of the network. One passenger later recalled that the embankment was also washed out just 20 yards in front of the train.[15]

The station was completely surrounded by floodwaters and Dorer later described how local residents from Aylsham tried to get a horse and cart through the flood waters with supplies but failed. Eventually people waded in waist-deep water along part of the track to get milk to the children onboard the train and later other provisions for all the passengers. Two of these residents were named in the local press as Mr Thomas Woods Purdy, a solicitor of Millgate House and Clerk to the Navigation Commissioners, and Mr Frank Edward Buckingham, a chemist in Red Lion Street. Some of the male passengers also waded across to bring provisions back and, as one passenger on the train noted, were unable to change out of their wet clothes since their luggage had been sent on ahead. Dorer also noted that babies, small children and their mothers were taken to the signal box near the station where a fire was burning but the rest of the passengers had to spend an uncomfortable night on the train. M&GN staff worked ceaselessly, some of them going for thirty six hours without a break.[16]

The stranded passengers were eventually evacuated from the train and many were ferried across the Bure at Ingworth by the fishing boat *Nelly*. They were then taken by road to Cromer where they spent Tuesday night before they were able to continue their train journey on Wednesday. Others were able to walk into Aylsham where they found lodgings before being taken by car to Melton Constable to continue their journeys. The Eastern Daily Press spoke to one unnamed lady from Sheffield who was on the train. She was one of those who walked to Ingworth and was ferried across the swollen Bure. She recounted her thoughts on arriving at the flooded pastures,

> I shall never forget the sight. It was terrible; nothing but water with
> wrecks of huts and gardens and trees floating, and it was as deep as the sea.

15 *Eastern Daily Press,* 31st August 1912
16 Dorer, A.L. (1953) 'Memories of the 1912 Flood' in *Norfolk Magazine*, vol. 6, no. 1.

The woman was driven by car to Cromer, and arrived at Leicester station at 10pm on Tuesday night, finally reaching her home town of Sheffield by 12.30am on Wednesday morning.[17]

By 5pm on Monday afternoon there were a dozen trains stopped on the network in the vicinity. Most were able to be redirected quite quickly but the Aylsham train was not so speedily recovered and remained at Aylsham station for six weeks until a temporary timber bridge over the Blackwater was opened. In his memoirs, William Marriott, an engineer for the M&GN railway, said that the flood cost the M&GN about £20,000.[18]

The mid-eighteenth century Great Bridge, otherwise known as Anchor Bridge, that bridged the Bure at Aylsham escaped without major damage as did the more recent Little Bridge that crossed the mill stream. The area around the staithe at Dunkirk suffered greater damage particularly Bullock's granaries where the earth walls of the basin were washed away. However, the granary had been noted as being in need of repair at the Commissioner's AGM in February 1912. The Mill at Aylsham seemed to escape major damage which perhaps suggests that the spread of the flood water across Millgate and Dunkirk had lessened the power of the surge from above Aylsham. The lock, which was situated some distance outside of the town, was flooded but subsequent reports from the Commissioners do not mention any major repairs or problems.

The damage was also relatively light at Burgh, although Woolsey's Bridge was damaged, and there was still 8 to 10 feet of water underneath it when the Commissioners inspected it on 6th September 1912. The Cradle Bridge, Burgh Lock, the Lock Bridge and Burgh Mill were left largely intact. A special meeting of the Commissioners on the 6th February 1913 reported that the right bank below Burgh Lock Bridge was swept away for 20 yards and the channel was filled with gravel and would require dredging for 200 yards. These were perhaps the first signs that the future of the canal was in jeopardy.

It was below the Mill at Burgh where the next tranche of damage was most evident. The reason for this may well be that the Bure is joined by its tributary, the Mermaid, in the flood plains south of Burgh Mill. The Mermaid rises in the grounds of Cawston Manor and flows due east through Fengate to join the Bure. In 1912 there was still a working mill at Bolwick which the Mermaid, diverted through a lake in the grounds of Bolwick Hall in 1810, powered. It is recorded that Marsham was flooded badly at the point where the Norwich Road passed through it so it is likely that the river, which runs just to the north of Marsham, was carrying a great weight of water as it headed towards the Bure. After heading roughly south from Burgh, the Bure turns east through Oxnead. Here there were several separate channels, including William Pepper's canal to power the breast-shot wheel at Buxton Mill.

The lock at Oxnead was also damaged and Oxnead Park Bridge certainly suffered some damage although it did not collapse. In fact it stood without repair for twelve years until further decay forced the Commissioners to place a notice on it

---

17 *Eastern Daily Press,* 26th Aug 1912 to 29th Aug 1912.
18 Marriott, W. (1974) *Forty Years of a Norfolk Railway – The Reminiscences of William Marriott from 1884 to 1924.*

warning the public that they crossed the bridge at their own risk. After flowing east from Oxnead, the river collected an additional influx from Kings Beck. This in turn is filled by Blackwater Beck, Hagon Beck, Stackbridge Beck and other unnamed streams which drain a huge corridor from Skeyton up to Roughton. As this stream joins the Bure it turns sharply south and heads down to Lammas.

It was at Buxton and Lammas that some of the most extensive damage was done. As the water went through Lammas it tore away the bank just before Lammas Bridge and Buxton Mill. When the water finally receded great chunks of the bank were left high and dry in the fields. The Anchor of Hope public house which stood just upstream of the bridge was badly damaged. The water crashed into the mill damaging the lock, but the critical damage here was to Lammas Bridge. The bridge at Lammas crossed a weir leading into the channel across the meadows to the south. The weir had been fitted with sluice gates which could be used to control the amount of water pooling up behind Buxton Mill. If the mill pond was filling too quickly the gates could be opened to let some water channel off down the cut. On the 26th August the surge destroyed the bridge and sluice gates with it allowing the torrent to cut across the land to the east and south of the mill and head onwards with great force. Once the weir bridge had burst the Bure now rushed away from Buxton Mill, and contemporary photographs show the millpond drained of water. At the time many local residents believed that if the weir gates had been opened when the heavy rain started, the flood waters would have dissipated earlier across the flood plains south of Buxton Mill and caused much less damage.

The floodwaters sweeping across the damaged bridge near the Anchor of Hope in Lammas.

The GER rail bridge to the south of Buxton Mill was not damaged but contemporary photographs show the waters up to the underside of the bridge.

> For many a mile the intervening valley of the Bure was no insignificant inland sea.[19]

---

19 *Eastern Daily Press,* 26th Aug 1912 to 29th Aug 1912.

The Great Eastern Railway bridge just south of Buxton.

The area around Hautbois was also affected but the waters had plenty of room to dissipate across the meadows here. Neither the sixteenth-century Mayton bridge over the old river, nor the canal bridge at Mayton were seriously damaged. It was below Hautbois, as the water channelled through Horstead, where some of the worst destruction to property occurred. As the deluge reached Horstead and Coltishall the Eastern Daily Press described events.

> The River Bure rose suddenly on Monday night or in the small hours of Tuesday morning in consequence of the weir at Buxton giving way. Houses near the river at Great Hautbois, Coltishall and Horstead were all flooded. Several houses in the parish of Great Hautbois collapsed. The river became an immense broad. Boats were washed adrift; wherries broke away and became stranded in the riverside meadows.[20]

Coltishall Bridge was dammed by sheaves of hay washed off the meadows at Lammas and Hautbois. The water thus flooded around the villages and caused some major destruction in the vicinity. The White Horse hotel at Great Hautbois was partly demolished and lost its well-known bowling green. At Horstead, eight cottages collapsed and Sarah Appleton, a widow aged 75, was buried in the debris and had to be rescued. Mrs Wilfred White received a head injury from a fall and the lock-keeper's widow had to be rescued by boat as did several other older and less mobile residents. One of those doing the rescuing was Edward George Wright, a local cycle engineer, who also gave up rooms in his home on The Street, Coltishall to accommodate some of the homeless.[21]

---

20   *Eastern Daily Press*, 26th Aug 1912 to 29th Aug 1912.
21   *Eastern Daily Press, Norfolk Chronicle, Norwich Mercury*, 26th Aug 1912 to 29th Aug 1912.

Coltishall Bridge finally gave way sometime on Tuesday afternoon, causing the water level at Buxton to finally drop, and surged onto the lock causing much damage to the bank between the two structures. The collapse of Coltishall Bridge was one of the most disruptive effects in the region as a detour of some five miles across the two Mayton bridges was required to get vehicles from Horstead to Coltishall. The flood had reached the end of the navigation where it dammed up against the lock.

> At Coltishall Lock the water was held up and then all of a sudden the
> Lock broke and swept away a wherry that was moored there, and washing
> it all over the marshes.[22]

Below the lock at Coltishall the water dissipated more evenly and the damage was lessened. However, the events of Monday 26th and Tuesday 27th August were only the beginning of the end as far as the Navigation was concerned.

The Community Recovers

In the days following the flood the community had to return to some sort of normality as quickly as possible. There were two immediate problems. Firstly, those that had directly suffered loss and damage in the floods and secondly the widespread effects on transportation throughout the county.

In response to the first of these issues a Norwich relief fund was set up almost immediately. A county wide Flood Relief Fund was established within a fortnight, as well as other local Relief Funds. At Aylsham, a meeting at the Black Boys on 9th September appointed Harry Proudfoot as Acting Chair whilst a similar fund in Horstead saw the local headmistress, Mrs Browne, elected as treasurer whilst Mr Frank Patteson chaired the Coltishall Relief Fund. Many local people had lost furniture, livestock and garden produce in the flood, and the Relief Funds were able to assist them. The British Red Cross also went into action and set up a centre in Aylsham Town Hall to receive parcels of clothing. The community's reaction to the post-flood assistance can be gauged by letters to the local press. The most common questions raised were why the army was not called in and why rural areas were not perceived to be getting the same level of help as Norwich. Some people suggested that Harvest Festival be cancelled given that so much of the local harvest was destroyed.[23]

The effects on transportation and infrastructure dominated the local reaction to the floods. With Ingworth bridge down and the area completely flooded Aylsham was cut off from Cromer. The connection was soon restored by the implementation of ferries between the two towns. A Cromer fishing dinghy called *Nelly* was strapped to the roof of Mr Arthur Gowing's motor coach, called *The Venture*, and driven to the scene where it was manned by two Cromer fishermen. This boat helped ferry people, including the passengers from the stranded M&GN train, across the water where Mr Gowing's coach could run them to Cromer. Another small boat was loaned and manned by Mr H.F. Proudfoot of Aylsham.

22 Wilson, A. (1996) *Wherries and Windmills: Barton Turf and District in the Early 1900s*.
23 Letters to the *Eastern Daily Press*, 30th Aug 1912 to 6th Sep 1912.

Temporary foot bridges were rigged up by locals across the river, as at Corpusty and Coltishall, but access for carts and motor vehicles was not immediately possible.

This rapid community-based response was not followed up by Norfolk County Council. Despite convening a meeting with some speed, the repairs to the infrastructure would take some time and would be obstructed by many arguments over ownership and responsibility. It was this uncertainty that would prolong the life of the Navigation for several years after the flood.

The flood at Millgate, with Mash's Row in the background. Photograph by Joseph Dester. Courtesy Aylsham Town Council Archive.

Infrastructure Repairs

The flood waters on the upper Bure quickly subsided leaving behind a substantial amount of damage and debris to be dealt with. The most significant after-effect to the county as a whole was clearly the mass destruction of bridges which disrupted travel on a widespread scale. The first report of damage had come at 5.40pm on Monday when a telegram for the District Surveyor was handed in at Aylsham. It stated simply that 'Hevingham Fox bridge is blown'.[24] The reports of damage then began to appear in the local press but the figure for damaged or destroyed bridges fluctuated wildly.

The County Council first met to discuss restoration of the bridges on Saturday 31st August. The county surveyor, Mr Heslop, acted quickly and submitted his first full report

---

24 Manning, D. (1996) 'Norfolk Bridges Part 2' in *Norfolk Industrial Archaeology Society Journal*, vol. 6, no. 1.

at this meeting. Whilst the press had prematurely reported the collapse of some bridges which had in fact withstood the onslaught, the damage was still considerable. Heslop was instructed not only to affect temporary repairs but also to ensure the rebuilt or restored bridges were improved to take both better road traffic and greater river flow. It seemed a positive and fast response to the emergency. A suggestion to ask the army to install pontoon bridges as an interim measure was rejected given the speed with which local contractors could put temporary structures in place.[25] By the time of the next full meeting of the Highways Committee on 5th October repair work was well underway and most bridges could take temporary weight-restricted traffic. The true total of damaged and destroyed bridges in the County is difficult to ascertain but the figure quoted at this meeting was 99, although this may have included culverts as well as full bridges.[26]

As noted above, the bridge at Coltishall was causing the most disruption on a local scale. Traffic was being diverted via Mayton Bridges, so the County Council decided that a temporary bridge was not required. Local residents were not happy with this decision and in the end a temporary, 2-ton limit, bridge was quickly built and was open by November 1913. In January 1913 it was also decided that the ford at Corpusty should finally be bridged, which was opened on 19th March 1914. Burgh Bridge proved more troublesome than some. It was reported as being damaged in the flood but the responsibility for repairing it was contested. In 1915 St Faith's Rural District Council asked the Navigation Commissioners to repair the road over the bridge. The Commissioners were unable to comply due to lack of funds so in May 1915 the bridge was declared unsafe. By August heavy loads were prevented from using the bridge and in February 1917 it was closed completely. A deck of clad tree trunks was laid across the old deck to strengthen it and restoration work eventually began. The bridge was fully restored by September 1919.[27] Most of the other bridges that needed replacing were rebuilt by 1913. These included Thurning Church Bridge, Little London, Calthorpe, Itteringham, Saxthorpe Elmerdale and Barningham. Thurning rail bridge had services restored in October 1912. A temporary wooden bridge had been erected in the first instance but this was then replaced with steel girders on brick abutments. The new bridge also had a central brick pier creating two arches. The stream could now flow normally through the west arch but could expand into the east arch in times of flooding. The other M&GN rail bridge near Barningham was also replaced. The line was shifted slightly and ran over a temporary bridge and embankment until the new bridge could be completed.

On the course of the Navigation itself the locks were all damaged to some extent and were effectively unusable without repair. One immediate effect of the flood was that several wherries were trapped upstream of Coltishall and unable to get back onto the main navigable river. The majority of the vessels above the locks were not thought worthy of rescue but the 20 ton *Zulu*, owned by Barclay, Pallett and Co., was rescued by a team of men from Allen's boatyard in Coltishall. She was winched out of the water above the lock at Buxton, hauled across the road on rollers and relaunched below the lock.

---

25 *Eastern Daily Press, Norfolk Chronicle, Norwich Mercury,* 26th Aug 1912 to 29th Aug 1912.

26 *Eastern Daily Press, Norfolk Chronicle, Norwich Mercury,* 26th Aug 1912 to 29th Aug 1912.

27 Manning, D. (1996) *Norfolk Industrial Archaeology Society Journal,* vol. 6, no. 1.

A special meeting of the Navigation Committee was convened on Wednesday 4th September with Mr W. Pallett taking the oath as Commissioner. A special committee comprising Pallett, Mr Sewell and Mr Patteson plus the clerk was formed to confer with the owners of Buxton and Oxnead mills, and Aylsham Rural District Council to see what steps could be taken to put the river in order and repair the extensive damage at Buxton and Lammas. It was carefully minuted that the appointment of such a committee was in no way an admission of liability. On Friday 6th September this committee met at Aylsham basin for their first survey, where they examined the damage that has been previously mentioned. The negotiations about the repairs then began.

Sir Edward Stracey, owner of the mill and land at Buxton and Lammas, agreed to build a dam across the broken weir provided that the Commissioners would pay him £200 if they received a grant from the government. This dam was eventually completed in early 1913 and the road reopened across it. The lock gates were a different matter and it was down to the Commissioners to make them good. Despite a survey by local builder Mr Bloom in December 1912 and a further quote from Blythe, a builder from Foulsham, in the summer of 1914, the repairs had not been carried out by the time the First World War broke out. Further down river, two temporary bridges were erected by the War Office across the canal and river at Mayton. These temporary timber bridges augmented the existing bridges in 1915 to provide additional facilities to evacuate Aylsham in the event of an enemy raid.

In April 1921 the Aylsham Rural District Council wrote to the county surveyor and asked for the two temporary bridges at Mayton to be removed. In 1925 it was noted that the temporary bridge alongside the county bridge had been removed, or at least closed, and the one by the Navigation bridge left in place since it had been thought that the Navigation bridge might need reconstruction. However it was soon found to be rotting and was torn down by Blythe of Foulsham. The original Navigation bridge was listed as unsafe for vehicular traffic in 1926 but was finally repaired in June and July 1926 by Aylsham Rural District Council for £58 plus £8 for fencing. The foundation and walls of the bridge were found to be good so only the decking and parapet walls were replaced.

The years taken for the repairs to be made boiled down to the fact that the original Act of Parliament laid responsibility for bridge and lock repairs with the Navigation Commissioners. Already indebted, the events of 26 August 1912 and the immediate stoppage of trade, and therefore tolls, put the Commissioners in an almost impossible position. They would make repairs to the Bridge at Brampton and the lock at Burgh but this was not until 1925. By this time the Navigation had been closed to vessels for over a decade and there was no apparent way of restarting the Navigation.

The Abandonment of the Navigation

The deluge of August 1912 sounded the death knell for the Navigation. Although the popularity of the railway and the growth in motor vehicles and slowly improving roads would have had a substantial effect on waterborne trade, the sudden closure of the Navigation to wherries and other boats due to the damaged locks and bridges was catastrophic. Tolls, the main source of income for the Navigation, dried up at once and the only source of income was from rentals of buildings owned at Aylsham Staithe and the lock-keeper's cottage at Coltishall. On the debit side of the balance sheet the Commissioners now faced huge bills to repair the bridges they were responsible for under the Act, at Burgh, Oxnead, Buxton and Brampton, as well as the dredging of the silted up stretches, the repair of damaged banks and other minor repairs. It was estimated that the total cost was in the region of £4,000 if the Navigation were to be restored to pristine condition or £1,500 for a remedial solution involving mending the broken locks and bridges, and dredging the channel of debris and mud.

Applications were made for grants from the Great Yarmouth Port and Haven Commission and from the government Development Commission. The latter party agreed a loan in principle but set certain conditions, including the proviso that the County Council should undertake future maintenance of the bridges, that the holders of the £5,000 loan shares should relinquish their interest and that the local landowners and millers should guarantee to make good any excess of expenditure on maintenance of the Navigation over and above the income from it, for a period of ten years. The County Council was not prepared to agree to take on the maintenance of the bridges and although the Commissioners had some success in persuading shareholders to give up their interest, without the Council's assent the loan could not be made.

Although efforts were made to make repairs from the limited income and assets of the Commissioners, these were largely to stop further damage to the river through leaks and to allow road traffic and pedestrians to cross the bridges. The prospect of wherries ever using the Navigation again seemed a distant dream. Eventually the Commissioners began to concede defeat.

At a meeting of the Commissioners on 19th October 1926 the Clerk was directed to write to the Board of Trade enquiring whether it would be prepared to close the Canal under the provisions of Section 45 of the Railway and Canal Traffic Act 1888. On the 11th March 1927 it was agreed to make an application and warrant under Section 45 of the Act. The application received objections from Norfolk County Council, Aylsham Rural District Council, and Horstead and Coltishall Parish Council. The crux of the objections seemed to revolve around the fact that these local authorities felt that abandoning the Navigation would mean responsibility for the upkeep of the bridges would fall upon them. The Clerk was directed to write to the objectors and explain that without toll income the repairs could not be made, the Navigation would fall into disrepair and become a charge on the local authorities in any case. Since the County Council were the biggest stumbling block to the closure, an agreement had to be reached with them whereby they would receive the balance of the Navigation's assets if they dropped their objection. This was agreed in late 1927 and eventually conveyed to Norfolk County Council at the Commissioners meeting on 8th January 1929.

With complex negotiations completed the application was finally made. The Minister of Transport authorised the abandonment on 20th September 1928 and under a further document dated the 8th November, released the Commissioners from all liabilities and obligations under the original Act. The Navigation was no more, in legal terms at least.

---

28 Additional information by Jim Pannell.

13. The Landscape Today

To the casual observer, the Bure above Coltishall resembles little more than a beautiful, winding river abounding with wildlife and traversed only by the occasional canoe. The remaining watermills at various towns and villages along its course are a reminder of its historical importance to local industry but the signs of its eighteenth-century canalisation can be harder to spot. The majority of the course of the Navigation, from Coltishall to Burgh, is accessible by public footpath. The following chapter highlights some of the man-made structures which are still extant along the river and canal between the current head of the navigable river at Coltishall, and the head of the Navigation at Aylsham.

Coltishall to Mayton Bridge

The Navigation began on the Bure between Horstead and Coltishall. Horstead Mill was the first watermill along the course of the Navigation, but is the only one which is no longer standing. The Mill was still operating commercially for Read's on 23rd January 1963 when a fire, probably started by an electrical fault, gutted the building beyond repair. The mill site is still clearly visible as the remains of the ground floor and the wheel channels straddle the Bure. On the parallel cut the Navigation lock still survives. Now, however, rather than being a gateway to the Upper Bure it firmly marks the end of the navigable river. The gates were sealed shut in 1930 as the Commissioners met one of the conditions of the official abandonment of the Navigation. Immediately adjacent to the lock are the ruins of the superintendent's cottage, built in the 1840s. The house was still standing in the 1970s, but has since been demolished. The brick foundations are now overgrown, but the layout of the house is still distinguishable.

Coltishall Bridge links the villages of Horstead and Coltishall, and was dramatically destroyed in August 1912. Like the other destroyed bridges it has been replaced, with a decorative concrete balustrade that differentiates it from the other repaired bridges with their flat concrete decks and simple railings. To the north of Coltishall Bridge is a range of former malthouses, since converted into a slaughterhouse. From the footpath on the opposite bank, the nineteenth century buildings are clearly visible amongst the numerous modern additions.

The nineteenth-century house called Great Hautbois House, a former rectory, can be seen from the river to the north of Coltishall Bridge. Philippa and Beth Patteson bequeathed the house to the Girl Guide movement in 1984 and since 1988 it has been a residential activity centre. A substantial cut now leads from the river towards the house. This is not original to the Navigation, and was constructed in the very late nineteenth century as part of the landscaping of the gardens.

The lock at Horstead. The cottage built by the Commissioners was situated in the trees to the right of the photograph.

Coltishall Bridge, as rebuilt after the flood of August 1912.

The former maltings near Coltishall Bridge.

The Navigation between Horstead and Mayton Bridge in October 2011.

After leaving Horstead there is comparatively little to see on this stretch of the river that relates to the Navigation itself. There are a number of marl and other extraction pits along this stretch of the river, however later tree growth means than they are difficult to see on the ground, and are best appreciated from the air. The stretch of river leading up to Mayton Bridge itself is one of the best visible new cuts of the Navigation. The open banks and meadows along the stretch gives a clear view of the scale and length of the new cut, all excavated by hand in the 1770s when the Navigation was under construction. Mayton Bridge was only slightly damaged in the flood of 1912, but was badly damaged by fire on 28th July 1965 and now has a concrete pad lying across earlier brick piers. Ten years later it was in need of further repair. The staithe, which was the cause of litigation in the 1790s and complaints in the nineteenth century, lies to the west side of the bridge, and is now completely overgrown with no visible traces from the period of the Navigation's operation. The original Mayton Bridge and the old course of the river lie along the road which crosses the Navigation bridge.

The straight cut to the south of Mayton Bridge in October 2011.

Mayton Bridge, with the post-fire concrete pad on top of the earlier brickwork.

Mayton Bridge to Buxton

After Mayton Bridge the Navigation continues on a straight course past Little Hautbois Hall, which dominates the skyline over the flat meadows to the north of the Navigation, whilst on the opposite bank stands Mayton Hall which is surrounded by a medieval moat. This stretch of the Navigation is also an excellent example of where the original course of the River Bure was straightened in the 1770s, although this is not a new cut like that below Mayton Bridge.

This stretch of the river is crossed by another bridge; the iron girder bridge of the Great Eastern Railway still crosses the river just below Buxton and is still used by the Bure Valley Railway, who reopened the line as a 15" railway in 1990, eight years after it had finally closed as a freight railway, and 38 years since the last passengers had been conveyed upon it. The bridge is a prominent reminder of the decline of the Navigation after the arrival of the railways in Aylsham in the 1880s. The bridge itself is now an important part of the industrial heritage of the area and was listed in 1998.

A straightened section of the Navigation between Mayton Bridge and Buxton Mill.

The GER railway bridge across the Bure near Buxton.

Buxton Mill is probably the most prominent of all those on the canal as it stands right on the public highway, and is an excellent example of a late eighteenth-century watermill. It has also been through the most transformations since its closure as a working mill in August 1970. In August 1971 Roger Ferris opened the mill as a tea room and later added a restaurant, and it was known as the Old Mill Hotel in the late 1970s. It also became an arts and crafts centre and a furniture showroom, and by 1988 it had become the Buxton Mill Tavern. In 1991 a fire engulfed the building, but it was magnificently restored under the supervision of architect Keith Reay and reopened. In 2002 it became the Rivierie hotel and restaurant but in that same year received planning permission for conversion into flats, and is now private residences. Alongside the mill itself is the Mill House, built by William Pepper in the late eighteenth century. The car park for the new flats, previously built for the hotel, stands on the infilled lock. The lock was filled in June 1933 to allow for road improvements between Lammas and Buxton. Along Mill Street are a number of nineteenth century houses and other buildings which grew up alongside the Navigation. In front of the mill is some evidence of its history during the Second World War when it was part of a stop line along the River Bure. A series of concrete tank traps now lie askew on the edges of the Navigation.

Buxton Mill and the Mill House (to the left of the mill).

Buxton to Oxnead

The road from Buxton to Lammas runs over the weir bridge, now fitted with sluice gates. The bridge was repaired after its destruction in 1912, and it is difficult today to picture the great fissure in the bank which happened when the great weight of water finally wiped out the bridge and sluice in August 1912. Next to the weir bridge is the old Anchor of Hope public house, which stopped selling beer in 1969 and is now a private residence.

The course of the river from Buxton Mill to Oxnead was relatively unaltered by the activities of the Navigation Commissioners, and walking along the footpath on this stretch certainly gives the impression of a natural watercourse as there are few other visible remains of the Navigation to be found on this bend of the river.

The Navigation near Lammas, with the church tower of St Andrew, Lamas, visible in the centre.

Oxnead Mill is now almost obscured by trees. In 1957 it was bought by Jim and Barbara Crampton, who founded the private charter airline Norfolk Airways in 1952, and who later started Rig Air (later Air Anglia) which flew aircraft supporting the North Sea rigs. The Cramptons restored cinema organs and three organs were stored in the mill with a water-turbine providing power for them. Today, the mill is still used as a store and has been partly renovated where the roof and lucum have been damaged. Oxnead lock lies beside the mill, and is now almost empty of water. The lock gates have been removed, but the brick sides of almost the whole chamber are visible. The lock was completed in 1778, but extensive repairs were carried out to the brickwork in the late nineteenth century, and much of the visible brickwork appears to be of this date. The section of river leading past Oxnead Hall has clearly been straightened, and Biedermann's map does not show this as one of the original proposed works, although the accounts do show payments for work on 'Oxnead Canal' in 1774 which may refer to this section of the river.

Beyond the meadows above Oxnead Mill stands Oxnead Bridge. The brick abutments are late eighteenth century and thus contemporary with the Navigation

The lock chamber at Oxnead, completed in 1778 and photographed in April 2011.

but a concrete deck, typical of the Highway departments early twentieth-century design, has replaced the original roadway. A few yards down the road from the bridge, a well-preserved Second World War pillbox stands as a reminder that in June 1940 the Bure was suddenly thrust into the frontline. There was a very real risk of invasion by German forces and although the main attack was expected on the south coast, diversionary or secondary landings on the Norfolk coast were thought to be a real possibility and plans to deal with such an event had to be made.

'Operational Order no. 4', prepared by the 287th Field Company of the Royal Engineers in June 1940 ordered that the River Bure was to be turned into a 'stop line' intended to hold up any German advance from Norfolk landing grounds, and to disrupt and delay the advance in order to buy time for the defence to organise itself for a counter attack.[1] The plan was simple but absolute; every bridge between Wroxham and Aylsham, including those used by the railways, and all bridges between Stalham and North Walsham would be blown in the event of invasion. These plans were promptly put into place, and backed up on July 21st 1940 by Operational Order number 6 in which the mined bridges were listed as being at Wroxham, Coltishall, Little Hautbois (possibly Mayton Bridge), Buxton, Buxton Mill, Oxnead, Brampton, Burgh, Aylsham and Ingworth; an apparent extension of the earlier order. If the Germans had invaded the army would have repeated with explosives the damage wrought by the flood 28 years earlier.

---

1   TNA, WO 166/3756.

Oxnead Bridge, built in the late eighteenth century with a twentieth-century concrete pad.

Oxnead to Burgh

The short stretch of river between Oxnead and Burgh flows past the sites of the brickyard and limekiln in Oxnead, and a nineteenth-century boathouse in Brampton, all of which have now disappeared from the landscape. Burgh Mill was one of the last working watermills in Norfolk, and was operated commercially by the Grix family until 1980. The whiteboard, multi-peaked and pantiled mill building is a particularly distinctive sight along the course of the Navigation. The nearby lock has now been fitted with a sluice and the gates removed. The original brickwork is still visible beneath more recent concrete and a low, flat bridge replaces the old raised footbridge which was of sufficient height for the wherries to pass. The new cut below the lock, excavated to allow wherries to bypass the mill, is another excellent example of a straight canalised cut on the Navigation.

Twisting underneath Burgh, the Bure is still bridged by a wooden Cradle Bridge allowing people on foot to cross from Brampton to Burgh. Burgh Bridge, which caused such arguments between the Navigation and the local authorities after it was damaged in the flood, retains some original brickwork. The Cradle Bridge in Burgh is also the last point along the course of the Navigation which can be accessed by public footpath, with the exception of a number of buildings in Aylsham itself.

Burgh Mill.

Burgh Bridge, showing the older brick piers and modern road bridge.

Burgh to Aylsham

After Burgh Bridge the course of the Navigation lies almost due north, with a new cut close to Burgh Hall. Aylsham Lock lies on this stretch of the river, on a silted up and overgrown portion of the Navigation. The lock was damaged in the flood and never repaired. A 1928 photograph clearly shows the pound full of water with the upper gates acting as a weir and the lower gates open to allow the water to flow. The lock is, in the photograph, already showing signs of decay with small bushes and weeds growing through the woodwork. Today the lock is virtually invisible from a distance as a small copse obscures it. The crumbling infrastructure is still there and there is normally water in and around it. The state of the eighteenth-century cuts along this stretch is a result of the decision by the Bure Drainage Board to divert the Navigation into the river about 1950.[2] The effect of this was to increase the flow in the canal, whereby the banks were seriously eroded, notably behind the Bone Mill. As a consequence it was necessary to put in a weir just below the meadow behind Maiden's Bower and shore up the banks behind the mill.[3] The junction of the canal and the old river is just above the bridge made for the bypass road, the vestige of the canal still visible down to the lock. Upstream the two channels run roughly parallel with each other through the Dunkirk industrial estate and into Aylsham itself.

Aylsham Lock in 1928. Courtesy of Norfolk County Council Library and Information Service.

---

2   Sapwell, J. (1960).

3   Ben Rust, personal communication.

Aylsham Lock.

The flour milling machinery in the Steam Mill survived the 1912 flood though many sacks of grain and flour were damaged.[4] In June 1914 Barclay Pallett & Co. bought the watermill using it for animal food and storage, while continuing to manufacture flour in the Dunkirk roller mills. After the Second World War the cutting from the canal into the flour mill was filled in to install four 50-ton bins. In 1959 a grain silo and dryer were built on adjacent land to the west. This necessitated demolishing a couple of cottages. In 1966 a new provender mill was built beside the silo on land previously used as allotments. The grain silo could supply both the flour mill and the new provender mill. With these new facilities business was centred in Dunkirk. Animal feed production ceased at the watermill, at Wroxham and North Walsham.

In 1967 the company was sold to British Oil and Cake Mills (BOCM), a subsidiary of Unilever. The new mill was doubled in size and the marketing side of the business combined with Tyrrell & Byford of Attleborough to form Tyrrell Byford & Pallett, with new offices on the old station yard and headquarters at Attleborough. Flour milling ceased in 1972. The machinery was removed and the building left empty. The local fire service used it for training purposes until the wooden structure of the building was demolished leaving the six foot high brick walls. Subsequently in around 1980 a new building was erected on these foundations for the manufacture of premixes. After a decision to close the plant in 1984 was revoked the mills became a special foods plant for BOCM Silcock. In the late 1980s the company was sold to R. & W. Paul, becoming BOCM Paul. They continued

---

4   Much of this section kindly provided by Ben Rust, who also contributed to the section on the history of the Aylsham mills in Gale, G. and Mollard, T. (2006), pp.29–45.

manufacture at Aylsham until 1994, when the plant was closed and the property sold to a developer, Ivan Daniels. The new building on the foundations of the flour mill is now Dunkirk Garage. Aylsham Farm Machinery occupy the adjacent yard and buildings including the Bone Mill with its original sack-hoist still intact. The small brick building in the yard just nosing on to the street once housed the steam engine. The street up to The Staithe and the cul-de-sac of Wherry Close is now lined with new houses. The cutting into the meadow of Maiden's Bower a little further downstream, where the Wright family had a boatyard in the nineteenth century and wherrymen would disembark for the Royal Oak, was filled in quite recently. On the other side of the road opposite the Bone Mill the Gothic miller's house, built in 1860, is a striking building amid the industrial buildings now developed between Dunkirk and Banningham Road.

Aerial view of Aylsham staithe looking upstream over Dunkirk. Wherry Close was still under construction when this photograph was taken. Reproduced with permission of Archant.

Aylsham Mill.

In 1969 the watermill was sold to Jim and Barbara Crampton and was Grade II listed later that same year. In 1975 planning permission was granted to convert part of it into one residential unit and four holiday flats. The front section over the river housed a theatre organ later removed, but much of the machinery was retained. Then in 2001 further permission for a residential conversion was granted along with change of use from holiday let to residential for the four converted flats. In 2007 the mill was bought by Jonathan and Martine Spalding with a view to further residential development. At the time of writing the mill remains partly converted and partly derelict. There is a sandbagged strongpoint appended to the north wall of the mill which was built during the Second World War to overlook the road bridges and the shallow crossing downstream from the mill pool. The bridge over the millstream, built by William Berry in 1759, and the one over the bypass stream, built in 1821, both escaped significant damage in the flood of 1912 and retain much original work. Just above the bypass stream can be seen the track that led down to a drift across the river that was used up to the 1930s by stock coming from the market in Aylsham or passing through, to replenish traction engines and water carts and no doubt staunch the wheels of carts in the summer.

The Granary and other warehouses around the basin and staithe were already in disrepair when the flood hit. It was not until 1929, when the Norfolk County Council acquired the land and buildings, following the demise of the Navigation Company that improvements were carried out. The County Council used the staithe and buildings for a Highways Depot. They let the Granary and the land behind it to Barclay Pallett & Co. The land belonging to Barclay Pallett west of the Dunkirk mill was used as allotments and the small buildings used for rearing pigs and poultry. At the start of the Second World War the County Council repossessed the land and buildings let to Barclay Pallett. They were upgraded and used for decontamination purposes, in case of a chemical/gas attack.

In the mid-1950s the County Council closed the Highways Depot and offered the land and buildings, including the Granary site, to Barclay Pallett, who purchased the lot. In 1974 BOCM Silcock sold the Granary to Tom Bishop, with a right of way across the Staithe from near the Great Bridge. He used the buildings for storage and sold them in 1990 to Alan Rowlands, who converted them into two private residences, Rivendell and Wherryhouse. Alan Rowlands made a new driveway to Dunkirk, The Staithe, in 1992. In June 1997 Aylsham Town Council bought the remainder of the land previously owned by the Navigation and known as Aylsham Staithe, thus safeguardong it for the town. Houses have been built on the former mill site and Ivan Daniels has also acquired from the Spaldings much of the island between the canal and the river below the water mill.

The mid-nineteenth century bone mill in Aylsham, photographed in January 2012.

Although the Aylsham Navigation did not produce a highly industrialised canal landscape like those found in the Midlands and the North, there are still substantial traces of this eighteenth-century scheme surviving in the modern landscape. The watermills, locks and bridges form the principal physical remains on the ground, many of which can be seen from public footpaths. However, the charm of this stretch of the Bure now lies in its solitude and tranquility, a far cry from the bustle of wherries and goods up and down the river when the Navigation was in operation.

14. Conclusion

From 1779 onwards the Navigation was a vital part of the economy of the Bure valley, providing an efficient, low cost alternative to road transport for heavy and bulky goods. It also revitalised the towns and villages along its length with new opportunities for trade and light industry. During the late eighteenth and the first half of the nineteenth century, coal, bricks, timber, grain and other produce was being moved up and down the Navigation, providing a link with both national and international trade routes. In the second half of the nineteenth century, after the reorganisation of the management structure in 1846, the Navigation continued to go from strength to strength, with a steady increase in the number of vessels using the waterway and the income generated from tolls.

The Aylsham Navigation was a typical example of the navigation schemes developed in this period, operated by a group of Commissioners drawn from the local towns and landed gentry, and financed by subscriptions and the income from tolls. The Commissioners also faced the same problems as other contemporary schemes, particularly the ongoing issue of maintenance and upkeep, both of the channel itself and of the infrastructure. They also had to deal with the growing competition of high speed, low cost transport offered by the railways in the second half of the nineteenth century. Canals and river navigations, by their very nature, could not be standardised or linked in the same way as the late Victorian railway network. Indeed, their variability in terms of infrastructure and management practices made them more vulnerable to the competition offered by the railway companies.[1] In 1888, a Royal Commission report on the state of inland waterways in England found that only eleven waterways were making a profit of over £10,000 per year.[2] The profits of the Aylsham Navigation were never in this league. In the same year, 1888, the income from tolls was just £370.

The steady decline of the Navigation in this period has already been discussed in depth in the chapters above, but this was a decline shared by the other navigations and canals in East Anglia. In the 1830s and 1840s the Commissioners of the Stour Navigation attempted to make the scheme more competitive against the railways, with new towpaths, a reformed toll system and the modernization of some of the locks. In 1848, the year before the railway between Sudbury and Marks Tey opened, the tolls brought in £3,400. By 1852 they had dropped to just £1,400.[3] There followed a long period of decline, and in 1914 the Stour Navigation Company went into liquidation and was finally dissolved in 1937.[4] In 1846 the trustees of the Ipswich and Stowmarket Navigation leased it to the Eastern Union Railway Company, who were then building a line along the Gipping valley. The trustees resumed control of the navigation in 1888, and struggled to maintain

---

1   Porteous, J.D. (1977) *Canal Ports: The Urban Achievement of the Canal Age*, p.17.

2   Ibid.

3   Boyes, J. and Russell, R. (1977) *The Canals of Eastern England*, p.85.

4   Ibid., p.89.

its viability until its closure in 1934.[5] In 1884 the Halesworth Navigation ceased to operate, and was formally abandoned in 1934.[6] The North Walsham and Dilham canal passed between a number of owners in the late nineteenth and early twentieth centuries, after an act permitting its sale had been passed in 1866. In the floods of August 1912 the canal was badly damaged and the bank breached above Bacton Wood Lock. Although attempts were made to rescue the canal and it gradually fell into disuse and silted up, the last wherry passing through in 1934.[7] Given the fate of other navigable waterways in East Anglia it is almost certain that had the floods of August 1912 not occurred then the Aylsham Navigation would nevertheless have continued its long, slow decline into eventual abandonment. The floods merely hastened the inevitable.

The Aylsham Navigation is an excellent example of a late eighteenth century scheme of river improvement in East Anglia, particularly because of the fortunate survival of a comprehensive set of minutes and accounts for the whole history of the Navigation. East Anglia is not a region which is often studied with regard to canals and navigable waterways, but the Navigation demonstrates that the landowners, merchants and farmers of the region were alive to the possibilities offered by water transport to expand their trading networks. Although some light industry did spring up alongside the Navigation, the main cargoes were closely linked to the region's agrarian output. Norfolk has never been famous as an industrial county, and lacks the dense networks of canals linking together factories and growing industrial centres which could be found in northern England and the Midlands. It was however, renowned in this period as a leader of agricultural innovation, with the produce of improved methods of farming being moved along the newly improved River Bure. The men who created the Navigation included local landowners and farmers, but the men who took the lead on the venture were businessmen, merchants, millers and solicitors; William Pepper, John Adey, John Repton and George Hunt Holley for example. These men did not, in general, possess large landed estates on which they could carry out the latest innovations in farming, but they could engage with the drive towards 'improvement' in the late eighteenth century by implementing schemes such as the Navigation, helping to link the local agrarian economy into wider networks of trade and communication. The Navigation, therefore, supported the 'agricultural revolution' in this part of Norfolk, which in turn, supported the 'industrial revolution' elsewhere in the country and contributed to the growth of the national economy.

---

5   Ibid., p.98.
6   Ibid., p.107.
7   Ibid., p.132.

Appendix 1: Summary of the Parliamentary Act

Para. 1. Commissioners. "All Persons having or who shall hereafter have Freehold or Copyhold Estates in the Hundreds of …..in the County of Norfolk, of the annual Value of One Hundred Pounds, or shall be possessed of a personal Estate to the Amount of Three Thousand pounds, and whose usual Place of Residence shall be One of the said Hundreds…..and their Successors ….are thereby appointed Commissioners."

Para. 2. Commissioners impowered to employ or contract with any Persons for performing the Works. Much detail about expected construction and need to respect local property.

Para. 3. First Meeting of Commissioners. Arrangements for first meeting on 4 August 1773 and subsequent General Meetings on first Wednesday in August each year at the Black Boys or some other convenient place, with conditions for adjournment. Notice of meetings to be placed in "*The Norwich* News Papers", Commissioners not to have other vested interests and to defray their own expenses.

Paras 4–6. Commissioners may act as Justices, qualifications and penalties on acting if not qualified. Commissioners to take an oath.

Para. 7. For purchase of Lands. "Full Power and Authority to agree with the Owners or Proprietors of and Persons interested in any Lands …. which the said Commissioners …shall judge necessary to be cut, digged, pulled down, removed, or otherwise made use of for the Purpose of the Act". Land could be bought or leased. If agreement could not be agreed a whole series of legal procedures to resolve matters up to Sheriff and jury.

Paras 8–14. Further requirements to record, arbitrate, define agreements and recompense.

Paras 15–17. Tolls. "there shall be paid to the Collector ….a Toll….not exceeding the Sums following: ..for every Ton Weight of Coals, Cinders, Bricks, Pavements, Tiles, Lime, and Terras, the Sum of One Shilling; and for every Ton Weight of Corn, Grain, Meal, Flour, Timber, Goods, wares, Merchandizes, or Commodities whatever…the Sum of One Shilling and Six Pence, and so in Proportion for any greater or lesser Weight than a Ton." Tolls reduced to two-thirds for goods to and from Skeyton Brook passing through the locks at Buxton and Horstead only. No toll to be charged on "Straw, Muck, Marle, Clay, or other Materials to be used in the improving or manuring of Lands only, nor for any such Boat, Barge or other Vessel laden with any materials for the Repair of any Mill or Mills upon the said River". Rules for failure to pay.

Para. 18–19. Tolls may be assigned for Money borrowed. The Commissioners were permitted to borrow up to £5,000, no work to be done until that sum subscribed, the subscribers to be paid 5% interest per annum from the toll receipts and the shares could be assigned or transferred to other persons; records of all transactions to be kept.

Para. 20. Appoint Officers. To appoint a Collector of Tolls, a Treasurer, a Clerk, a Surveyor and any other officers the Commissioners shall think fit, to take an oath and be paid out of the "Monies to be raised", and shall be "removable at the Will and Pleasure of the Commissioners".

Para. 21. Disbursements to be entered in a Book. Accounts to be recorded, annually verified by the Commissioners and Treasurer under oath, terms for keeping accounts and penalties for default.

Para. 22. Owners of Vessels to give Account of Lading. Boat owners to report in writing content and destination of goods laden and penalties for default, including seizure.

Para. 23–25. Commissioners to set up and maintain Gates, Bridges, &c. Commissioners to cause to be made and kept in repair substantial gates, bridges, passages and stiles in and over all parts of the waterway, deepen the river where needed, and if necessary raise banks for towing paths or otherwise and create tunnels to drain overflow. Commissioners to be indemnified for such works and held to account for any subsequent damage, any unresolved cases to be taken before a jury, the costs defrayed by the losing party.

Paras 26–30. Owners of Vessels to be answerable for their Servants. Owners answerable to a Justice of the Peace for "any Damage, Spoil or Mischief …. done by …. their Boat, Barge or Vessel" or by anyone employed by them and penalties for default. Vessels obstructing the Navigation to be fined £5. Vessels sunk to be raised or expenses charged. Owners "shall cause …. their Names, Place and Place of Abode at full Length to be placed and set in large Capital Letters, Four Inches long and broad in Proportion, on the upper Part of the Boat on both Sides …. and painted White…and at all Times legible". They must allow the vessel to be measured and "cause Figures to be placed on the Head and Stern …. to denote the Draught of Water, and how deep such a ….Vessel is laden". Offences in these respects and also leaving open gates, locks or hindering other vessels subject to a fine of £5. Anyone else "maliciously or wantonly open or cause to be opened any Lock, Sluice, Staunch, or Floodgate" or in other way "waste the Water" subject to a fine of £5.

Paras 31–34. Penalty on Millers not opening or shutting Locks after Notice. A fine of £20 to millers not opening or closing locks upon reasonable request with 48 hours notice. Recompense to be paid by the hour for such inconvenience to be determined from time to time by a Jury, but no allowance made for loss of water during periods of repair to the waterway. Millers also liable to a fine of 40s for obstructing the Navigation.

Paras 35–36. Locks to be opened on Tender of Money. Lock keepers liable to a fine of 40s for not operating locks in specified manner. If Commissioners fail to repair locks immediately then after 14 days notice a Justice of Peace can order the repair to be made.

Para. 37. Drains to be made into the River or Canal to convey the Water from the Lands adjoining. Likewise if Commissioners fail to maintain drains they can be ordered to do so by a Justice of the Peace after due notice.

Para. 38. Posts to be erected to distinguish the Height the Water is to stand in the River. To prevent disputes between the Commissioners and the Millers "Stones or Posts shall be set up, whereupon shall be marked in visible Letters or Figures the Height to which such Water shall and may be allowed to be raised, and that when such Water shall be raised to the Height marked on such Stone or Post the same may flow waste over such Pen or Staunch".

Para. 39. Power to make Bye-laws. The Commissioners empowered to "have full Power to make Bye-laws, Orders and Constitutions for the good and orderly using of the said Navigation, and for the well-governing of the Keelmen, Watermen and Boatmen who shall convey or carry any Goods, Wares, Merchandizes, or Commodities on any Part thereof, and from time to time to alter or repeal the same, and to impose such reasonable Fines, Forfeitures or Punishments upon all persons offending". Recourse to courts of law if necessary.

Para. 40. Upon Payment of Tolls Navigation to be free. "That the Navigation Works and Towpaths hereby authorized to be made .... shall be free for the Use of all Persons .... upon Payment of such Tolls". The next subparagraph makes special provision for lowering the wooden pipe across the river on the land of Thomas Anson and maintaining it so that it continues to drain his meadows.

Para. 41. For paying the Expenses of the Act. Cost of Act to be defrayed from subscriptions raised.

Paras 42–45. For recovery of Penalties. A subsidiary statement to allow seizure of offender's goods and chattels if not covered by previous directions and arrangements to commit such offenders to the "common Gaol, there to remain without Bail or Mainprize, for any Time not exceeding Three Months, or until such Fines, penalties, and Forfeitures shall be paid". All subject to appeal.

Paras 44 and 45 outline penalties for giving false evidence and damaging the works.

Para. 46. Navigation not to be subject to Commissioners of Sewers.

Para. 47. Navigation to be exempt from Taxes.

Para. 48. Proceedings to be entered in a Book. Minutes to be kept and witnessed.

Para. 49. Writings to be without Stamps. Warrants, assignments, etc. to be free of stamp duty.

Para. 50. Lands not used to be reconveyed to former Proprietors.

Para. 51–51. Preservations of Rights. Landowners adjoining the waterway retain right to use pleasure boats, and exercise their other rights such as fishing and wildfowling, so long as it does not interfere with the Navigation. Landowners also free to erect any structures and use their land in any way that does not obstruct the Navigation.

Para. 53. Constables to execute Warrants. Warrants under this Act to be directed to the Constable or other proper officer enforcing the law.

Paras 54–55. Distress not unlawful for Want of Form. Redress for wrongful prosecution.

Para. 56. Public Act. That the Act be recognised by all Judges, Justices and others.

Appendix 2: Donors and Subscribers to the Navigation

List of donors (D), subscribers to the Old Loan (OL), the abatement to less indicated by ">", the New Loan (NL) and the Loan in Aid (LA).

Adey, John £100(>80) OL + £100 NL

Andrews, John £20 D

Anson, Thomas exs £100 (>£85) OL

Astley, Sir Edward £100(>70) OL

Bacon, William £20 D

Baldra, Nicholas £100 OL

Barber, James £100(>85) OL

Barnard, Thomas £20 D

Bedingfield, John £100(>80) OL + £100 NL

Bell, Coulson £21 D + £100(>70) OL

Bell, William £50 NL

Berry, William £5 D + £50 NL

Blomefield, Henry £10 D

Blomefield, John £10 D + £100(>0) OL

Buckingham, Earl of £100(>0) OL

Bulwer, Thomas £10 D

Bulwer, William Wiggett £50 D + £100(>50) OL

Carter, William £10 D

Clarke, John £20 D

Clarke, Robert £5 D

Clarke, Samuel £20 D

Clover, Thomas £50 NL

Colls, Robert £100 NL

Collyer, Rev. Daniel £150 NL

Cooke, Bell £5 D

Cooke, John £100 NL

Cooke, Robert £10 D

Cook, Stephen £100(>85) OL

Cooper, William £20 D

Cubitt, Woolmer £20 D

Curties, James £50 D

Dix, Thomas £10 D

Durrant, Thomas £10 D + £100(>70) OL + £100 NL + £20 LA

Eaton, William £10 D + £100(>75) OL + £50 NL

Fish, Thomas £10 D

Francis, Robert £20 D + £50 NL

Gill, William £5 D

Green, John £5 D

Harbord, Sir Harbord £10 D + £100(>85) OL

Harriman, Richard £5 D

Harvey, Thomas £50 NL

Holley, George Hunt £50 D + £100(>70) OL + £100 NL + £20 LA

Hurry, George £100(>75) OL + £100 NL

Hurry, John £100(>75) OL + £100 NL

Hurry, Samuel £100(>75) OL + £100 NL

Hurry, Thomas £100(>75) OL

Hurry, William £100(>75) OL + £100 NL

Ives, John £100(>75) OL + £50 NL

Jewell, Rev William £100(>85) OL

Kemp, Henry £5 D

Kent, Nathaniel £100(>80) OL

Kerrison, Roger £100 NL

Lane, Benjamin £100(>75) OL

Lubbock, William £20 D

Marsham, Robert sen £50 D + £100(>50) OL + £20 LA

Marsham, Robert jun £20 LA

Miller, John £50 NL

Page, Joseph £5 D

Palgrave, William £50 NL

Parmeter, Robert £50 D + £100 OL + £100 NL + £20 LA

Partridge, Francis £20 D

Partridge, Thomas £20 D

Pepper, William & Co. £50 D + £100(>80) OL

Peterson, John £100(>85) OL

Piggon, Edward £10 D + £100(>80) OL + £100 NL

Rackham, Peter £20 D + £50 OL + £50 NL

Ray, Rev George £20 D

Repton, John £10 D + £100(>85) OL

Robins, James £10 D

Robins, Thomas £30 D + £100(>80) OL

Rumbelow, James & Co. £40 D

Rumpe, Thomas £10 D

Sharp, Elizabeth £100(>75) OL

Smith, John £40 D + £100(>80) OL + £200 NL + £20 LA

Smyth, James £100(>85) OL

Soame, Mary £10 D

Suffield, Thomas £100(>80) OL

Walpole, Lord £100(>0) OL + £20 LA

West, Christopher £5 D

Wickes, John £20 D + £100 NL

Windham, William £100(>70) OL

Woolsey, John £20 D

Wymark, James £5 D

Appendix 3: Wherries owned on the Aylsham Navigation

Aylsham

Eighteenth Century (recorded in Yarmouth register of 1795–1798)[1]

BROTHERS, 18 tons, owned Robert Parmeter; skipper John Maidstone.

BUCKENHAM, 12 tons, built in 1780, owned Robert Parmeter; skipper Edward Roofe

DEFIANCE, 42 tons, possibly owned Robert Parmeter; skipper George Tuck.

MAY FLOWER, 16 tons, owned Burr, brick maker, skipper William Sago.

NORFOLK FARMER, 30 tons, owned Willliam Lubbock, farmer and marl dealer; skipper John Rous.

OLIVE BRANCH, 36 tons, possibly owned Robert Parmeter; skipper Clement Cook.

THREE SISTERS, 18 tons, owned Robert Parmeter; skipper John Lovorick.

Mid-Nineteenth Century

ASLACTON, owned Frederick Copeman, Steam Mill, skipper Ted Brown.

AYLSHAM, 24-25 tons, owned Barber & Ingram, corn, coal and timber merchants. Crew George Gibbs and John Forster in Wherryman's Appeal 1859.[2] Later owned by Stanley Bullock, Water Mill, skipper B. Wright. In 1871 census at Great Yarmouth harbour with John Palk as mate.

BOLWICK[3], 24 tons, owned Tom Shreeve of Bolwick Mill in Marsham and later by Barber & Ingram in Aylsham – unusually she had a square stern. Skipper James Wright in 1887.[4]

BURE, built mid-C19 by Bob Wright, Aylsham, for Dr William Wynne. John Money master in 1871 census of Yarmouth harbour; Robert Bircham wherryman in 1881 census at Acle. Later renamed *Laura*, then *Rachel*. Unusually she had a square stern.

DOVE, crew Silas Watson & George Bircham according to mid-century Wherrymen's appeal. John Gilding was owner and skipper in 1887.

---

1   NRO Y/C38/3. The 1795–1798 records were made by the Town Clerk of Yarmouth, 149 vessels were listed.

2   NRO MC634/24.

3   Misspelt Baldwich in Clark (1961).

4   NRO YPH253, River Bure Tolls Ledger 1887, copy kindly provided by Michael Sparkes.

GLEANER, 25 tons, owned George Bircham, coal and coke merchant c.1875–1887. At Wroxham in 1902–1905.

JENNY LIND, crew William Harris according to mid-century Wherrymen's appeal.

LOTHIAN, crew William Wright and Isaac Bussey according to mid-century Wherrymen's appeal.

MAYFLOWER, based Aylsham but owned and operated from Burgh at one time by Isaac Helsdon, timber merchant, a relative of the Birchams. James Helsden is listed as skipper in 1887. Owned by Cross & Co. and skippered by Strike in 1907–1908.

PRINCE OF WALES, owned Frederick Copeman & George Soame, millers.

PROSPECT, 13 tons, owned George Bircham, coal and coke merchant c1875–1883, skipper Mr Parsons.

UNION, 28 tons, owned Robert Mayston, coal merchant 1846–1856; later under skipper John Reynolds from Horstead.

ZULU, 15 tons, probably built in Coltishall, recorded 1871 census at Yarmouth harbour with John Money as master. Owned Ben Cook and successors Barclay Pallett c.1880–1912; skipper Jimmy Wright. She was manhauled across and around obstructions at Buxton lock after the flood in 1912, then owned in Catfield by John George Riches.

Late Nineteenth to Early Twentieth Century

ALBERT, owned Tom Shreeve, miller, skipper William Bircham in 1881 census at Acle.

ALEXANDRA, 22 tons, owned Stanley Bullock, skipper was 'Sink' Collier; Bunn was wherryman in 1907–1908.

CYPRUS, 24 tons. Clark says she was owned by A.R. Amies, coal, coke and timber merchant at Horstead; skippered by Joe Bircham, but she was owned by Stanley Bullock in Aylsham in 1907–1908 with Bircham as wherryman.

ELIZABETH, 27 tons, owned Barclay, Pallett & Co., North Walsham, possibly used at Aylsham 1908–1912 – unusually she had a square stern.

ERNEST, owned Stanley Bullock.

ETHNIE, 22 tons, owned Barclay, Pallett & Co., North Walsham, possibly used at Aylsham 1908–1912.

GIPSY, built Aylsham by Elijah Wright in 1875 and traded for c. ten years before bought from Shreeve by Henry Doughty and converted to a pleasure wherry.

KATE, 22 tons, owned Ben Cook and finally skippered by "Shiner" Wright. She once did 8 round trips from Aylsham to Yarmouth in one month.

PALMERSTON, built 1898 in Aylsham and owned by Stanley Bullock. William Balls and William Wright crew in 1881 census at Acle. Bircham was responsible as wherryman for her as well as *Cyprus* in 1907–1908.

PARAGON, 24 tons, owned in Aylsham according to Tom Catchpole family archive, but at one time owned by B. Barnard, Horstead Roller Mills, bought after 1912 by Hobrough of Norwich and converted into a lighter.

Burgh-next-Aylsham

Eighteenth Century (recorded in Yarmouth register of 1795–1798)

ENDEAVOUR, 16 tons, owned Burr, brick maker; skipper Matthew Bidney. In 1887 owned by Robert Lockett and skippered by Gedge.

Late Nineteenth to Early Twentieth Century

HILDA, 22 tons, last owned by Cross & Co., malsters, Horning; skipper Charles Rump. Built in 1898 she spent her early years with Isaac Helsdon at Burgh. Escaped flood by being out of service.

Buxton

Mid Nineteenth Century

DISPATCH, crew John Southgate according to mid-century Wherrymen's appeal.

Late Nineteenth to Early Twentieth Century

BERTHA, 20 tons, owned Ling & Co., Buxton Roller & Water Mills, converted for cruising in summer months in 1890s.

BLANCHE, 22 tons, owned Tom Shreeve, miller at Buxton, Acle and Aylsham.

BRITANNIA, 20 tons, owned by Ling & Co.; skipper Barnes in 1907–1908. Converted for cruising in summer months in 1890s.

EMILY owned by Ling & Co; skipper Rivett in 1907–1908.

ETHELBERT – see Coltishall.

Coltishall – a number of these were too large to use the Aylsham Navigation.

Eighteenth Century (recorded in Yarmouth Register for 1795–1798)

BARLEYCORN, 20 tons, skipper Samuel Parson.

BARLEY CORN, 36 tons, skipper Gazeley Kettle.

FRIENDS' ADVENTURE, 35 tons, skipper William Horn.

HARVEST HOME, 20 tons, skipper John Fox.

INDUSTRY, 37 tons, skipper James Willins.

JOHN AND MARY, 38 tons, skipper Joseph Chamberlain.

WHEATSHEAF, 42 tons, skipper Gould Scott.

WILLIAM AND BETSEY, 43 tons, skipper Edward Smith.

Mid Nineteenth Century

ALARM, 30 tons, owned by Mrs Wright, who was a coal merchant and kept the Rising Sun inn, skipper Jack Barnes.

LEANDER, 28 tons, also owned by Mrs Wright. In 1887 owned by Robert Amies and skippered by James Bunn.[11]

LITTLE MARGARET, crew James Edridge & James Rope according to mid-century Wherrymen's appeal.

LORD EXMOUTH, 28 tons, owned by Mealing & Mills, maltsters; Henry and James Wright crew in Wherryman's Appeal 1859; skipper 'Flea' Wright.

MARY ANN, crew Henry Haylett according to mid-century Wherrymen's appeal.

SHEPHERD, owned by Ling & Co., Coltishall.

WIDGEON, John Money and family of Coltishall masters in 1881 census for Wroxham.

Late Nineteenth to Early Twentieth Century

ETHELBERT, possibly built in Aylsham, but later owned at Coltishall (according to Clark) or Buxton (according to Best) by Ling & Co.; skipper Bob Bates.

VIOLET, owned by Robert Amies and sold to Mrs Elizabeth Bircham in 1900.

Hautbois

TRADER or HORSTEAD TRADER. James Bunn and Mary Ann Bunn of Aylsham master and wife in 1881 census of Acle. She was owned at Hautbois by a Rev. J.D. Girling in 1888.

Horstead

Eighteenth Century (recorded in Yarmouth register of 1795–1798)

COLTISHALL, 42 tons, owned Colls & Watts, Horstead Mill; skipper Samuel Thaxter.

CROSTWICK, 21 tons, possibly owned by Colls & Watts; skipper Edmund Reynolds.

FANCY, 25 tons, possibly owned by Colls & Watts, operated by Robert Blyth.

UNION, 28 tons, owned Colls & Watts; skipper John Reynolds.

Mid Nineteenth Century

HOPE, crew Henry and Robert Neve according to mid-century Wherrymen's appeal

LITTLE SPARK later Maid of the Mist, 12 tons, she spent her working life at the Horstead Marl pits.

Late Nineteenth to Early Twentieth Century

CYPRUS, 24 tons, owned A.R. Amies, coal, coke and timber merchant, Horstead, later at Aylsham.

PARAGON, 24 tons, owned by B. Barnard, Horstead Roller Mills.

Oxnead

Eighteenth Century (recorded in Yarmouth register of 1795–1798)

OXNEAD, 18 tons, owned William Spinks.

Mid to Late Nineteenth Century

ROYAL CHARLIE owned in the 1880's by Charles Browne.

VOLUNTEER, 26 tons, owned Tom Shreeve of Marsham, but trading from Oxnead Mill, skipper H. Powley in 1887 and presumably later by Mr Rivett. Owned by Charles Browne and skippered by George Strike in 1907–1908; she was acquired by George Strike c.1910; bought by F.H. Dove of Yarmouth in 1915 for £85; Allens carried out repair work early the following year.

<u>Glossary</u>

Archimedes Screw device of ancient origin for raising water by means of a spiral within a tube.

balk or baulk a roughly squared timber beam.

billet thick piece of wood cut to length and split for fuel.

bombazine a twilled dress material of worsted with or without an admixture of silk or cotton, especially when black, formerly use for mourning.

buck or **buckwheat** *Fagopyrum esculentum*, introduced into Europe by the Turks in the thirteenth century. The seeds were eaten, and used for animals and poultry.

burthen archaic variation of **burden.**

calimancoes Flemish woollen cloth with glossy surface, woven with a satin twill and chequered on one side.

chaldron a measure of capacity, originally of 32 bushells, but 36 bushells from 1664/5. In 1695 a chaldron of coal = 53 cwt = 3 wagon loads = 6 cart loads. This is the official weight in the Act of Parliament.

cofferdam or coffin dam watertight enclosure pumped dry to permit work below the waterline.

crome a long-shafted tool with three or four tines bent at 90°, for pulling about muck, clay, soil, etc.

crome or **chrome** leather tanned with chromium salts making it more supple and pliable than vegetable-tanned leather and less liable to damage by water. Invented in 1858.

dydling or **didling** term for removing the weeds and deposits in the channels using special tools.

drug low truck, with small, wide, solid wheels, for transporting timber.

duck strong untwilled linen cloth.

flash lock early lock, dating back to Roman times, designed with a single gate, known as a flash lock or staunch lock and commonly built into small dams or weirs where a head of water was used for powering a mill. The lock allowed boats to pass the weir while still allowing the mill to operate when the gate was closed.

hacks racks holding fodder for cattle.

holland tile the early name for pantiles, imported from Holland from the seventeenth century.

hoves or **hovers** floating islands of vegetation.

journeyman one who works for another on daily basis.

lamp black almost pure carbon collected from soot mixed with gum to form a pigment.

leat an open watercourse conducting water to a mill, etc.

marl clay with a variable percentage of carbonate of lime. Used from Roman times to condition and fertilise the soil. Many Norfolk parishes contain Marl-pits. Marl was also used in brick-making.

melton cloth with a close-cut nap, used for overcoats, etc. Melton Mowbray, a town in central England, formerly a centre of manufacture.

neat's foot oil oil made from boiled cow-heel and used to dress leather.

oilcake a mass of compressed linseed etc., left after oil has been extracted, used as fodder or manure.

pea jacket sailor's short double-breasted overcoat of coarse woollen cloth – from Dutch *pijjakker*, 'coat of coarse cloth'.

pen solid construction for holding back water, see also staunch.

pightle a small field or enclosure.

pollard the bran sifted from flour.

pound lock a lock with two gates to confine water and often a side reservoir to maintain the water level.

quant a punting pole with a prong or knob at the bottom to prevent it sinking into the mud, as used by Norfolk wherrymen.

scantling measuring rod or ruler; dimensions, particularly cross-section of timber.

shoal submerged sandbank.

shoddy an inferior cloth made partly from the shredded fibre of old woollen cloth

staunch a strong or solid construction

strake continuous line of planking or plates from the stem to the stern of a ship.

tares vetch; the cultivated vetch is *Vicia sativa,* used as a fodder crop.

tarras or **terras** earth.

trunk pipe or a cut.

wharfinger owner or keeper of a wharf.

worsted fine smooth yarn from combed long staple wool; fabric made from this; originating from parish of Worstead in Norfolk.

Bibliography

Adderson, R. and Kenworthy, G. (2011) *Country Railway Routes: Melton Constable to Yarmouth Beach*, Middleton Press, Midhurst.

Alderton, D. and Booker, J. (1980) *The Batsford Guide to the Industrial Archaeology of East Anglia*, Batsford, London.

Armstrong, M. (1781) *History and Antiquities of the County of Norfolk*, Norwich.

Austin, J., Greenacre, J. & Grint, B. (2011) *The Search for Eugenia Fynch: The story of Norfolk's unknown Victorian photographers*, Acle Community Archive Group.

Bayne, A.D. (1873) *Royal Illustrated History of Eastern England, Volume One*, Great Yarmouth.

Best, D. (1976) *The Aylsham Navigation*, unpublished dissertation, Keswick Hall College of Education.

Bircham, N. (1979) *By the Last Wherryman*, unpublished.

Bird, M. (forthcoming), *The Diary of Mary Hardy 1773–180: Public house and Waterway.*

Bond, R. (1986) *Coltishall – Heyday of a Broadland Village,* Poppyland Publishing, North Walsham.

Boyes, J. and Russell, R. (1977) *The Canals of Eastern England*, David and Charles, Newton Abbot.

Bradshaw, G. (1904) *Bradshaw's Canals and Navigable Rivers of England and Wales*, London.

Brittain, H. (1889) *Notes on the Broads and Rivers of Norfolk and Suffolk.*

Burton, A. (2005) *The Canal Builders*, Tempus, Stroud.

Church, R. (1986) *The History of the British Coal Industry, vol. 3: 1830-1913 Victorian Pre-eminence*, Clarendon Press, Oxford.

Clark, R. (1961) *Black Sailed Traders: The Keels and Wherries of Norfolk and Suffolk*, David Charles, Newton Abbot.

Colman Green, G. (1944) *The Norfolk Wherry*, No. 1, 6 June 1944.

Cossons, N. (1975) *The BP Book of Industrial Archaeology*, David and Charles, Newton Abbot.

Cox, A. (1979) *Brickmaking: a history and gazetteer,* Bedfordshire County Council and the Royal Commission on Historical Monuments.

Daniels, S. (1999) *Humphry Repton: Landscape Gardening and the Geography of Georgian England*, Yale University Press, New Haven & London.

Dorer, A.L. (1953) 'Memories of the 1912 Flood' in *Norfolk Magazine*, vol. 6, no. 1.

Doughty, H.M. (1891) *Our Wherry in Wendish Lands*, Ashford, Southampton.

Eden, P. (1976) 'Land surveyors in Norfolk 1550–1850' in *Norfolk Archaeology*, vol. 35, pp.480–1.

Emerson, P.H. (1893) *On English Lagoons*, David Nutt.

Evans, N. (1985) *The East Anglian Linen Industry: Rural Industry and Local Economy, 1500–1850*, Gower, Aldershot.

Flinn, M.W. (1984) *The History of the British Coal Industry, vol. 2: 1700–1830 The Industrial Revolution*, Clarendon Press, Oxford.

Fuller, M. (unknown date) *How to Build a Wherry*.

Glover, F.J. (1961) 'Philadelphia Merchants and the Yorkshire Blanket Trade 1820–1860' in *Pennsylvania History*, Vol. 28, pp.121–141.

Horn, P. (1982) 'An Eighteenth-Century Land Agent: The Career of Nathaniel Kent (1737–1810)' in *Agricultural History Review*, vol. 30, pp.1–16.

Jenkins, D. and Ponting, K. (1982) *The British Wool Textile Industry 1770–1914*, Heinemann, London,

Jones, J. and Manning, M. (1993) 'Limeburning and Extractive Industries' in P. Wade Martins ed., *An Historical Atlas of Norfolk*, Norfolk Museums Service, Norwich.

Kendon, M. and Prior, J. (2011) 'Two Remarkable British Summers – 'perfect' 1911 and 'calamitous' 1912' in *Weather*, vol. 66, no. 7, pp. 179–184.

Ketton-Cremer, R.W. (1944) *Norfolk Portraits*, Faber & Faber, London.

Loudon, J.C., ed. (1840) *The Landscape Gardening and Landscape Architecture of the late Humphry Repton Esq.*, London.

Lucas, R. (1993) 'Brickmaking' in P. Wade Martins ed., *An Historical Atlas of Norfolk*, Norfolk Museums Service, Norwich.

Nolan, J. (1995) 'No. 1, Market Place' in *Aylsham Local History Society Journal*, vol. 4, pp.244–245.

Malster, R. (1971) *Wherries and Waterways*, Terence Dalton, Lavenham.

Malster, R. (1999) *The Mardler's Companion: A Dictionary of East Anglian Dialect*, Malthouse Press, Holbrook, Suffolk.

Manning, D. (1996) 'Norfolk Bridges Part 2' in *Norfolk Industrial Archaeology Society Journal*, vol. 6, no. 1.

Marriott, W. (1974) *Forty Years of a Norfolk Railway – The Reminiscences of William Marriott from 1884 to 1924*, M&GNJRS Publications.

Millican, P. (1937) *A History of Horstead and Stanninghall Norfolk*, Hunt, Norwich.

Palmer, C.J. (1872) *The Perlustration of Great Yarmouth*, Great Yarmouth.

Peabody, R. (2000) *Memories of Aylsham: The memoirs of William Frederick Starling 1851–1937*, Aylsham Local History Society.

Polhill, R. (2012) 'Mr Biedermann's Invention' in *Aylsham Local History Society Journal*, vol. 9, pp.141–145.

Porteous, J.D. (1977) *Canal Ports: The urban Achievement of the Canal Age*, Academic Press, London.

Priestley, J. (1967) *Historical Account of the Navigable Rivers, Canals and Railways throughout Great Britain*, Frank Cass, London.

Reade, A. (1923) *Johnsonian Gleanings*, Part 4, London.

Robert Mill, H. (1912) *British Rainfall*, London.

Rye, W. (1885) *A History of Norfolk*.

Seward, D. (1972) 'The Wool Textile Industry 1750–1960' in J. Geraint Jenkins ed. *The Wool Textile Industry in Great Britain*, Routledge, London.

Sinclair, O. (1987) *When Wherries Sailed By*, Poppyland Publishing, North Walsham.

Skempton, A.W. (2002) *A Biographical Dictionary of Civil Engineers in Great Britain and Northern Ireland, Volume 1: 1500–1830*, Thomas Telford Publishing, London

Smeaton, J. (1814) *The Miscellaneous Papers of John Smeaton, Civil Engineer*, London.

Stoker, D. (1976) 'The Early History of Papermaking in Norfolk' in *Norfolk Archaeology*, vol. 36, pp.224–251.

Vince, J. (1970) *Discovering Watermills*, Shire, Princes Risborough.

Wenham, P. (1989) *Watermills*, Robert Hale, London.

Wilson, A. (1996) *Wherries and Windmills: Barton Turf and District in the Early 1900s*.

White, W. (1836) *White's History, Gazetteer, and Directory of Norfolk,* London.

White, W. (1845) *White's History, Gazetteer, and Directory of Norfolk*, London.

Willan, T.S. (1964) *River Navigation in England: 1600 – 1750*, Frank Cass & Co., London.

Williams, R. (1989) *Limekilns and Limeburning*, Shire, Princes Risborough.

Young, A. (1813) *General View of the Agriculture of the County of Norfolk*, London.

INDEX

Names of wherries in italics.